The AI Revolution

Dedication

To the pioneers of artificial intelligence, whose relentless pursuit of knowledge and innovation laid the foundation for this transformative technology. Their dedication to pushing the boundaries of what's possible has reshaped our world, and this book is a testament to their remarkable contributions. This work is also dedicated to the future generation – the students, researchers, and innovators who will continue to shape the AI revolution and ensure that its benefits are shared equitably by all. May this book serve as a guidepost on their journey, illuminating the path towards a future where artificial intelligence empowers humanity and enhances the human experience, solving the world's biggest problems and pushing the boundaries of human knowledge. Finally, to my family and friends, whose unwavering support has been instrumental in the completion of this project. Your understanding, encouragement, and belief in me have been a constant source of strength and inspiration.

Preface

Artificial intelligence is no longer a futuristic fantasy; it is a rapidly evolving reality that is reshaping our world at an unprecedented pace. From healthcare to finance, education to manufacturing, AI is transforming industries and impacting our lives in profound ways.

Yet, this transformative technology presents both incredible opportunities and significant challenges. This book aims to provide a comprehensive and accessible overview of the AI revolution, exploring its historical development, current applications, and future implications. Written for a broad audience – from general readers to professionals to students – it delves into the complex world of AI without sacrificing clarity or engagement. We explore the technical foundations of AI, such as machine learning and deep learning, using clear language and real-world examples, making even the most complex concepts readily understandable. The book also addresses the ethical, societal, and economic ramifications of AI, encouraging critical reflection on its potential impact on humanity. We examine the need for responsible AI development, fair and unbiased algorithms, and robust regulatory frameworks. Ultimately, this book seeks to empower readers with knowledge and understanding, enabling them to navigate the AI revolution confidently and contribute to shaping a future where this powerful technology serves humanity's best interests. The book hopes to provide a roadmap for individuals and businesses to thrive in an increasingly AI-driven world, encouraging adaptability and the strategic harnessing of AI's transformative potential. It is my hope that readers will finish this book not only informed about the current state of artificial intelligence, but also inspired to engage with its future possibilities.

Introduction

The rise of artificial intelligence is arguably the most significant technological advancement of our time, comparable in its transformative potential to the invention of electricity or the internet. This book provides a journey through the landscape of AI, beginning with its historical roots and charting its remarkable progress to the sophisticated applications we see today. We examine the evolution of AI, from early conceptualizations and the initial bursts of enthusiasm to the "AI winters" and the subsequent resurgence driven by deep learning and big data. The narrative unfolds through a series of chapters, each focusing on a key aspect of the AI revolution. We explore the core algorithms and techniques of machine learning, providing accessible explanations of complex concepts like neural networks, supervised and unsupervised learning, and reinforcement learning. The practical applications of AI are showcased through in-depth case studies across diverse sectors: healthcare, finance, education, manufacturing, and more.

We delve into specific areas such as natural language processing, computer vision, and robotics, exploring their capabilities and limitations. This book also confronts the crucial ethical and societal considerations that accompany this technological progress. We discuss the potential for bias in AI systems, the importance of data privacy and security, and the need for transparent and accountable AI decision-making. The economic implications are also explored, examining the impact on productivity, employment, and the global economy. We analyze investment trends, the global competition for AI supremacy, and the potential for AI to exacerbate existing economic inequalities. Finally, the book provides actionable advice for individuals and businesses navigating this transformative era, encouraging proactive strategies for adaptation and harnessing the opportunities presented by this powerful technology. It is my aim that this book will serve as a valuable resource for anyone seeking a comprehensive understanding of the AI revolution and its implications for our future.

The Genesis of AI Early Concepts and Dreams

The very notion of artificial intelligence, the creation of machines capable of thought and action akin to humans, has captivated humanity for millennia. Long before the advent of computers, the dream of artificial minds found expression in myths, legends, and philosophical inquiries. Ancient Greek automatons, intricate mechanical devices designed to mimic human or animal movements, hinted at a fascination with creating artificial life. These early examples, though lacking the computational power of modern AI, represent the seeds of a persistent human desire to replicate intelligence in artificial forms.

Philosophical discussions about the nature of mind and intelligence laid further groundwork. The works of thinkers like René Descartes, with his exploration of the mind-body duality, and Gottfried Wilhelm Leibniz, who envisioned a calculus ratiocinator (a calculating machine capable of reasoning), sparked debate about the possibility of creating artificial minds. These early thinkers wrestled with questions that remain central to AI research today: What constitutes intelligence? Can it be replicated in machines? And what are the ethical implications of creating artificial minds?

The 18th and 19th centuries saw the development of increasingly sophisticated mechanical devices, fueled by the industrial revolution. These advancements, though not directly related to AI as we know it today, fostered crucial technological progress. The development of programmable looms, for example, demonstrated the potential for machines to execute complex sequences of instructions, a precursor to the stored-program computers that would become the foundation of modern AI. The invention of the telegraph and the telephone brought about new forms of communication and information processing, paving the way for the development of more advanced computational systems.

The true genesis of AI as a formal scientific discipline is generally attributed to the Dartmouth Workshop of 1956. Organized by John McCarthy, Marvin Minsky, Claude Shannon, and Nathaniel Rochester, this pivotal event brought together a group of leading researchers from diverse backgrounds, including mathematics, computer science, and engineering. The workshop's ambitious goal was to explore the possibility of creating machines capable of "thinking," marking the official commencement of AI as a field of research.

The Dartmouth Workshop was not only a landmark event but also a catalyst for significant early advancements. The participants laid out a detailed research agenda, outlining various approaches to AI, including symbolic reasoning, game playing, and natural language processing. The workshop also helped to establish a common vocabulary and set of goals for the nascent field, fostering collaboration and driving progress in the years that followed.

One of the most significant achievements of the early AI era was the development of the first AI programs. Allen Newell and Herbert A. Simon, two key figures at the Dartmouth Workshop, created the Logic Theorist, a program capable of proving mathematical theorems. This early success demonstrated the potential of computers to perform tasks previously considered exclusive to human intelligence. Later, they created the General Problem Solver (GPS), which expanded on the Logic Theorist's capabilities by tackling a wider range of problems using a more general approach.

The success of the Logic Theorist and GPS generated considerable excitement and optimism about the future of AI. The belief that machines could soon match or exceed human intelligence in a wide range of tasks spurred significant investment in research and development. Early AI research focused on developing symbolic reasoning systems, which relied on representing knowledge and reasoning in a symbolic form. This approach proved effective in tackling certain problems, like playing chess and solving mathematical puzzles, but it struggled with more complex and real-world challenges.

During this era, several key figures made significant contributions to the development of AI. John McCarthy developed LISP, a programming language widely used in AI research, and contributed significantly to the development of time-sharing systems that facilitated collaborative research. Marvin Minsky, a pioneer of neural networks and cognitive science, contributed heavily to both theoretical and practical aspects of AI. Claude Shannon, known for his work in information theory, played a crucial role in establishing the theoretical foundations of AI.

Despite the initial progress and optimism, the early years of AI research also revealed limitations. The symbolic reasoning systems, while capable of solving specific problems, proved brittle and struggled to adapt to new situations or handle uncertainty. Many early AI programs were limited by the computational resources available at the time, hindering their ability to tackle more complex problems. The complexity of natural language processing and the challenges of understanding and representing real-world knowledge also posed significant hurdles.

The initial enthusiasm for AI was followed by periods of disillusionment, often referred to as "AI winters." These periods were characterized by reduced funding and interest in AI research as the field struggled to meet its overly optimistic early predictions.

The limitations of early AI systems and the failure to deliver on ambitious promises led to a decline in funding and a shift in research priorities.

However, each "AI winter" was followed by a resurgence of interest and new breakthroughs, driven by advancements in computing power, new algorithms, and the availability of vast amounts of data.

The development of powerful computers allowed researchers to tackle more complex problems and develop more sophisticated AI systems. New algorithms, such as backpropagation for training neural networks, and the availability of massive datasets enabled the development of deep learning models, transforming the field of AI. These advancements laid the groundwork for the current AI boom, which has seen remarkable progress in diverse applications ranging from image recognition to natural language processing to robotics. The story of AI's early years is not merely one of technical progress, but a testament to the enduring human fascination with creating intelligent machines and the enduring challenges in fulfilling that vision. The journey from ancient myths to the Dartmouth Workshop and beyond is a fascinating chronicle of intellectual ambition, scientific innovation, and the ongoing quest to understand and replicate intelligence itself. The subsequent chapters will explore the specific techniques and applications that have emerged from these early foundations, showcasing the profound and transformative impact AI is having on the world today.

The Dawn of Machine Learning Early Algorithms and Their Limitations

The seeds of what we now know as machine learning were sown long before the term itself gained widespread currency. The perceptron, invented by Frank Rosenblatt in 1957, stands as a pivotal early example. This single-layer neural network, a remarkably simple architecture by today's standards, could learn to classify inputs based on training data. Imagine a rudimentary image recognition system: a perceptron could be trained to distinguish between images of cats and dogs, albeit with significant limitations.

The perceptron's learning process relied on adjusting the weights associated with its connections, a process akin to fine-tuning the sensitivity of different detectors. If a perceptron incorrectly classified an image, the weights were adjusted to improve its performance on subsequent inputs. This seemingly straightforward mechanism represented a breakthrough – a demonstration that a machine could, in a rudimentary way, learn from experience.

The initial enthusiasm surrounding the perceptron was substantial.

Its ability to learn, albeit in a restricted context, fueled hopes of creating truly intelligent machines. However, these hopes would soon be tempered. Minsky and Papert's influential 1969 book, *Perceptrons*, exposed critical limitations in the perceptron's architecture. They demonstrated mathematically that single-layer perceptrons were incapable of solving certain seemingly simple problems, such as the XOR problem (exclusive OR). This problem, which requires distinguishing between two distinct input patterns, exposed a fundamental weakness: a single layer could not efficiently delineate complex, non-linearly separable patterns. This critique had a profound impact on the field, significantly dampening enthusiasm and contributing to the first "AI winter."

The limitations highlighted by Minsky and Papert were not merely theoretical; they reflected the practical challenges of the time. The computational power available in the 1960s and early 1970s was severely restricted. Training even relatively simple neural networks required substantial computational resources, and the available hardware simply couldn't keep pace with the demands of more complex architectures. The size of the datasets that could be effectively processed was also severely limited, further hindering progress. This confluence of factors – theoretical limitations, computational constraints, and data scarcity – contributed to a period of reduced funding and diminished interest in neural network research.

This period, however, was not a complete standstill. While research on perceptrons and early neural networks waned, other approaches to machine learning flourished. Symbolic AI, focused on representing knowledge and reasoning using symbolic logic, continued to advance. Expert systems, programs designed to mimic the decision-making abilities of human experts in specific domains, emerged as a promising application. These systems relied on extensive knowledge bases, encoding rules and facts within a specific domain, allowing them to provide expert-level advice or make predictions. Medical diagnosis, financial forecasting, and geological exploration were just a few of the areas where expert systems saw application. While successful in their niche applications, expert systems suffered from inherent limitations. Their performance was heavily dependent on the completeness and accuracy of their knowledge bases, making them brittle and difficult to adapt to new situations or unforeseen circumstances.

The development and refinement of decision tree algorithms provided another avenue for progress in machine learning. Decision trees, with their hierarchical structure, offered a relatively intuitive and interpretable approach to classification and prediction. They could handle both numerical and categorical data, making them adaptable to a range of problems. Algorithms like ID3 and CART (Classification and Regression Trees) provided efficient methods for building and pruning decision trees, minimizing overfitting and improving generalization performance. Despite their advantages, decision trees, like other early machine learning algorithms, were not without limitations. They could be susceptible to overfitting, particularly with noisy or high-dimensional data. The tendency to favor features with many levels also presented a challenge.

Bayesian methods, rooted in probability theory, offered a different approach to machine learning. These methods provided a principled framework for incorporating prior knowledge and updating beliefs based on new evidence. Naive Bayes classifiers, a simplified form of Bayesian networks, gained popularity due to their computational efficiency and surprisingly good performance on various tasks, even with the strong independence assumption. However, the assumption of feature independence, a cornerstone of the naive Bayes approach, often limits the accuracy in real-world scenarios where feature dependencies are common. Despite this limitation, Bayesian methods provided a robust and theoretically well-founded approach to machine learning, laying groundwork for future advancements.

The limitations of early machine learning algorithms highlighted the need for more sophisticated techniques and more powerful computational resources. The "AI winters" were not just periods of stagnation, but rather periods of reflection and recalibration.

Researchers sought to address the shortcomings of existing methods, exploring new algorithms and architectures, and patiently awaiting the advancements in computing power that would eventually unlock the potential of more complex models. The stage was set for the resurgence of neural networks and the rise of deep learning, a story that would unfold in the following decades. The early history of machine learning is not just a chronicle of successes and failures, but also a testament to the iterative nature of scientific progress. Each setback, each "winter," fueled innovation and laid the foundation for the remarkable progress witnessed in the latter part of the 20th century and beyond. The lessons learned from these early algorithms, their limitations, and the challenges they posed, continue to shape the development of machine learning even today. The journey from single-layer perceptrons to the sophisticated deep learning models of today is a story of incremental progress, driven by both theoretical insights and technological advancements.

Expert Systems and the Rise of Symbolic AI

The limitations of early neural networks, vividly exposed by Minsky and Papert, didn't halt the pursuit of artificial intelligence. Instead, the field pivoted, focusing on a different paradigm: symbolic AI.

This approach, rather than mimicking the biological processes of the brain, emphasized the manipulation of symbols and logic to represent knowledge and perform reasoning. The core idea was to encode human expertise into computer programs, creating systems capable of mimicking the decision-making process of human experts. This led to the development of expert systems, a significant milestone in the history of AI.

Expert systems weren't designed to be general-purpose intelligence.

Instead, they focused on narrow, well-defined domains. The system's knowledge was meticulously encoded in a knowledge base, often using rule-based systems. These rules, expressed in a formal language, captured the relationships between different facts and concepts within the domain. For example, an expert system designed for medical diagnosis might contain rules like: "IF patient has fever AND cough THEN suspect influenza." The system used an inference engine to apply these rules to new cases, arriving at a conclusion or recommendation.

The construction of these knowledge bases was a laborious, expert-intensive process. Knowledge engineers, specialists trained to elicit and formalize expert knowledge, worked closely with domain experts to translate their expertise into a computer-understandable format. This involved painstakingly identifying key concepts, relationships, and decision-making rules. The resulting knowledge base, though complex, provided the foundation for the expert system's reasoning capabilities.

The 1970s and 80s witnessed a surge in the development and deployment of expert systems across various fields. MYCIN, a medical diagnosis system developed at Stanford University, was a pioneering example. Designed to diagnose bacterial infections, MYCIN demonstrated the potential of expert systems to provide valuable assistance to medical professionals. It could analyze patient symptoms, medical history, and lab results to propose likely diagnoses and recommend treatment plans. While not a replacement for human doctors, MYCIN showed the potential to improve diagnostic accuracy and efficiency.

Other notable expert systems emerged in different domains. PROSPECTOR, developed for mineral exploration, aided geologists in identifying promising sites for mining operations. DENDRAL, focusing on organic chemistry, helped researchers analyze the structure of complex molecules. These systems showcased the versatility of the symbolic AI approach and its capacity to address complex problems in specialized domains. The success of these early expert systems fueled significant investment in the field, leading to the development of sophisticated software tools and methodologies for knowledge acquisition and representation.

However, the limitations of expert systems soon became apparent. The knowledge bases, while representing a significant body of expertise, were inherently brittle. They could handle only the situations explicitly encoded in their rules. Any deviation from the pre-defined scenarios could lead to unexpected or erroneous results. The systems lacked the ability to learn from new data or adapt to changing circumstances. They were essentially static representations of knowledge, unable to evolve or improve their performance through experience.

The problem of knowledge acquisition proved to be particularly challenging. Extracting and formalizing expert knowledge was a time-consuming and expensive process. Domain experts often found it difficult to articulate their tacit knowledge—the intuitive, often implicit understanding that guides their decision-making—in a structured, formal way. The knowledge acquisition bottleneck became a major impediment to the wider adoption of expert systems.

Furthermore, the reliance on handcrafted rules made expert systems difficult to maintain and update. As new knowledge emerged or existing rules became outdated, the entire knowledge base had to be revised, a laborious and error-prone task. This lack of adaptability and the difficulties in maintenance contributed to the limitations of expert systems.

The inherent difficulty in handling uncertainty and incomplete information also hampered the performance of expert systems. The rule-based approach struggled to cope with situations where information was ambiguous or missing. The lack of probabilistic reasoning mechanisms made it hard for these systems to account for uncertainty inherent in many real-world problems. This was a significant limitation, especially in domains like medical diagnosis, where uncertainty is pervasive.

Despite these limitations, the development of expert systems had a profound impact on the field of AI. They pushed forward research in knowledge representation, reasoning, and inference. The techniques and methodologies developed for building and deploying expert systems influenced subsequent developments in knowledge-based systems and AI in general. Expert systems highlighted the importance of incorporating domain-specific knowledge into AI systems, a lesson that remains relevant today.

The successes and failures of expert systems provided invaluable lessons, shaping the future trajectory of AI research and development. The limitations of these early systems paved the way for new approaches that addressed the inherent challenges of knowledge acquisition, uncertainty handling, and adaptability. The shift towards more flexible and data-driven approaches, exemplified by the resurgence of neural networks and the rise of machine learning, was partly a consequence of the shortcomings exposed by the symbolic AI paradigm.

The decline of expert systems in the late 1980s and early 1990s wasn't a sudden demise, but rather a gradual shift in focus within the AI community. The limitations of these systems, coupled with the increasing availability of computational power and the rise of data-driven approaches, led to a decline in investment and research. While expert systems found niche applications in specific domains, their dominance as a central paradigm in AI research faded.

Nevertheless, the fundamental principles of knowledge representation and reasoning developed during the era of expert systems continue to inform contemporary AI research, demonstrating the enduring legacy of this important chapter in the history of artificial intelligence. The shift towards data-driven approaches, while seemingly a departure from the symbolic paradigm, actually built upon some of its key concepts, integrating symbolic methods with statistical techniques to create more powerful and robust AI systems. This integration continues to be a key area of research and development in the ongoing evolution of artificial intelligence.

The Deep Learning Revolution Neural Networks and Big Data

The limitations of symbolic AI, particularly the brittleness of expert systems and the challenges of knowledge acquisition, created a fertile ground for a paradigm shift. This shift, fueled by advancements in computing power and the explosion of available data, led to the resurgence of neural networks and the rise of deep learning. While neural networks had been explored since the 1950s, their early iterations lacked the computational resources and data volume necessary to achieve significant breakthroughs. The seminal work of Frank Rosenblatt on the perceptron in the late 1950s, while groundbreaking, showcased the limitations of single-layer networks in solving complex problems, a vulnerability expertly exposed by Minsky and Papert's critique in the 1960s. This criticism, although insightful, prematurely dimmed the enthusiasm for neural networks, pushing the field towards the symbolic approach for several decades.

The revival of neural networks wasn't a sudden event but a gradual evolution. The late 20th and early 21st centuries witnessed a confluence of factors that made their resurgence possible. First and foremost was the dramatic increase in computing power. The development of faster processors, parallel processing techniques, and the advent of GPUs (Graphics Processing Units) provided the computational horsepower needed to train complex neural networks with millions or even billions of parameters. GPUs, initially designed for rendering graphics, proved surprisingly well-suited for the parallel computations required by neural network training, significantly accelerating the learning process. This computational revolution was crucial because training large neural networks is computationally intensive, requiring massive amounts of processing power and time.

Secondly, the explosion of data availability played a pivotal role. The digital revolution generated an unprecedented amount of data in diverse forms—text, images, audio, video, sensor readings, and more. This massive dataset provided the "fuel" for training sophisticated neural networks. Deep learning models, with their numerous parameters, thrive on large datasets, improving their performance as the amount of training data increases. The availability of this data, coupled with efficient data storage and retrieval systems, created an environment ripe for the development of powerful deep learning models. The internet, social media, and various sensor technologies contributed to this deluge of data, offering a rich source of information for training neural networks across a wide range of applications. The rise of cloud computing further facilitated access to this data, allowing researchers and developers to leverage vast computational resources and datasets without needing expensive on-premise infrastructure.

Thirdly, algorithmic advancements played a significant role. Researchers developed innovative training algorithms, such as backpropagation, that made it possible to effectively train deep neural networks. Backpropagation is a crucial algorithm that efficiently calculates the gradient of the loss function, providing a way to adjust the network's weights to minimize errors during training. Furthermore, refinements in network architectures, including the development of convolutional neural networks (CNNs) for image processing and recurrent neural networks (RNNs) for sequential data, expanded the capabilities of neural networks.

The invention of deep learning frameworks like TensorFlow and PyTorch further democratized the application of deep learning, providing user-friendly tools and libraries that simplified the process of developing and deploying neural networks. These frameworks have been instrumental in reducing the technical barriers to entry for researchers and developers, fostering a collaborative and rapidly evolving ecosystem of deep learning tools and resources.

The combination of increased computational power, abundant data, and improved algorithms resulted in a series of breakthroughs in deep learning. Image recognition, once a formidable challenge for AI systems, experienced dramatic improvements with the advent of deep CNNs. These networks, inspired by the visual cortex of the brain, excelled at extracting features from images, achieving superhuman performance in various image classification tasks. Similarly, deep learning revolutionized natural language processing (NLP), enabling significant advances in machine translation, text summarization, and sentiment analysis. Recurrent neural networks, particularly Long Short-Term Memory (LSTM) networks, proved adept at processing sequential data, capturing long-range dependencies in text and speech.

These breakthroughs led to a wide range of practical applications across diverse fields. In healthcare, deep learning models are used for medical image analysis, disease diagnosis, and drug discovery. In finance, they're used for fraud detection, risk assessment, and algorithmic trading. In autonomous vehicles, deep learning plays a vital role in object recognition, path planning, and decision-making. In manufacturing, it enables predictive maintenance, quality control, and process optimization. These are just a few examples of the many applications where deep learning has had a transformative impact, showcasing its versatility and potential to solve complex real-world problems.

However, the success of deep learning also brought forth challenges. The "black box" nature of deep neural networks, the difficulty in interpreting their decisions, raised concerns about transparency and explainability. The massive computational resources required for training and deploying these models presented environmental considerations relating to energy consumption. Furthermore, biases in training data can lead to biased predictions, raising ethical concerns regarding fairness and accountability. The potential for misuse, for example, in the creation of sophisticated deepfakes or in perpetuating existing societal biases, demands careful consideration of the ethical implications of this technology. Addressing these issues, including the development of explainable AI (XAI) and techniques for mitigating bias, is crucial for ensuring responsible development and deployment of deep learning systems.

The deep learning revolution is an ongoing process. Research continues to push the boundaries of what's possible, with ongoing exploration of novel architectures, training algorithms, and applications. The quest for more efficient models, capable of running on less powerful hardware, is also a major focus. The development of techniques for enhancing transparency and explainability will be essential for ensuring trust and broader adoption of deep learning technologies. Furthermore, the intersection of deep learning with other areas of AI, such as reinforcement learning and knowledge representation, promises even more sophisticated and powerful AI systems in the future. The deep learning revolution is not just a technological advancement but a societal transformation, reshaping industries, economies, and even the way we interact with technology itself. Understanding its capabilities, limitations, and implications is crucial for navigating this transformative era and ensuring a future where AI benefits all of humanity.

AI Today A Landscape of Applications and Technologies

The dramatic breakthroughs in deep learning, detailed in the previous section, have propelled artificial intelligence into a new era of unprecedented capabilities and widespread adoption. AI is no longer confined to the realm of research laboratories; it's actively reshaping industries, influencing our daily lives, and prompting crucial societal discussions about its ethical implications. This section delves into the current landscape of AI applications and technologies, exploring the diverse ways AI is being deployed and the key technological advancements driving this transformation.

One of the most visible and impactful areas of AI application is natural language processing (NLP). NLP empowers computers to understand, interpret, and generate human language. This has led to remarkable advancements in several areas, including machine translation. Services like Google Translate, powered by sophisticated neural machine translation models, have significantly improved the accuracy and fluency of translations between numerous languages, breaking down communication barriers across cultures and facilitating global interactions. Beyond translation, NLP fuels chatbots and virtual assistants like Siri, Alexa, and Google Assistant, which are becoming increasingly sophisticated in understanding and responding to complex user requests. These virtual assistants are not just simple query processors; they are learning to anticipate needs, personalize responses, and even engage in more nuanced conversations. The progress in NLP is also evident in sentiment analysis, which allows businesses to gauge customer opinions from social media posts, reviews, and other textual data, informing crucial business decisions. Similarly, NLP powers advanced text summarization tools, capable of condensing lengthy documents into concise and informative summaries, boosting productivity in various sectors like research, journalism, and legal proceedings. The continued advancements in NLP are driven by transformer-based models like BERT and GPT-3, which demonstrate remarkable abilities in understanding context, generating coherent text, and even engaging in creative writing tasks.

Computer vision, another crucial area of AI, empowers computers to "see" and interpret images and videos. This technology has revolutionized image recognition, enabling applications like facial recognition in security systems and smartphones, automated image tagging on social media platforms, and medical image analysis for disease detection. Self-driving cars heavily rely on computer vision to navigate roads, detect pedestrians and obstacles, and make crucial driving decisions. Object detection, a key component of computer vision, allows systems to identify and locate specific objects within an image or video, enabling applications like quality control in manufacturing, retail inventory management, and agricultural monitoring. The advancements in computer vision are largely fueled by convolutional neural networks (CNNs), which excel at extracting meaningful features from visual data, driving improvements in accuracy and efficiency. The continued development of more robust and efficient CNN architectures, along with the availability of massive labeled datasets, is propelling further advancements in this field.

Robotics is another area undergoing a significant transformation due to AI. While robots have been used in industrial settings for decades, the integration of AI is empowering robots with greater autonomy, adaptability, and dexterity. AI-powered robots are increasingly capable of performing complex tasks in unstructured environments, making them suitable for diverse applications ranging from warehouse automation and surgery to exploration and disaster relief. AI algorithms enable robots to learn from their experiences, adapt to changing conditions, and improve their performance over time, moving beyond pre-programmed instructions to a more dynamic and intelligent behavior.

Reinforcement learning, a type of machine learning where robots learn through trial and error, is proving to be particularly effective in training robots to perform intricate and nuanced tasks, such as manipulating delicate objects or navigating complex terrains. The advancements in robotics are not limited to industrial applications; they are extending into personal robotics, with the emergence of more sophisticated household robots capable of assisting with daily tasks.

Beyond these core areas, AI is also making significant strides in other domains. In healthcare, AI is being used for drug discovery, personalized medicine, and disease prediction. Machine learning algorithms can analyze vast datasets of patient information to identify risk factors for various diseases, enabling proactive interventions. AI is also being employed in financial services for fraud detection, risk management, and algorithmic trading, enhancing efficiency and reducing risk. In agriculture, AI-powered systems can optimize irrigation, monitor crop health, and predict yields, leading to improved efficiency and sustainability. The applications of AI are truly ubiquitous, impacting nearly every aspect of modern life.

The technologies powering this AI revolution are constantly evolving. Deep learning, as discussed earlier, remains a cornerstone, driving advancements in NLP, computer vision, and robotics. However, other key technologies are also contributing significantly. Reinforcement learning, with its focus on training agents to make optimal decisions in dynamic environments, is proving invaluable in robotics and game playing. Generative models, capable of creating new content such as images, text, and music, are pushing the boundaries of creativity and design. Explainable AI (XAI) is gaining traction, aiming to improve the transparency and interpretability of AI models, addressing concerns about the "black box" nature of deep learning. Federated learning, which allows models to be trained on decentralized data sources without directly sharing the data itself, is addressing privacy concerns in collaborative AI development.

The landscape of AI applications and technologies is dynamic and rapidly evolving. New breakthroughs are constantly emerging, leading to innovative applications and expanding the possibilities of what AI can achieve. The continued convergence of these technologies, coupled with the exponential growth of data and computing power, promises even more remarkable advancements in the years to come. Understanding this landscape is crucial for navigating the challenges and opportunities presented by this transformative technology. The ethical implications of AI, particularly concerning bias, transparency, and accountability, will require careful consideration and proactive measures to ensure that this powerful technology is used responsibly and benefits all of humanity. The future of AI is not predetermined; it will be shaped by the choices we make today, balancing its potential benefits with the need for responsible innovation and ethical deployment.

Supervised Learning Training Models with Labeled Data

Supervised learning stands as a cornerstone of machine learning, a paradigm where algorithms learn to map inputs to outputs based on a labeled dataset. This means the data used for training explicitly provides both the input features and the corresponding correct output, allowing the algorithm to learn the underlying relationships and make predictions on new, unseen data. This contrasts with unsupervised learning, where the algorithm explores the data without pre-defined labels, and reinforcement learning, where an agent learns through trial and error by interacting with an environment. The essence of supervised learning lies in its ability to generalize from the training data to accurately predict outcomes for data it hasn't encountered before.

One of the simplest yet widely used supervised learning algorithms is linear regression. This algorithm models the relationship between a dependent variable and one or more independent variables by fitting a linear equation to the data. The goal is to find the line (or hyperplane in higher dimensions) that best fits the data points, minimizing the difference between the predicted and actual values. This difference is typically measured using a cost function, such as mean squared error (MSE), which calculates the average squared difference between predicted and actual values. Linear regression is particularly useful for predicting continuous values, such as house prices based on size and location, or stock prices based on various market indicators. The simplicity of linear regression allows for easy interpretation, as the coefficients of the linear equation directly reflect the impact of each independent variable on the dependent variable. However, its simplicity also limits its applicability to situations where the relationship between variables is truly linear; non-linear relationships require more sophisticated models.

Moving beyond linear relationships, logistic regression is a powerful algorithm used for binary classification problems. Instead of predicting a continuous value, logistic regression predicts the probability of an instance belonging to a particular class. It uses a sigmoid function to transform the linear combination of input features into a probability score between 0 and 1. A threshold is then applied to classify the instance into one of the two classes. For instance, logistic regression can be used to predict whether a customer will click on an advertisement based on their demographic information and browsing history, or whether an email is spam or not spam based on its content and sender information. The effectiveness of logistic regression lies in its ability to handle probabilistic outcomes and its relative ease of implementation and interpretation. However, like linear regression, it assumes a linear relationship between the input features and the log-odds of the output, limiting its accuracy in scenarios with complex, non-linear relationships.

Support Vector Machines (SVMs) offer a more robust approach to classification and regression problems, particularly in high-dimensional spaces. SVMs aim to find the optimal hyperplane that maximizes the margin between different classes. The margin represents the distance between the hyperplane and the nearest data points of each class, also known as support vectors. By maximizing this margin, SVMs aim to create a decision boundary that is as far as possible from the data points, improving generalization and reducing the risk of overfitting. SVMs can handle both linear and non-linear relationships through the use of kernel functions, which map the data into a higher-dimensional space where a linear separation might be possible. Different kernel functions, such as polynomial or radial basis function (RBF) kernels, offer flexibility in handling various types of data and relationships.

SVMs are known for their strong generalization performance and their ability to handle high-dimensional data effectively. However, they can be computationally expensive for very large datasets, and the choice of the appropriate kernel function can significantly impact performance.

Decision trees are another popular supervised learning algorithm that offers a visually intuitive and easy-to-interpret approach to classification and regression. A decision tree builds a tree-like structure where each internal node represents a test on an attribute, each branch represents the outcome of the test, and each leaf node represents a class label or a continuous value. The algorithm recursively partitions the data based on the attribute that best separates the classes or minimizes the prediction error. Decision trees are effective in handling both categorical and numerical data, and they are relatively easy to interpret because the decision-making process is clearly represented by the tree structure.

However, decision trees are prone to overfitting, especially when the tree becomes too deep and complex. Techniques like pruning, which removes unnecessary branches, are commonly used to mitigate overfitting. Ensemble methods, such as random forests and gradient boosting machines, combine multiple decision trees to improve predictive accuracy and robustness.

Ensemble methods represent a powerful approach in supervised learning that leverages the collective wisdom of multiple base learners, such as decision trees. Random forests, for example, create a large number of decision trees, each trained on a random subset of the data and a random subset of features. The final prediction is made by aggregating the predictions of all the trees, typically through voting for classification or averaging for regression. This approach reduces overfitting and improves the robustness and accuracy of the model compared to using a single decision tree.

Gradient boosting machines (GBMs) take a different approach, sequentially building trees where each subsequent tree corrects the errors made by the previous trees. GBMs are known for their high predictive accuracy and their ability to handle complex relationships in data. However, both random forests and GBMs can be computationally intensive, particularly for large datasets.

The choice of the appropriate supervised learning algorithm depends on several factors, including the type of problem (classification or regression), the size and characteristics of the data, the desired level of interpretability, and the computational resources available. Linear and logistic regression are suitable for simpler problems with linear relationships, while SVMs offer a more robust approach for higher-dimensional data and non-linear relationships. Decision trees are appealing for their interpretability, while ensemble methods like random forests and GBMs generally offer superior predictive accuracy but at the cost of increased computational complexity. Regardless of the algorithm chosen, careful consideration of data preprocessing, model evaluation, and hyperparameter tuning is crucial for achieving optimal performance and ensuring the model generalizes well to unseen data. The process of selecting and fine-tuning the model often involves iterative experimentation, comparing the performance of different algorithms and evaluating their predictions using appropriate metrics such as accuracy, precision, recall, F1-score for classification problems, and MSE or RMSE for regression problems.

Furthermore, techniques like cross-validation are employed to assess the model's generalization ability and prevent overfitting to the training data.

Beyond the core algorithms, several advanced techniques enhance the effectiveness of supervised learning. Regularization, for example, adds a penalty term to the cost function to prevent overfitting by discouraging overly complex models. Different regularization techniques exist, such as L1 and L2 regularization, each with its own properties and effects on model complexity and performance. Feature scaling and selection are also critical preprocessing steps that can significantly improve model performance. Feature scaling transforms the features to have similar scales, preventing features with larger values from dominating the model, while feature selection identifies the most relevant features, reducing model complexity and improving generalization. These advanced techniques, along with careful consideration of model architecture and hyperparameters, are crucial for building effective and robust supervised learning models. The ongoing research in supervised learning continues to push the boundaries of what's possible, with new algorithms and techniques constantly emerging to improve accuracy, efficiency, and robustness in handling increasingly complex datasets and real-world problems. The future of supervised learning is likely to involve even more sophisticated models, capable of handling massive datasets, extracting intricate patterns, and providing even more accurate and reliable predictions. The development of explainable AI (XAI) techniques will also play a crucial role, increasing transparency and trust in the predictions made by these complex models.

Unsupervised Learning Discovering Patterns in Unlabeled Data

Unsupervised learning represents a significant departure from its supervised counterpart. Instead of relying on pre-labeled data to guide the learning process, unsupervised learning algorithms delve into raw, unlabeled datasets to uncover hidden patterns, structures, and relationships. This exploration allows for the discovery of insights that might be missed by human analysts or overlooked in supervised approaches where the focus is solely on predefined target variables. The power of unsupervised learning lies in its ability to reveal unexpected correlations, identify anomalies, and generate new hypotheses based purely on the inherent characteristics of the data. This makes it particularly valuable in exploratory data analysis and tasks where labeled data is scarce or expensive to obtain.

One of the most fundamental tasks in unsupervised learning is clustering, where the goal is to group similar data points together. K-means clustering, a widely used algorithm, exemplifies this approach. The algorithm begins by randomly selecting 'k' centroids, which represent the initial centers of the clusters. Each data point is then assigned to the closest centroid based on a distance metric, typically Euclidean distance. The centroids are then recalculated as the mean of all data points assigned to each cluster. This iterative process of assignment and centroid recalculation continues until the centroids converge or a predefined number of iterations is reached. The outcome is a partitioning of the data into 'k' clusters, with each cluster containing data points that are relatively close to each other and far from data points in other clusters. The choice of 'k' significantly influences the results, often requiring experimentation and evaluation techniques like silhouette analysis or the elbow method to determine the optimal number of clusters for a given dataset. For instance, k-means can be applied to customer segmentation, grouping customers with similar purchasing behaviors or demographics. In image processing, k-means can be used for image compression by clustering similar pixels, representing them with the centroid of the cluster. The effectiveness of k-means lies in its relative simplicity and computational efficiency, but it's important to note that its performance can be sensitive to the initial choice of centroids and the presence of outliers, which can significantly influence the cluster formations.

Hierarchical clustering offers a different perspective on clustering, building a hierarchy of clusters instead of a flat partitioning. There are two main approaches to hierarchical clustering: agglomerative and divisive. Agglomerative clustering, also known as bottom-up clustering, starts with each data point as a separate cluster and iteratively merges the closest clusters until a single cluster remains. The distance between clusters is typically measured using linkage criteria such as single linkage (shortest distance between points in two clusters), complete linkage (longest distance), or average linkage (average distance between all pairs of points). This creates a dendrogram, a tree-like diagram visualizing the hierarchical relationship between clusters at different levels of merging. Divisive clustering, or top-down clustering, takes the opposite approach, starting with a single cluster containing all data points and recursively splitting the clusters until each data point forms its own cluster. Hierarchical clustering is particularly useful for visualizing the relationships between clusters and identifying the hierarchical structure within the data, providing a richer understanding than the flat partitioning of k-means. The choice between agglomerative and divisive methods depends on the specific dataset and the desired level of granularity in the hierarchical structure. For example, hierarchical clustering can be useful for analyzing phylogenetic relationships in biology, organizing documents based on topic similarity, or identifying different stages in a complex process.

Dimensionality reduction is another crucial aspect of unsupervised learning, focusing on reducing the number of variables in a dataset while retaining as much relevant information as possible. This is particularly important when dealing with high-dimensional data, where the sheer number of variables can hinder computational efficiency and introduce noise. Principal Component Analysis (PCA) is a widely used technique for dimensionality reduction. PCA identifies the principal components, which are orthogonal linear combinations of the original variables that capture the most variance in the data. The first principal component captures the maximum variance, the second principal component captures the maximum remaining variance orthogonal to the first, and so on. By projecting the data onto a lower-dimensional subspace spanned by the top 'k' principal components, we can reduce the dimensionality while retaining a significant portion of the original variance. This technique is useful for visualizing high-dimensional data, reducing noise in datasets, and improving the performance of machine learning algorithms that are sensitive to the curse of dimensionality.

For instance, PCA can be used in image recognition to reduce the number of features extracted from images while maintaining important discriminatory information. In financial modeling, it can be used to reduce the dimensionality of financial time series data to better understand market movements and construct efficient portfolios. It's crucial to carefully select the number of principal components to retain, balancing the reduction in dimensionality with the preservation of essential information.

Beyond k-means, hierarchical clustering, and PCA, the field of unsupervised learning encompasses a broad range of techniques addressing diverse problems. Self-organizing maps (SOMs) create a low-dimensional representation of high-dimensional data, preserving topological relationships. Autoencoders, a type of neural network, learn compressed representations of data, useful for denoising and feature extraction. Anomaly detection techniques, such as isolation forests and one-class SVMs, aim to identify data points that deviate significantly from the norm, crucial in fraud detection and system monitoring. Generative models, like generative adversarial networks (GANs) and variational autoencoders (VAEs), learn the underlying probability distribution of the data, allowing them to generate new data points similar to the training data. These models have found applications in image generation, drug discovery, and various other creative and scientific endeavors.

The selection of the most appropriate unsupervised learning technique depends on the specific goals of the analysis and the characteristics of the data. Clustering methods are best suited for grouping similar data points, dimensionality reduction techniques for simplifying high-dimensional data, and anomaly detection methods for identifying outliers. Generative models excel at generating new data points similar to the training data. The iterative nature of unsupervised learning often involves experimentation with different techniques and parameters to determine the best approach for uncovering hidden patterns and insights within the data. Visualizations and evaluation metrics play crucial roles in understanding the results and interpreting the discovered structures. The continuous evolution of unsupervised learning algorithms and the ever-increasing availability of computational power promise to unlock even deeper insights from data in the years to come, furthering our understanding of complex systems and phenomena. The integration of unsupervised learning with other machine learning paradigms, such as supervised and reinforcement learning, is also expected to lead to powerful hybrid approaches capable of addressing complex real-world problems with unprecedented accuracy and efficiency. The future of unsupervised learning is bright, promising transformative advancements across diverse fields.

Reinforcement Learning Learning Through Trial and Error

Reinforcement learning represents a paradigm shift from the supervised and unsupervised learning approaches we've explored.

Instead of learning from labeled data or uncovering patterns in unlabeled data, reinforcement learning focuses on training an agent to make optimal decisions within a dynamic environment. The core principle is simple yet powerful: an agent interacts with its environment, takes actions, and receives rewards or penalties based on the consequences of those actions. Through trial and error, the agent learns a policy – a strategy for selecting actions – that maximizes its cumulative reward over time.

This learning process is fundamentally different from supervised learning, where the agent is explicitly told the correct actions for each situation. In reinforcement learning, the agent must discover the optimal actions through exploration and exploitation.

Exploration involves trying out different actions to learn about the environment's dynamics, while exploitation involves using the knowledge gained to select the actions that are expected to yield the highest rewards. The balance between exploration and exploitation is a critical aspect of reinforcement learning, as too much exploration can lead to suboptimal performance, while too much exploitation can prevent the agent from discovering better strategies.

The mathematical framework for reinforcement learning is often based on Markov Decision Processes (MDPs). An MDP defines a system where an agent interacts with an environment through a sequence of states, actions, and rewards. The state represents the current situation, the action is the agent's choice, and the reward is the feedback received from the environment. The key assumption of an MDP is the Markov property, which states that the future state depends only on the current state and action, not on the past history. This simplifies the problem considerably, allowing for the development of efficient algorithms.

One of the most widely used algorithms in reinforcement learning is Q-learning. Q-learning is a model-free algorithm, meaning it doesn't require a model of the environment's dynamics. It learns a Q-function, which estimates the expected cumulative reward for taking a particular action in a particular state. The Q-function is updated iteratively based on the rewards received and the estimated Q-values of subsequent states. The update rule is based on the Bellman equation, a fundamental equation in dynamic programming that expresses the optimal Q-value in terms of the immediate reward and the optimal Q-values of future states.

The process of Q-learning involves repeatedly interacting with the environment, observing the current state, selecting an action (often using an epsilon-greedy strategy that balances exploration and exploitation), receiving a reward, and updating the Q-function. This iterative process continues until the Q-function converges to an optimal solution, at which point the agent can select actions that maximize its expected cumulative reward. The convergence of Q-learning is guaranteed under certain conditions, but in practice, it can be slow, especially in large state spaces.

The combination of reinforcement learning and deep learning, known as deep reinforcement learning (DRL), has revolutionized the field. Deep neural networks provide a powerful way to approximate the Q-function, even in very high-dimensional state spaces. This allows DRL agents to learn complex policies in challenging environments, such as playing games, controlling robots, and managing complex systems. Deep Q-Networks (DQNs), for example, use a convolutional neural network to represent the Q-function, allowing them to handle visual inputs directly. Other DRL algorithms, such as actor-critic methods, learn both a policy (actor) and a value function (critic), allowing for more efficient and stable learning.

DRL has achieved remarkable success in various domains. In the gaming world, AlphaGo, developed by DeepMind, defeated the world champion Go player, demonstrating the potential of DRL to master complex games with vast state spaces. Other notable examples include AlphaStar, which mastered StarCraft II, and OpenAI Five, which defeated professional Dota 2 players. These achievements highlight the power of DRL to learn highly sophisticated strategies and outperform human experts in challenging tasks.

Beyond games, DRL has found applications in robotics, enabling robots to learn complex motor skills, navigate challenging environments, and interact with humans in more natural ways. For instance, DRL has been used to train robots to perform tasks such as grasping objects, assembling products, and walking on uneven terrain. In healthcare, DRL is being explored for personalized treatment planning, drug discovery, and robotic surgery. In finance, DRL can be used for algorithmic trading, risk management, and fraud detection.

The application of DRL to real-world problems requires careful consideration of several factors. The design of the reward function is crucial, as it dictates the agent's learning goals. A poorly designed reward function can lead to unexpected and undesirable behavior, a phenomenon known as reward hacking. The choice of the neural network architecture and the training parameters also significantly influence the agent's performance. Moreover, the computational cost of training DRL agents can be substantial, requiring powerful hardware and efficient algorithms.

Despite these challenges, the field of reinforcement learning is rapidly evolving, with new algorithms and techniques continuously being developed. The integration of reinforcement learning with other machine learning paradigms, such as supervised and unsupervised learning, is also expected to lead to powerful hybrid approaches capable of addressing complex real-world problems. The potential applications of reinforcement learning are vast, ranging from autonomous vehicles and personalized medicine to climate change mitigation and sustainable resource management. As the field matures and computational resources improve, we can expect to see even more impressive achievements in the years to come, transforming various aspects of our lives. The future of reinforcement learning is indeed bright, brimming with possibilities for addressing some of humanity's most pressing challenges and unlocking new frontiers of innovation. The ongoing research into improving the efficiency, robustness, and scalability of reinforcement learning algorithms promises to further expand its reach and impact.

One area of active research focuses on developing more robust and interpretable reinforcement learning models. Current DRL models often lack transparency, making it difficult to understand why they make certain decisions. This lack of interpretability limits their applicability in critical domains such as healthcare and finance, where understanding the reasoning behind a decision is crucial. Researchers are exploring methods to improve the interpretability of DRL models, making them more trustworthy and easier to deploy in real-world applications.

Another important area of research is developing more sample-efficient reinforcement learning algorithms. Training DRL agents often requires a massive amount of data, which can be time-consuming and expensive. Researchers are investigating ways to reduce the amount of data required to train effective agents, making DRL more accessible and applicable to a wider range of problems. This includes exploring techniques like transfer learning, where knowledge gained in one environment is transferred to a new environment, and curriculum learning, where the agent is trained on progressively more difficult tasks.

Furthermore, the development of more efficient algorithms for handling continuous action spaces is crucial. Many real-world problems involve continuous actions, such as controlling the steering wheel of a car or adjusting the temperature of a chemical process. Traditional Q-learning approaches struggle with continuous action spaces, and researchers are exploring new techniques such as actor-critic methods with continuous action spaces, to address this challenge. These advancements will pave the way for broader applications of reinforcement learning in robotics, control systems, and other domains where continuous control is essential.

The ethical considerations of reinforcement learning are also gaining increasing attention. As DRL agents become more powerful and capable of making decisions with significant consequences, it's crucial to ensure that they are aligned with human values and do not cause harm. Research into fairness, accountability, transparency, and ethics in AI (FATE) is essential to ensure responsible development and deployment of reinforcement learning systems. This involves designing algorithms that are robust to bias, transparent in their decision-making processes, and accountable for their actions. The interplay between technological advancements and ethical considerations will shape the future trajectory of reinforcement learning, ensuring that its immense potential is harnessed for the benefit of humanity. The responsible development and deployment of this powerful technology will be key to its successful integration into our society.

Deep Learning Architectures Convolutional and Recurrent Networks

Deep learning, a subfield of machine learning, has revolutionized numerous applications through its powerful architectures. Two prominent architectures stand out: Convolutional Neural Networks (CNNs) and Recurrent Neural Networks (RNNs). These networks leverage the power of deep learning to excel in processing distinct types of data, leading to breakthroughs in diverse fields.

CNNs are specifically designed for processing grid-like data, primarily images and videos. Their unique strength lies in their ability to automatically learn hierarchical features from raw input data. Unlike traditional image processing techniques that rely on handcrafted features, CNNs employ convolutional layers that extract features directly from the pixels. These layers use filters, or kernels, which are small matrices of weights that slide across the input image, performing element-wise multiplication and summation. This process, called convolution, creates a feature map highlighting the presence of specific patterns in the input.

The beauty of CNNs is their ability to detect various features at different scales. Early convolutional layers identify simple features like edges and corners, while subsequent layers combine these simple features to create more complex features, such as shapes and textures. This hierarchical feature extraction allows CNNs to learn increasingly abstract representations of the input image, ultimately leading to accurate classification or object detection. Pooling layers further reduce the dimensionality of the feature maps, making the network more robust to variations in the input and reducing computational cost. Finally, fully connected layers map the extracted features to the output layer, producing the final classification or detection results.

The success of CNNs is evident in numerous real-world applications. In medical imaging, CNNs are used for disease detection, assisting radiologists in identifying cancerous tumors, diagnosing heart conditions, and analyzing brain scans. Self-driving cars heavily rely on CNNs for object recognition, enabling them to detect pedestrians, vehicles, and traffic signs. In facial recognition systems, CNNs accurately identify individuals, playing a crucial role in security and access control. Furthermore, CNNs power image search engines, helping users find relevant images based on visual content. The development of increasingly sophisticated CNN architectures, including those incorporating residual connections and attention mechanisms, continues to drive progress in image recognition and related tasks. Efficient architectures like MobileNet and ShuffleNet have also been developed to address the computational constraints associated with deploying CNNs on resource-limited devices, enabling their integration into mobile applications and edge devices.

Recurrent Neural Networks (RNNs), on the other hand, excel at processing sequential data, such as text, time series, and speech. Unlike feedforward neural networks, where information flows in one direction, RNNs incorporate loops, allowing information to persist across time steps. This ability to retain past information is crucial for understanding context in sequential data. At each time step, an RNN receives an input, combines it with its internal state (memory), and updates its state accordingly. The updated state influences the output at that time step, capturing dependencies between elements in the sequence.

The most basic type of RNN is the Elman network, which has a simple recurrent connection from the hidden layer to itself. However, the vanishing gradient problem, where gradients during backpropagation become exponentially small, limits the ability of basic RNNs to learn long-range dependencies in sequences. This limitation led to the development of more sophisticated RNN architectures, such as Long Short-Term Memory (LSTM) and Gated Recurrent Units (GRUs).

LSTM networks address the vanishing gradient problem by introducing a sophisticated mechanism involving gates that control the flow of information within the network. These gates, namely the input, forget, and output gates, regulate the updates to the cell state, a crucial memory component of the LSTM unit. This intricate mechanism enables LSTMs to effectively learn long-range dependencies, making them particularly powerful for tasks involving long sequences.

GRUs are a more simplified version of LSTMs, combining the forget and input gates into a single update gate. This simplification leads to a more computationally efficient network while still retaining the ability to capture long-range dependencies. Both LSTMs and GRUs have found widespread applications in natural language processing (NLP).

In NLP, RNNs, particularly LSTMs and GRUs, are essential for tasks such as machine translation, text summarization, sentiment analysis, and question answering. Machine translation involves translating text from one language to another, leveraging RNNs to capture the context and nuances of the source language. Text summarization uses RNNs to extract the most important information from a long text, generating a concise summary.

Sentiment analysis uses RNNs to determine the emotional tone of a text, identifying whether it's positive, negative, or neutral. And question answering utilizes RNNs to understand the context of a question and provide accurate answers based on given information.

Beyond NLP, RNNs are widely used in time series analysis for tasks such as stock price prediction, weather forecasting, and anomaly detection. In stock price prediction, RNNs analyze historical stock prices to predict future price movements. In weather forecasting, RNNs model atmospheric conditions to predict future weather patterns. And in anomaly detection, RNNs identify unusual patterns in time series data, flagging potential issues or outliers.

The advancements in RNN architectures and training techniques continue to push the boundaries of their capabilities. Attention mechanisms, which allow the network to focus on specific parts of the input sequence, further enhance the performance of RNNs. The development of transformers, which leverage attention mechanisms without recurrent connections, has also revolutionized NLP, achieving state-of-the-art results in various tasks. Transformers are particularly well-suited for parallel processing, allowing for faster training and inference compared to traditional RNNs.

The choice between CNNs and RNNs depends on the nature of the data being processed. For grid-like data such as images and videos, CNNs are the preferred architecture, while for sequential data such as text and time series, RNNs (or transformers) are more appropriate. Hybrid architectures, combining CNNs and RNNs, are also employed for tasks involving both spatial and temporal information, such as video analysis and action recognition.

Furthermore, the increasing computational power and the availability of large datasets have fueled the development of ever more complex and capable deep learning models. This includes the emergence of hybrid models that combine the strengths of both CNNs and RNNs, leading to even more powerful and versatile systems. For instance, models used in video analysis often integrate CNNs to extract spatial features from individual frames and RNNs to model the temporal evolution of these features across the video sequence. These hybrid approaches have yielded impressive results in tasks such as action recognition, video captioning, and video question answering.

The future of deep learning architectures is likely to involve even greater sophistication and specialization. We can anticipate the development of more efficient and resource-friendly architectures, particularly important for deploying deep learning models on mobile and embedded devices. Research into improved training techniques and the exploration of novel architectural designs will continue to push the boundaries of what's possible, leading to advancements across a wide range of applications. The ongoing integration of deep learning with other areas of artificial intelligence, such as reinforcement learning and symbolic reasoning, will further broaden the scope and impact of these powerful tools. The evolution of deep learning is a continuous process of innovation and refinement, promising to shape the future of technology in profound ways. This continuous evolution makes deep learning a constantly exciting and dynamic field to follow. The ongoing exploration of novel architectures and training techniques promises to deliver even more impressive results and applications in the years to come.

Evaluating and Improving Machine Learning Models

Evaluating and improving the performance of a machine learning model is crucial for ensuring its effectiveness and reliability in real-world applications. The process isn't simply about achieving high accuracy; it's about understanding the nuances of model performance and identifying areas for improvement. This involves a multifaceted approach, encompassing rigorous evaluation using appropriate metrics and strategic techniques to enhance the model's capabilities.

One of the fundamental steps in evaluating machine learning models is selecting the right performance metrics. The choice of metrics depends heavily on the specific problem being addressed.

For classification problems, common metrics include accuracy, precision, recall, and the F1-score. Accuracy, while seemingly straightforward, represents the overall correctness of the model's predictions. It's calculated as the ratio of correctly classified instances to the total number of instances. However, accuracy can be misleading in scenarios with imbalanced datasets, where one class significantly outnumbers others. A model might achieve high accuracy by simply predicting the majority class, even if its performance on the minority classes is poor.

Precision, on the other hand, measures the proportion of correctly predicted positive instances out of all instances predicted as positive. It addresses the issue of false positives—instances incorrectly classified as positive. Recall, also known as sensitivity, quantifies the proportion of correctly predicted positive instances out of all actual positive instances. It focuses on the issue of false negatives—instances incorrectly classified as negative. The F1-score provides a balanced measure combining precision and recall, offering a single metric that considers both false positives and false negatives. It's particularly useful when dealing with imbalanced datasets or situations where minimizing both types of errors is crucial.

Beyond these primary metrics, other evaluation measures might be relevant depending on the context. For regression problems, common metrics include mean squared error (MSE), root mean squared error (RMSE), and R-squared. MSE calculates the average squared difference between the predicted and actual values, while RMSE is the square root of MSE, providing a measure in the same units as the target variable. R-squared, also known as the coefficient of determination, represents the proportion of variance in the target variable explained by the model. A higher R-squared value generally indicates a better fit.

The choice of evaluation metrics is crucial, and the best approach often involves using a combination of metrics to gain a comprehensive understanding of model performance. For instance, in medical diagnosis, high recall is often prioritized to minimize the risk of missing positive cases, even if it might lead to a slightly lower precision. Conversely, in spam detection, high precision might be preferred to reduce the number of false positives, even if it leads to a few more false negatives.

Once the appropriate evaluation metrics have been chosen, the next step is to utilize effective evaluation techniques. Cross-validation is a powerful technique for assessing model generalization performance. It involves splitting the dataset into multiple folds, training the model on some folds, and evaluating it on the remaining fold(s). This process is repeated multiple times, with different folds used for training and testing, providing a more robust estimate of the model's performance than a single train-test split. K-fold cross-validation, where the data is divided into k folds, is a widely used approach. Leave-one-out cross-validation (LOOCV), an extreme case of k-fold cross-validation where k equals the number of data points, is useful for small datasets but can be computationally expensive.

Another crucial aspect of model evaluation is handling overfitting and underfitting. Overfitting occurs when the model performs exceptionally well on the training data but poorly on unseen data. This indicates that the model has memorized the training data rather than learning generalizable patterns. Underfitting, on the other hand, occurs when the model performs poorly on both training and testing data, suggesting that it's too simple to capture the underlying patterns in the data. Techniques such as regularization (L1 and L2 regularization) can help mitigate overfitting by adding penalty terms to the model's loss function, discouraging excessively complex models. Early stopping, a technique where training is stopped before the model starts overfitting, is another effective approach.

Hyperparameter tuning is a critical step in improving model performance. Hyperparameters are parameters that control the learning process, such as the learning rate, the number of hidden layers in a neural network, or the regularization strength. Finding the optimal set of hyperparameters is often challenging and typically involves techniques like grid search, random search, or Bayesian optimization. Grid search exhaustively explores a predefined set of hyperparameter combinations, while random search randomly samples hyperparameter combinations. Bayesian optimization utilizes a probabilistic model to guide the search, efficiently identifying promising hyperparameter settings.

Feature engineering is another powerful tool for improving model performance. It involves creating new features from existing ones or selecting a subset of relevant features. Effective feature engineering can dramatically improve a model's ability to learn patterns in the data. Techniques like feature scaling (standardization or normalization) and dimensionality reduction (principal component analysis or linear discriminant analysis) are commonly used to preprocess features before feeding them into the model.

The iterative nature of model improvement is key. The process of evaluating a model, identifying weaknesses, and applying improvement techniques is often iterative. Careful monitoring of performance metrics across different stages of the process allows for data-driven decisions regarding model adjustments. Visualizations, such as learning curves, can help understand the learning process and identify potential issues.

In conclusion, the evaluation and improvement of machine learning models involve a range of techniques and considerations. Selecting appropriate evaluation metrics, employing robust evaluation methods like cross-validation, managing overfitting and underfitting, tuning hyperparameters, and performing feature engineering are all critical steps in building high-performing and reliable machine learning models. The iterative and data-driven nature of this process ensures continuous refinement and improvement, leading to models that are better equipped to tackle real-world challenges. The advancements in computational power and the development of sophisticated algorithms continue to push the boundaries of what's achievable, promising even more powerful and reliable machine learning models in the years to come. The interplay between theoretical advancements and practical applications drives continuous innovation in this rapidly evolving field. The field's dynamic nature necessitates a constant adaptation to new techniques and methodologies to stay ahead of the curve.

This ongoing evolution ensures that the application of machine learning continues to expand, impacting various facets of our lives in increasingly significant ways. The future of machine learning is likely to be shaped by a synergistic blend of theoretical breakthroughs, advancements in computing power, and the development of more efficient algorithms. The potential applications are vast and far-reaching, making the pursuit of improving machine learning models an ongoing and vital endeavor.

The Challenges of Understanding Human Language

The seemingly effortless way humans communicate belies the immense complexity of natural language. For machines, understanding human language is a Herculean task, far exceeding the challenges presented by structured data like numbers or images. The inherent ambiguity, context-dependency, and subtle nuances of human expression pose significant hurdles for even the most advanced natural language processing (NLP) systems.

One of the most fundamental challenges lies in the inherent ambiguity of language. Words, phrases, and even sentences can have multiple meanings depending on the context. Consider the sentence, "I saw the man with the telescope." This seemingly straightforward sentence is actually ambiguous. Did the speaker use the telescope to see the man, or did the man possess the telescope?

The sentence itself provides no clear answer. Humans effortlessly resolve this ambiguity based on their understanding of the world and the broader context of the conversation. However, an NLP system needs explicit rules or sophisticated contextual understanding to make the correct interpretation. This requires far more than simple keyword matching; it necessitates a deep understanding of semantics and pragmatics – the meaning of words and the implied meaning behind them.

Beyond lexical ambiguity, there's syntactic ambiguity where the grammatical structure of a sentence can lead to multiple interpretations. For instance, consider the sentence, "Visiting relatives can be a nuisance." Does this mean that the act of visiting relatives is bothersome, or that relatives who are visiting are a nuisance? The ambiguity stems from the grammatical structure, which allows for both interpretations. This illustrates the difficulty NLP systems face in parsing sentences correctly and deriving the intended meaning.

Context plays an equally vital role in understanding language. The same sentence can have vastly different meanings in different contexts. Consider the phrase "That's cool." In one context, it could express admiration for something stylish; in another, it could simply mean something is literally cold. The context, whether it's the surrounding text, the speaker's tone, or the overall situation, dictates the true meaning. Replicating this nuanced contextual understanding in NLP systems requires advanced techniques such as incorporating external knowledge bases, modeling conversational history, and using deep learning models that can capture complex relationships between words and their context.

Sarcasm, irony, and humor represent even greater challenges. These linguistic devices rely heavily on implied meaning and often contradict the literal interpretation of words. Understanding sarcasm, for example, necessitates recognizing the mismatch between the literal meaning of a statement and the speaker's intended meaning. This requires an NLP system to not only understand the literal meaning but also to infer the speaker's intent, which often involves recognizing emotional cues and situational context. Current NLP models struggle significantly with these nuanced aspects of language, frequently misinterpreting sarcasm or irony as literal statements.

The variability of human language adds another layer of complexity. People express themselves in diverse ways, employing different dialects, accents, slang, and writing styles. These variations can significantly affect the accuracy of NLP systems, which are often trained on standardized language corpora. A system trained on formal written English might struggle with informal spoken language containing colloquialisms or grammatical errors. Addressing this necessitates training NLP models on diverse datasets that represent the full range of human linguistic variation. This includes incorporating data from various dialects, social media conversations, and other sources that capture the diversity of human expression.

The challenges are further compounded by the evolution of language. New words and phrases constantly emerge, while the meanings of existing words can shift over time. Keeping NLP systems up-to-date with these changes is an ongoing challenge that requires continuous retraining and adaptation. The dynamic nature of language necessitates the development of robust methods for incorporating new data and adjusting the models accordingly.

Overcoming these challenges requires a multi-faceted approach. Significant progress has been made in recent years with the advent of deep learning models, especially transformer architectures. These models have shown remarkable abilities in tasks such as machine translation, text summarization, and question answering. However, limitations persist, particularly in handling nuanced linguistic phenomena like sarcasm and ambiguity.

One promising approach involves incorporating external knowledge bases into NLP systems. By connecting NLP models to large knowledge graphs or encyclopedias, we can provide them with access to factual information and world knowledge, which can help in resolving ambiguities and understanding context. This approach moves beyond simply analyzing the text itself to incorporating external information to enrich the understanding.

Another avenue of research focuses on developing more robust methods for handling context. This includes incorporating conversational history, modeling the speaker's intentions, and using sophisticated contextual embedding techniques that capture the relationship between words and their surrounding context. The development of more advanced models that can effectively integrate context will be crucial in improving the accuracy and robustness of NLP systems.

Furthermore, the development of more diverse and comprehensive training datasets is essential. This involves gathering data from a wider range of sources, including various dialects, social media conversations, and other informal communication channels. By training models on more diverse data, we can improve their ability to handle the variations in human language and reduce bias.

Ethical considerations are paramount in the development and deployment of NLP systems. Bias in training data can lead to biased outputs, perpetuating and amplifying existing societal inequalities. Careful attention must be paid to ensuring fairness and mitigating bias in both the data and the models themselves. This requires rigorous evaluation and ongoing monitoring to identify and address potential biases. Transparency in model development and deployment is also crucial to building trust and accountability.

The quest for truly understanding human language remains a significant challenge. While impressive progress has been achieved, the intricacies of human communication continue to push the boundaries of NLP capabilities. The ongoing research into more sophisticated models, improved training techniques, and the incorporation of external knowledge promises a future where machines can more effectively navigate the richness and complexity of human language, leading to a wide array of applications across various domains. From more accurate machine translation and improved chatbots to enhanced medical diagnosis tools and more efficient search engines, the potential benefits of overcoming these challenges are vast and far-reaching. The ongoing pursuit of this challenging goal represents one of the most exciting frontiers in artificial intelligence research.

Text Preprocessing and Feature Extraction

Before an NLP system can begin to understand the nuances of human language, the raw text data needs to be prepared. This preparatory stage, known as text preprocessing, is crucial for the success of any NLP application. It involves a series of transformations designed to clean, standardize, and structure the text, making it more suitable for analysis by algorithms. Think of it as preparing ingredients before cooking a meal – the better the preparation, the better the final result.

One of the first steps in text preprocessing is **tokenization** . This involves breaking down the text into individual units, or tokens. These tokens can be words, phrases, or even individual characters, depending on the specific application and the chosen tokenization method. Consider a sentence like, "The quick brown fox jumps over the lazy dog." A simple word-based tokenizer would produce the following tokens: ["The", "quick", "brown", "fox", "jumps", "over", "the", "lazy", "dog"]. However, more sophisticated tokenizers might handle punctuation differently, creating separate tokens for commas, periods, or other punctuation marks. The choice of tokenization method significantly impacts the subsequent analysis, affecting the representation of the text and the performance of the NLP model. Furthermore, handling contractions (like "don't" or "wouldn't") requires careful consideration, with some methods opting to split them into two tokens ("do" and "not") while others treat them as single units. This decision depends on the specific requirements of the NLP task. For example, sentiment analysis might benefit from treating "don't" as a single unit to capture the negative sentiment more effectively.

Following tokenization, **normalization** techniques are frequently employed. This process aims to reduce words to their base or root form, helping to eliminate redundancy and improve the efficiency of the NLP model. Two common normalization techniques are stemming and lemmatization. **Stemming** is a crude heuristic process that chops off the ends of words to obtain a stem, often producing non-existent words. For example, stemming "running" might yield "run," which is correct, but stemming "better" might give "bett," which is not a valid word. Despite this potential for inaccuracy, stemming is computationally efficient and works well in some applications, especially when speed is a priority.

Lemmatization , on the other hand, is a more sophisticated approach that uses morphological analysis to reduce words to their dictionary form, or lemma. This process considers the context and part-of-speech of the word, resulting in more accurate and meaningful reductions. For instance, lemmatizing "better" correctly yields "good," providing a far more semantically relevant representation. Lemmatization, while more accurate, is computationally more expensive than stemming. The choice between stemming and lemmatization depends on the specific application and the trade-off between accuracy and efficiency.

Another important preprocessing step is **stop word removal** . Stop words are common words like "the," "a," "an," "is," and "are," which often carry little semantic meaning in the context of many NLP tasks. Removing these words can reduce the dimensionality of the data, improve efficiency, and focus the analysis on more meaningful terms. However, the decision to remove stop words should be carefully considered, as they can sometimes contribute to the overall context, particularly in sentiment analysis or topic modeling. For example, the frequency of "not" can significantly impact sentiment. Therefore, removing stop words should be tailored to the specific needs of the task. Furthermore, the set of stop words may vary depending on the language and the specific application.

After cleaning and normalizing the text, the next crucial step is **feature extraction** . This process converts the textual data into numerical representations that can be understood and processed by machine learning algorithms. This is often necessary because most machine learning algorithms are not designed to work directly with raw text. Several techniques exist for feature extraction, each with its own strengths and weaknesses.

One of the simplest and most commonly used techniques is the **Term Frequency-Inverse Document Frequency (TF-IDF)** . TF-IDF measures the importance of a word in a document relative to a corpus of documents. The term frequency (TF) represents how frequently a word appears in a given document, while the inverse document frequency (IDF) reflects the rarity of that word across the entire corpus. Words that appear frequently in a specific document but infrequently across the whole corpus are assigned high TF-IDF scores, indicating their importance in characterizing that document. TF-IDF is computationally efficient and widely applicable but can be sensitive to word order and doesn't capture semantic relationships between words.

A more sophisticated approach involves using **word embeddings**, which represent words as dense vectors in a high-dimensional space. These vectors capture semantic relationships between words, meaning that words with similar meanings are closer together in this vector space. Popular word embedding techniques include Word2Vec, GloVe, and FastText. Word2Vec, for example, learns word embeddings by predicting a word based on its surrounding context. These techniques capture contextual information, allowing for more nuanced understanding of text compared to TF-IDF. Word embeddings can capture synonyms, analogies, and other semantic relationships between words, making them powerful features for various NLP tasks like text classification, sentiment analysis, and machine translation. For instance, the vectors for "king" and "queen" will be closer together in this space than the vectors for "king" and "table," reflecting the semantic similarity between "king" and "queen."

Beyond word embeddings, more advanced techniques like **document embeddings** are gaining popularity. These techniques represent entire documents as vectors, capturing the overall meaning and context of the document as a whole. Sentence-BERT is an example of a model that generates high-quality sentence embeddings, which can then be used to represent entire documents by averaging or pooling the embeddings of individual sentences.

These techniques are particularly useful for tasks that involve comparing the similarity of documents or clustering documents based on their semantic content.

The choice of feature extraction technique depends on the specific NLP task, the size of the dataset, and the computational resources available. For simple tasks with limited data, TF-IDF might be sufficient. However, for more complex tasks requiring nuanced semantic understanding, word embeddings or document embeddings are preferred. The complexity and computational cost associated with these techniques should be carefully weighed against the potential benefits in accuracy and performance.

Furthermore, advancements in deep learning have led to the emergence of techniques that combine feature extraction with model training. Models like transformers (BERT, RoBERTa, etc.) learn contextualized word embeddings directly within the model architecture. These models simultaneously learn representations and perform the downstream NLP task, often achieving superior performance without requiring explicit feature engineering. This integrated approach eliminates the need for separate feature extraction steps, streamlining the entire NLP pipeline. However, these models often require substantial computational resources for training and inference.

In conclusion, text preprocessing and feature extraction are fundamental steps in any NLP pipeline. The careful selection and application of appropriate techniques are essential for obtaining accurate and meaningful results. The choice between simple techniques like TF-IDF and more sophisticated methods like word embeddings and contextualized embeddings depends on the specific needs of the task and the trade-offs between accuracy, computational cost, and interpretability. The continuous evolution of NLP techniques, especially in deep learning, presents researchers and practitioners with an ever-expanding toolkit to tackle the multifaceted challenge of understanding human language. The best approach is often an iterative process, experimenting with different techniques to determine the optimal balance between accuracy and efficiency for a given task.

Sentiment Analysis and Opinion Mining

Sentiment analysis, also known as opinion mining, is a crucial application of Natural Language Processing (NLP) that focuses on automatically identifying and extracting subjective information from text. This subjective information reflects the opinions, sentiments, emotions, and attitudes expressed by the author or speaker. Unlike tasks focused on factual information extraction, sentiment analysis delves into the emotional undercurrents of language, revealing the nuanced perspectives embedded within text. This ability to gauge emotional tone has far-reaching implications across numerous fields, revolutionizing how we understand and interact with vast quantities of textual data.

The core objective of sentiment analysis is to classify text into predefined categories, typically positive, negative, or neutral. However, more sophisticated approaches incorporate finer-grained classifications, including categories such as anger, joy, sadness, fear, and surprise. The level of granularity depends on the specific application and the desired level of detail. For instance, a social media monitoring tool might only need to differentiate between positive and negative sentiment to track overall brand perception, while a customer service chatbot might require more granular sentiment analysis to understand the specific nature of customer complaints.

The techniques used in sentiment analysis range from simple rule-based systems to complex deep learning models. Rule-based approaches rely on a predefined set of lexicons—dictionaries containing words and phrases annotated with their corresponding sentiment polarity (positive, negative, or neutral). These systems work by matching words in the input text against the lexicon and aggregating the sentiment scores to determine the overall sentiment. While computationally efficient, these approaches often suffer from limitations. They struggle with sarcasm, negation, and contextual nuances, which can significantly alter the intended meaning. For example, the sentence "That's just great!" might be interpreted as positive by a simple lexicon-based system, while in reality, it could express sarcasm and negative sentiment.

More sophisticated methods leverage machine learning algorithms to learn patterns in the data and improve accuracy. These methods often employ supervised learning techniques, training models on large annotated datasets of text labeled with their corresponding sentiment polarity. This allows the algorithms to learn complex relationships between words, phrases, and sentence structures, and their associated sentiments. Support Vector Machines (SVMs), Naive Bayes classifiers, and logistic regression are commonly used
algorithms in supervised sentiment analysis. These models often outperform rule-based approaches in terms of accuracy, especially when dealing with ambiguous or nuanced language.

However, even supervised learning methods struggle with the complexities of human language. Context is king. The same word can express vastly different sentiments depending on the context. For example, "amazing" generally conveys positive sentiment, but in the sentence "That's an amazing disaster," it clearly takes on a negative connotation. The successful interpretation relies on the understanding of irony and the interplay between words in a sentence.

To address these challenges, researchers have developed more advanced techniques, such as deep learning models based on Recurrent Neural Networks (RNNs) and, more recently, Transformer architectures. RNNs, particularly Long Short-Term Memory (LSTM) networks, are particularly well-suited for processing sequential data like text because they can capture the long-range dependencies between words in a sentence. LSTM networks can effectively model the context in which words appear, making them robust to the effects of negation and sarcasm. For example, an LSTM would be more likely to correctly interpret "That's not bad" as a positive statement, understanding the role of the negation word "not."

The advent of Transformer architectures, such as BERT and its variants, has further revolutionized sentiment analysis. Transformers utilize attention mechanisms, allowing the model to focus on the most relevant parts of the input text when determining the overall sentiment. This attention mechanism is particularly useful in capturing long-range dependencies and contextual nuances. BERT and its successors have demonstrated state-of-the-art performance on various sentiment analysis benchmarks. These pre-trained models are often fine-tuned for specific tasks, adapting their knowledge to the nuances of the particular domain or application. This fine-tuning approach significantly improves performance and reduces the need for large annotated datasets.

Beyond the classification of text into broad categories, sentiment analysis extends to more granular tasks. Aspect-based sentiment analysis, for example, aims to identify sentiments toward specific aspects or features of a product or service. Instead of simply determining whether a review is overall positive or negative, aspect-based sentiment analysis seeks to pinpoint the opinions expressed about individual aspects, such as the price, design, or performance of a product. For instance, a review might state, "The camera is excellent, but the battery life is too short." Aspect-based sentiment analysis would correctly identify "camera" as having positive sentiment and "battery life" as having negative sentiment.

Another important aspect is the detection of emotions, going beyond simple positive/negative classifications to identify specific emotions like joy, sadness, anger, fear, and surprise. This involves more complex models that are trained on datasets annotated with a wider range of emotional labels. Emotion detection has numerous applications, particularly in areas such as mental health monitoring, customer relationship management, and social media analysis.

Sentiment analysis finds widespread applications across various industries. In market research, it allows companies to gauge consumer opinions about their products and services, enabling data-driven decision-making. Social media monitoring utilizes sentiment analysis to track brand reputation and identify potential crises, allowing companies to respond swiftly to negative sentiment.

Customer service departments leverage sentiment analysis to automatically categorize and prioritize customer inquiries, improving response times and enhancing customer satisfaction. In the finance industry, sentiment analysis can be applied to news articles and social media posts to predict stock market movements.

The accuracy and effectiveness of sentiment analysis are constantly evolving, driven by improvements in NLP techniques and the increasing availability of large annotated datasets. However, challenges remain. Sarcasm, irony, and the inherent ambiguity of human language continue to pose challenges for even the most sophisticated models. Furthermore, cross-lingual sentiment analysis, which aims to analyze text in multiple languages, requires careful consideration of language-specific nuances and cultural contexts.

The future of sentiment analysis is bright. Ongoing research focuses on developing more robust and accurate models capable of handling the complexities of human language. Improvements in deep learning architectures, coupled with advancements in data augmentation and transfer learning techniques, are pushing the boundaries of what's possible. As these models become increasingly sophisticated, their applications will expand even further, impacting various aspects of our lives in ways we are only beginning to imagine. The ability to understand and analyze the emotional undercurrents of human language is no longer a futuristic fantasy but a powerful tool shaping the technological landscape of today and tomorrow.

Machine Translation and Crosslingual Understanding

Machine translation represents a significant leap forward in cross-lingual communication, enabling the automated translation of text from one language to another. This technology has the potential to break down language barriers, facilitating global collaboration, information access, and cultural exchange. However, the complexity of human language presents considerable challenges in achieving truly accurate and nuanced translations.

Early approaches to machine translation relied on rule-based systems. These systems employed dictionaries and grammatical rules to directly translate words and phrases from one language to another. While conceptually straightforward, these methods proved brittle and struggled to handle the subtleties of language. They often produced grammatically incorrect and semantically nonsensical translations, failing to capture the nuances of meaning embedded within the original text. The limitations of these rule-based systems became increasingly apparent as the complexity of the translation tasks increased. For instance, idioms and expressions, which are highly language-specific, often yielded inaccurate and misleading translations. The contextual understanding required to accurately translate ambiguous phrases was simply beyond the capabilities of these early systems.

The advent of statistical machine translation (SMT) marked a significant turning point. Instead of relying solely on explicit rules, SMT leveraged statistical models trained on massive bilingual corpora—collections of texts paired in two different languages. These models learned probabilistic relationships between words and phrases in the source and target languages, enabling them to make more informed translation decisions. Hidden Markov Models (HMMs) and probabilistic context-free grammars were commonly employed in SMT systems. These models calculated the probability of different translation options based on the statistical patterns observed in the training data, effectively learning the statistical regularities of language. While SMT significantly improved the quality of machine translation, it still suffered from limitations in handling long-range dependencies and complex syntactic structures.

The accuracy of translation was still heavily reliant on the availability and quality of the training data. Furthermore, SMT models often struggled with out-of-vocabulary words and rare phrases not present in the training corpus.

The emergence of neural machine translation (NMT) revolutionized the field, utilizing deep learning architectures, particularly recurrent neural networks (RNNs) and more recently, transformer networks. NMT models learn to map entire sentences, rather than individual words or phrases, from the source language to the target language. This holistic approach allows them to capture contextual information and long-range dependencies more effectively than SMT systems. RNNs, particularly Long Short-Term Memory (LSTM) networks, proved particularly adept at processing sequential data like text, capturing the temporal dependencies within a sentence.

LSTMs' ability to maintain context over long sequences proved crucial in producing more fluent and accurate translations.

However, the computational cost of training LSTMs on large datasets could be substantial.

The introduction of the transformer architecture, and specifically models like Google's Transformer and BERT, marked another significant advance. Transformers leverage self-attention mechanisms, allowing the model to weigh the importance of different parts of the input sentence when generating the translation. This attention mechanism enables the model to capture complex relationships between words, even those far apart in the sentence, leading to more accurate and nuanced translations. The parallelizable nature of the transformer architecture allows for significantly faster training compared to recurrent networks, enabling the training of larger and more powerful models.

Furthermore, the ability to pre-train these models on massive multilingual corpora allows for greater generalization and performance across a wide range of language pairs. These pre-trained models can then be fine-tuned on smaller datasets for specific language pairs or domains, resulting in improved translation quality and reduced training time.

Despite the impressive progress in NMT, challenges remain. One significant hurdle is the handling of low-resource languages.

Training effective NMT models requires large amounts of parallel data, which is often scarce for less widely spoken languages. Techniques such as transfer learning, where knowledge acquired from high-resource languages is transferred to low-resource languages, are being actively investigated to address this issue.

Another challenge lies in the accurate translation of ambiguous expressions and idiomatic phrases. The contextual understanding required to correctly translate these expressions often exceeds the current capabilities of even the most sophisticated NMT models.

Furthermore, cultural nuances and differences in language use across various regions can pose significant difficulties. A direct word-for-word translation might not convey the intended meaning or even be grammatically correct in the target language.

The future of machine translation lies in addressing these challenges. Research is focusing on developing more robust models capable of handling low-resource languages, ambiguous expressions, and cultural nuances. Ongoing work involves incorporating external knowledge sources, such as encyclopedias and knowledge graphs, into the translation process. This would allow the models to leverage factual information to resolve ambiguities and improve the accuracy of translations. Furthermore, research into incorporating multi-modal information, such as images and audio, could significantly enhance the quality of machine translation, particularly in scenarios where context is crucial. The development of more efficient training algorithms and the use of specialized hardware, such as GPUs and TPUs, are also accelerating the progress in machine translation. In the coming years, we can expect further advancements in NMT, leading to increasingly accurate, fluent, and nuanced translations across a wider range of language pairs.

The implications of highly accurate machine translation are far-reaching. It has the potential to revolutionize fields such as global communication, education, and international business. For instance, it could facilitate cross-cultural understanding and collaboration by making information readily available in multiple languages. In education, it could provide learners with access to a broader range of learning resources, regardless of language barriers. Machine translation could also dramatically improve the efficiency and effectiveness of international trade and diplomacy, by enabling seamless communication between individuals and organizations across different linguistic backgrounds. However, the ethical considerations associated with machine translation also deserve careful attention. The potential for misuse, such as the spread of misinformation or the perpetuation of biases present in training data, necessitates the development of responsible and ethical guidelines for its use. The ongoing development of this technology will require a careful balance between innovation and responsible deployment to ensure its beneficial impact on society. The progress in machine translation is a compelling demonstration of the transformative power of artificial intelligence in facilitating human communication and understanding across linguistic boundaries. The continuous refinement and improvement of this technology will continue to shape the way people interact and collaborate on a global scale. The future of machine translation promises a world where language is no longer a barrier to communication, facilitating greater understanding and cooperation amongst diverse cultures and communities.

Chatbots and Conversational AI

The evolution of Natural Language Processing (NLP) has birthed a new generation of interactive AI systems: chatbots and conversational AI. These systems, far beyond simple keyword-based responses, aim to mimic human conversation, understanding context, intent, and even emotion to provide a more natural and engaging user experience. This capability relies heavily on advancements in both natural language understanding (NLU) and natural language generation (NLG). NLU focuses on enabling machines to comprehend human language, while NLG empowers machines to generate human-like text responses.

The journey of chatbots began with simple rule-based systems. These early chatbots, often found in early websites or online games, relied on pre-programmed responses triggered by specific keywords. Their limitations were stark: they could only handle a narrow range of inputs and failed miserably when confronted with anything outside their predefined scripts. A user asking a question slightly different from the programmed keywords would receive a nonsensical or irrelevant answer, highlighting the inflexibility of these rudimentary systems. These early chatbots served as a primitive demonstration of the potential but underscored the substantial challenges in creating truly conversational AI.

The next stage saw the introduction of statistical approaches. These methods leveraged statistical models trained on large datasets of conversations. These models learned probabilistic relationships between user inputs and appropriate responses, allowing for a more flexible and adaptable system. While an improvement, these statistical chatbots still suffered from a lack of true understanding. Their responses were often based on statistical correlations rather than a genuine comprehension of the user's intent. The system might provide a statistically likely response, but it might not always be the most appropriate or logical one given the context of the conversation.

The breakthrough came with the advent of deep learning. Deep learning architectures, particularly recurrent neural networks

(RNNs) and transformers, revolutionized chatbot development. These models, trained on massive datasets of text and conversation, learned complex patterns and relationships in language. RNNs, especially LSTMs, proved particularly effective at handling the sequential nature of language, maintaining context across extended conversations. However, the training process for RNNs could be computationally expensive and time-consuming.

The introduction of the transformer architecture dramatically altered the landscape. Transformers, with their self-attention mechanisms, allowed the model to process the entire input sentence simultaneously, rather than sequentially. This enabled a much more efficient and parallel processing approach, significantly reducing training time while enhancing the ability to capture contextual information and long-range dependencies within a conversation. Models like BERT and GPT-3, based on the transformer architecture, demonstrated a remarkable ability to understand nuanced language and generate coherent and contextually appropriate responses.

The impact of these advancements is evident in the widespread adoption of chatbots across various industries. Customer service is a prime example. Many companies now utilize chatbots to handle routine inquiries, freeing up human agents to focus on more complex issues. These chatbots can answer frequently asked questions, provide product information, and even guide users through troubleshooting steps. The ability of these AI-powered systems to handle a large volume of requests simultaneously has proven invaluable for improving customer service efficiency and reducing wait times.

Beyond customer service, conversational AI is transforming virtual assistants. Virtual assistants like Siri, Alexa, and Google Assistant rely heavily on NLP and conversational AI to understand voice commands and respond appropriately. These assistants can perform a wide range of tasks, from setting reminders and playing music to controlling smart home devices and providing information from the internet. Their increasing sophistication reflects the continuous improvements in NLU and NLG. The ability to maintain context across multiple interactions is key to the functionality of these virtual assistants; they need to remember previous requests and interactions to provide relevant and helpful responses.

The healthcare sector is also witnessing the transformative power of chatbots. Chatbots are being used to provide patients with basic medical information, schedule appointments, and even offer mental health support. These applications highlight the potential of chatbots to improve access to healthcare, particularly in remote areas or for patients with limited mobility. However, the ethical considerations surrounding the use of chatbots in healthcare are crucial and require careful attention. The potential for misdiagnosis or the provision of inaccurate information must be minimized through rigorous testing and validation.

The education sector is another area where chatbots are finding increasing applications. Chatbots can be used as interactive tutoring systems, providing personalized learning experiences tailored to the individual needs of students. They can offer immediate feedback, answer questions, and provide targeted support to help students master concepts. Furthermore, chatbots can automate administrative tasks, freeing up teachers to focus on providing more individualized attention to their students.

The development of conversational AI is not without its challenges. One significant hurdle is the handling of ambiguity and sarcasm. Human language is often imprecise, and interpreting the intended meaning of a user's statement can be difficult, especially when sarcasm or humor is involved. Developing chatbots that can accurately understand and respond appropriately to such nuanced language remains a significant research challenge. Another challenge is ensuring the ethical and responsible use of chatbots. Concerns about bias in training data, privacy violations, and the potential for manipulation necessitate the development of robust ethical guidelines and regulations.

The future of chatbots and conversational AI lies in addressing these challenges and pushing the boundaries of what is possible. Research is ongoing in areas such as improved context modeling, emotion recognition, and personalized interaction. The development of more sophisticated models capable of handling complex conversational scenarios and providing truly human-like interaction is a key focus. Furthermore, the integration of chatbots with other AI technologies, such as computer vision and robotics, holds immense potential for creating more intelligent and versatile systems.

The integration of multimodal interactions is also a promising area of development. This involves combining text with other forms of communication, such as images and voice, to enhance the richness and understanding of the conversation. Imagine a chatbot that not only understands your written query but also analyzes an image you upload to provide a more comprehensive and accurate response. This ability to process multiple modalities of input dramatically expands the potential applications of conversational AI.

As advancements in NLP continue, we can expect even more sophisticated and capable chatbots and conversational AI systems. These systems will become increasingly integrated into our daily lives, transforming the way we interact with technology and each other. However, the ethical considerations surrounding the development and deployment of these systems must be addressed proactively to ensure their responsible and beneficial use. The future of conversational AI holds both immense promise and significant responsibility. The development and application of this technology will require ongoing vigilance and ethical considerations to ensure it contributes positively to society. The journey toward truly natural and intelligent conversational AI is ongoing, but the progress made thus far is remarkable and the potential for future impact is transformative.

Image Acquisition and Preprocessing Techniques

The journey from raw visual data to meaningful information in computer vision begins with image acquisition and preprocessing. This crucial initial phase directly impacts the accuracy and efficiency of subsequent image recognition and analysis tasks. The quality of the acquired image, along with the effectiveness of preprocessing techniques, fundamentally determines the success of the entire computer vision pipeline. A poorly acquired or preprocessed image can lead to inaccurate results, no matter how sophisticated the subsequent algorithms are.

Image acquisition involves capturing the visual data using various methods and devices. The simplest method is capturing images using digital cameras, ranging from low-resolution smartphone cameras to high-resolution professional-grade DSLR cameras. The choice of camera depends on the specific application and required image quality. High-resolution cameras are essential when fine details are crucial, such as in medical imaging or satellite imagery analysis. Conversely, lower-resolution cameras may suffice for applications where precise details are less critical, such as basic object recognition in a controlled environment.

Beyond standard digital cameras, other image acquisition methods exist. Medical imaging employs specialized techniques like X-ray, ultrasound, magnetic resonance imaging (MRI), and computed tomography (CT) scans. These produce images representing internal structures of the body, providing crucial information for diagnosis and treatment. Satellite imagery, captured by sensors on satellites orbiting the Earth, provides wide-area coverage, essential for environmental monitoring, urban planning, and disaster response.

Microscopy offers incredibly detailed images of microscopic structures, crucial for biological research and material science. Each method generates images with specific characteristics, influencing the subsequent preprocessing steps.

The format of the acquired image is also critical. Common image formats include JPEG, PNG, TIFF, and RAW. JPEG, a lossy compression format, prioritizes file size reduction over image quality. This makes it suitable for web applications and situations where storage space is limited, but it's not ideal for applications requiring high image fidelity, like medical imaging or scientific research. PNG, a lossless compression format, preserves image quality but results in larger file sizes. It is better suited for applications where preserving every detail is paramount, such as graphics and images with sharp text. TIFF, another lossless format, offers high image quality and supports various color depths and compression schemes. It's often the preferred format for high-resolution images and archival purposes. RAW image formats capture uncompressed sensor data, allowing for maximum flexibility in post-processing and adjustments. They provide the greatest control over the final image but require specialized software for processing and occupy significantly more storage space. The selection of an appropriate image format should consider the specific requirements of the application, balancing image quality, file size, and processing ease.

Once the image is acquired, preprocessing techniques are employed to improve its quality and suitability for further analysis. This step is crucial because raw images often contain imperfections that can interfere with the accuracy of subsequent computer vision tasks.

Preprocessing involves a variety of techniques, each addressing specific image imperfections. One common issue is noise, which manifests as unwanted variations in pixel values, potentially obscuring important features. Noise reduction techniques, such as median filtering, Gaussian filtering, and wavelet denoising, aim to reduce this noise while preserving important image features. Median filtering replaces each pixel with the median value of its neighboring pixels, effectively suppressing impulsive noise spikes.

Gaussian filtering uses a Gaussian kernel to smooth the image, reducing noise while blurring sharp edges to a lesser extent than median filtering. Wavelet denoising decomposes the image into different frequency components, allowing for selective noise removal in specific frequency bands. The choice of noise reduction technique depends on the type and level of noise present in the image.

Image resizing is another essential preprocessing step, adjusting the image dimensions to match the requirements of the computer vision algorithm or the desired output format. Enlarging an image (upscaling) can be achieved through interpolation techniques like bilinear interpolation or bicubic interpolation, which estimate the values of new pixels based on the surrounding pixels. Reducing the image size (downscaling) often involves techniques like averaging or decimation, reducing the number of pixels while minimizing information loss. The appropriate resizing method depends on the application and desired level of detail preservation. Oversampling and over-sharpening can introduce artifacts.

Image normalization aims to standardize the pixel values, improving the robustness and performance of many computer vision algorithms. Normalization involves adjusting the range of pixel values to a specific range, typically [0, 1] or [-1, 1]. This ensures that different images, potentially captured under varying lighting conditions, are treated consistently by the algorithm.

Normalization techniques include min-max scaling, z-score standardization, and histogram equalization. Min-max scaling scales the pixel values to the specified range by linearly mapping them, ensuring that the minimum and maximum values are mapped to 0 and 1, respectively. Z-score standardization centers the pixel values around zero and scales them by their standard deviation, making the distribution of pixel values have a mean of 0 and a standard deviation of 1. Histogram equalization enhances contrast by distributing pixel values more uniformly across the entire range, often improving the visibility of subtle features.

Other preprocessing techniques include geometric transformations (like rotation, scaling, and translation) to align images to a standard orientation or compensate for camera perspective, and color space conversion. Color space conversion involves transforming the image from one color space (e.g., RGB) to another (e.g., HSV, YUV), which may be better suited for specific algorithms or tasks. For example, HSV (Hue, Saturation, Value) is often more robust to lighting variations than RGB.

The selection of appropriate preprocessing techniques depends heavily on the specific application and the characteristics of the acquired images. In medical imaging, for example, noise reduction is often crucial, as noise can obscure subtle details vital for diagnosis. In satellite imagery, geometric corrections are essential to account for the Earth's curvature and satellite positioning. In object recognition, image resizing and normalization are often necessary to standardize the input data for the algorithm.

The goal of preprocessing is not simply to improve the visual appearance of the image; it's to enhance the features that are relevant to the subsequent computer vision task, making the image more amenable to accurate analysis. Efficient and appropriate preprocessing significantly improves the accuracy, robustness, and efficiency of the entire computer vision system. A well-preprocessed image forms a solid foundation for the subsequent stages of image recognition and analysis, allowing for more accurate and reliable results. Careful consideration of the acquisition method, image format, and preprocessing techniques is essential for any successful computer vision application. Ignoring these foundational steps can lead to significant limitations and inaccuracies in the final analysis.

Feature Extraction and Object Detection

Having established the groundwork of image acquisition and preprocessing, we now delve into the heart of computer vision: feature extraction and object detection. These stages transform the raw pixel data into a representation that a computer can understand and use for higher-level tasks like image classification and scene understanding. Feature extraction involves identifying and quantifying salient characteristics within an image, while object detection aims to locate and classify specific objects within the image. These two processes are often intertwined, with features playing a critical role in effective object detection.

Feature extraction is a crucial step that bridges the gap between raw image data and meaningful information. Instead of relying on the entire image, algorithms focus on specific features that best represent its content. These features can be low-level, such as edges, corners, and textures, or high-level, representing more complex patterns and shapes. The choice of features depends heavily on the specific application. For example, in medical image analysis, subtle texture variations might be crucial for identifying cancerous cells, while in object recognition, edge detection might be sufficient to delineate object boundaries.

One common approach to low-level feature extraction is edge detection. Edges represent significant changes in image intensity, often corresponding to object boundaries. Numerous algorithms exist for edge detection, each with its strengths and weaknesses. The Sobel operator, for instance, employs convolution with a kernel that emphasizes intensity differences, effectively highlighting edges.

The Canny edge detector, a more sophisticated approach, uses multiple stages to minimize noise and accurately detect edges of varying strengths. It involves Gaussian smoothing to reduce noise, gradient calculation to identify potential edge points, non-maximum suppression to thin the edges, and hysteresis thresholding to connect fragmented edges. The result is a refined set of edges representing the significant boundaries within the image.

Corner detection is another vital technique, identifying points where two edges intersect. Corners are robust features, resistant to small variations in image scale and rotation. The Harris corner detector, a widely used method, identifies corners by calculating the second-moment matrix, which measures the local intensity variations in different directions. Corners correspond to regions with significant variations in all directions. The Shi-Tomasi corner detector, a variation of the Harris detector, offers improved performance by considering only the eigenvalues of the second-moment matrix. These corner points serve as stable landmarks for various computer vision applications, including image registration, object tracking, and 3D reconstruction.

Texture analysis is another crucial component of feature extraction. Textures describe the surface properties of objects, characterized by repetitive patterns and variations in intensity. Many techniques exist for quantifying textures. One common approach is to use local binary patterns (LBP), which assign a binary code to each pixel based on its relationship to its neighbors. This produces a histogram representing the texture distribution. Gabor filters are another effective tool for capturing texture information. These filters respond selectively to different orientations and frequencies, providing a rich description of the textural content. Wavelet transforms can also be used to decompose images into different frequency bands, allowing for detailed texture analysis across multiple scales.

Beyond these low-level features, high-level features represent more abstract concepts, often learned through machine learning techniques. Convolutional neural networks (CNNs), for instance, are powerful architectures adept at automatically learning hierarchical representations of images. The initial layers detect basic features like edges and corners, while deeper layers learn more complex features such as object parts and their spatial relationships. This hierarchical representation allows CNNs to capture complex patterns and structures essential for tasks like object recognition and image classification. Pre-trained CNN models, such as ResNet, Inception, and VGG, have achieved state-of-the-art results on various image recognition benchmarks, showcasing the power of learning high-level features from data.

Object detection, building upon feature extraction, aims to identify and locate specific objects within an image. Early approaches relied on handcrafted features and sliding window techniques. A sliding window method systematically scans the image with a window of a fixed size, extracting features within each window and classifying them. This approach, although conceptually simple, is computationally expensive and suffers from limitations in handling variations in object scale and aspect ratio.

Region-based convolutional neural networks (R-CNNs) represent a significant advancement in object detection. These methods combine the power of CNNs for feature extraction with region proposal mechanisms to identify potential object locations. Region proposal methods, such as Selective Search, identify regions of interest that are likely to contain objects. These regions are then processed by a CNN to extract features and classify them. Faster R-CNNs further optimize this process by integrating the region proposal network directly into the CNN architecture, significantly improving efficiency. Mask R-CNN extends this approach by adding a branch to generate pixel-level segmentation masks, providing more detailed information about the location and shape of detected objects. You Only Look Once (YOLO) represents another significant advancement, offering a highly efficient single-stage detection approach.

The performance of object detection models is often evaluated using metrics like precision and recall. Precision measures the proportion of correctly detected objects among all detected objects, while recall measures the proportion of correctly detected objects among all actual objects present in the image. The intersection over union (IoU) is frequently used to assess the accuracy of object localization, measuring the overlap between the predicted bounding box and the ground-truth bounding box. High precision indicates fewer false positives, while high recall indicates fewer false negatives. A high IoU value indicates accurate localization. Achieving a balance between precision and recall is crucial for building effective object detection systems.

Modern object detection techniques rely heavily on deep learning models, particularly CNNs. These models have demonstrated remarkable progress in achieving high accuracy in object detection tasks across various domains. However, challenges remain, particularly in handling occluded objects, objects with significant variations in appearance, and situations with complex backgrounds.

Recent research focuses on addressing these challenges through improved architectures, more robust training techniques, and the incorporation of contextual information. Furthermore, real-time object detection remains a crucial area of development, especially for applications like autonomous driving and robotics. The need for efficient algorithms that can process images in real time continues to drive innovation in this field.

The combination of sophisticated feature extraction techniques and powerful object detection models has enabled remarkable progress in computer vision. These methods have found widespread applications in various fields, including autonomous driving, medical image analysis, surveillance systems, robotics, and facial recognition. As research continues, we can anticipate even more advanced and robust methods capable of handling increasingly complex visual data. The future of computer vision lies in developing systems that can not only detect and classify objects but also understand the relationships between them and interpret scenes in a more human-like way. The development of explainable AI (XAI) techniques to improve the transparency and interpretability of these complex systems is also crucial for wider adoption and trust. The journey from pixels to understanding continues, and the innovations in feature extraction and object detection are paving the way for a future where computers can truly "see" and interact with the world around us.

Image Classification and Recognition

Image classification, a cornerstone of computer vision, tackles the challenge of assigning predefined labels to images. This seemingly simple task belies a significant computational hurdle: transforming the raw pixel data—a vast, unstructured array of numbers—into a meaningful representation that accurately reflects the image's content. The effectiveness of image classification hinges on the ability of algorithms to extract relevant features and learn the relationships between these features and the assigned labels.

Historically, image classification relied heavily on handcrafted features. Researchers painstakingly engineered algorithms to extract specific features, such as color histograms, texture descriptors, and edge orientations. These features, often based on domain expertise, were then fed into classical machine learning models, such as Support Vector Machines (SVMs) or k-Nearest Neighbors (k-NN), to perform the classification task. While these approaches yielded reasonable results for specific, well-defined tasks, they suffered from several limitations. The hand-engineered features were often brittle, failing to generalize well to variations in lighting, viewpoint, or object pose. Moreover, the design and selection of appropriate features required significant expertise, often necessitating extensive experimentation and fine-tuning.

The advent of deep learning revolutionized image classification. Convolutional Neural Networks (CNNs), a specific type of deep learning architecture, proved remarkably adept at automatically learning hierarchical representations of images. Instead of relying on handcrafted features, CNNs learn these features directly from the raw pixel data. The network architecture consists of multiple layers, each performing a specific transformation on the input data. Early layers typically detect low-level features, such as edges and corners, while deeper layers learn progressively more complex and abstract features, representing object parts and their spatial relationships.

This hierarchical feature learning is a key advantage of CNNs. By learning features at multiple levels of abstraction, CNNs can capture subtle variations in appearance and effectively generalize to unseen images. The learning process involves training the network on a large dataset of labeled images, adjusting the network's parameters to minimize the discrepancy between its predicted labels and the true labels. This process, known as backpropagation, allows the network to iteratively refine its feature representations and improve its classification accuracy.

Several seminal CNN architectures have achieved breakthroughs in image classification. AlexNet, a relatively early CNN architecture, demonstrated the power of deep learning in image classification, achieving a significant performance boost over previous methods in the ImageNet Large Scale Visual Recognition Challenge (ILSVRC). This success spurred further research and innovation, leading to the development of more sophisticated architectures, such as VGGNet, GoogLeNet (Inception), and ResNet. These architectures incorporated innovations like deeper networks, residual connections, and inception modules, further improving classification accuracy and efficiency.

ResNet, in particular, introduced the concept of residual connections, allowing for the training of significantly deeper networks without encountering the vanishing gradient problem. This breakthrough enabled the development of networks with hundreds or even thousands of layers, capable of learning highly complex feature representations. The depth of these networks allows them to capture increasingly subtle distinctions between image categories. This depth also confers a degree of robustness against noise and variations in image quality.

The success of deep CNNs in image classification is not solely attributable to their architecture. The availability of massive labeled datasets, such as ImageNet, played a crucial role. These datasets provide the raw material for training deep CNNs, enabling the networks to learn effective feature representations. The sheer size of these datasets ensures that the networks are exposed to a wide range of variations in object appearance, lighting conditions, and viewpoints. This broad exposure is essential for learning robust and generalizable features. The computational power required to train these deep networks is another critical factor, requiring specialized hardware like GPUs or TPUs to handle the computational demands.

While CNNs have dominated image classification in recent years, other methods continue to be explored and refined. Support Vector Machines (SVMs), despite their relative simplicity compared to deep CNNs, remain a viable option, particularly for smaller datasets or computationally constrained environments. Their ability to handle high-dimensional feature spaces and their inherent capacity for efficient classification makes them a valuable tool in specific applications. Other techniques, such as Random Forests and boosted decision trees, also offer alternative approaches to image classification, although their performance often lags behind that of state-of-the-art CNNs.

The performance of image classification models is typically evaluated using metrics such as accuracy, precision, and recall. Accuracy represents the overall correctness of the classifications, while precision and recall assess the performance of the model for specific classes. Precision measures the proportion of correctly classified instances among all instances predicted as belonging to a particular class, while recall measures the proportion of correctly classified instances among all actual instances of that class. The F1-score, a harmonic mean of precision and recall, provides a balanced measure of performance, considering both false positives and false negatives. The choice of evaluation metric depends on the specific application and the relative importance of minimizing false positives versus false negatives.

Image classification is not a solved problem. Ongoing research focuses on addressing limitations such as robustness to adversarial attacks, generalization to unseen data, and interpretability of model predictions. Adversarial attacks involve subtle perturbations to input images that can cause the model to make incorrect predictions, highlighting the vulnerability of some models to manipulation. Improving generalization capability is crucial for deploying models in real-world scenarios where the test data may differ significantly from the training data. The lack of interpretability in many deep learning models is a significant obstacle to wider adoption, particularly in high-stakes applications where understanding the reasoning behind a model's predictions is critical. Research efforts are underway to develop more explainable

AI (XAI) techniques that can shed light on the decision-making process of deep CNNs.

The future of image classification likely involves a combination of deeper networks, more sophisticated training techniques, and the incorporation of domain-specific knowledge. The development of more efficient and robust models, capable of handling increasingly complex visual data, remains a key focus of research. The ongoing quest for more interpretable models will also be crucial for fostering trust and wider adoption of these powerful technologies. The ability to classify images with high accuracy is not just a technical achievement; it's a fundamental building block for a wide array of applications, from medical diagnosis to autonomous driving, shaping the future of how we interact with the visual world.

Image Segmentation and Object Tracking

Image segmentation, a crucial step beyond simple image classification, delves into the intricate task of partitioning an image into multiple meaningful regions. Unlike classification, which assigns a single label to an entire image, segmentation aims to delineate specific objects or areas within the image, assigning a unique label to each distinct region. This granular level of analysis unlocks a much richer understanding of the image content, enabling applications far beyond simple identification. The resulting segmentation mask, a pixel-wise labeling of the image, provides a detailed map of the image's components.

Several approaches exist for achieving image segmentation, each with its strengths and weaknesses. One fundamental technique is thresholding, a relatively straightforward method that partitions an image based on pixel intensity values. By selecting a threshold value, pixels above the threshold are assigned to one class, while those below are assigned to another. This method is particularly effective for images with a clear contrast between the foreground and background, such as separating a black object on a white background. However, its simplicity also limits its effectiveness when dealing with complex images containing subtle variations in intensity or multiple objects with overlapping intensity ranges. Adaptive thresholding techniques attempt to address this limitation by adjusting the threshold based on local image characteristics, adapting to variations in illumination and contrast.

Region growing, another common segmentation approach, starts with a seed pixel and iteratively expands the region by incorporating neighboring pixels that share similar characteristics. The similarity criterion can be based on intensity, color, texture, or a combination of these features. This method is effective in grouping pixels belonging to a cohesive region, but it can be sensitive to noise and the selection of initial seed pixels. The choice of seed pixels significantly influences the final segmentation result, and inappropriate selection can lead to inaccurate or fragmented regions. Variants of region growing, such as seeded region growing and marker-controlled watershed segmentation, aim to improve robustness and accuracy by incorporating multiple seed points or using additional constraints based on image features.

More sophisticated segmentation techniques leverage the power of machine learning. Similar to image classification, deep learning architectures, particularly Convolutional Neural Networks (CNNs), have dramatically improved the accuracy and robustness of image segmentation. Fully Convolutional Networks (FCNs) are a class of CNNs specifically designed for dense prediction tasks, such as segmentation. Unlike traditional CNNs that produce a single output for the entire image, FCNs produce a pixel-wise output, creating a segmentation map. FCNs use upsampling layers to recover spatial information lost during the convolutional operations, allowing them to generate high-resolution segmentation masks.

U-Net, a popular architecture for biomedical image segmentation, extends the FCN architecture with a U-shaped structure that combines contracting and expanding paths. The contracting path captures contextual information, while the expanding path refines the segmentation at a finer resolution. This architecture has been highly successful in various applications, including medical imaging, where accurate and detailed segmentation is crucial for diagnosis and treatment planning. Variations on U-Net, such as Attention U-Net and DeepLab, incorporate mechanisms like attention mechanisms and atrous convolutions to further enhance performance and detail.

Beyond these architectures, other approaches leverage graph-based methods, treating the image as a graph where nodes represent pixels and edges represent the relationships between them. Graph cuts, for example, optimize a global energy function to partition the graph into distinct regions, representing the segmentation. This method often requires careful design of the energy function to accurately reflect the desired segmentation properties.

The choice of segmentation technique depends heavily on the specific application and the nature of the image data. For simple images with clear contrasts, thresholding may suffice. For more complex images with subtle variations, region growing or more advanced machine learning methods are often necessary. The accuracy of these methods also depends on the quality of the input image and the careful selection of parameters. In many real-world scenarios, a combination of techniques or a multi-stage process may be required to achieve optimal results.

Object tracking builds upon image segmentation by addressing the dynamic aspect of image sequences. Given a sequence of images, object tracking aims to identify and follow the trajectory of specific objects across consecutive frames. This continuous monitoring of object movement is crucial for numerous applications, including video surveillance, autonomous driving, and robotics.

Tracking algorithms typically rely on feature extraction and motion estimation. Feature extraction involves identifying distinguishing characteristics of the object, such as its shape, color, or texture. These features are then used to track the object's position across frames. Motion estimation involves determining the displacement of the object between frames, allowing the tracker to maintain its position across the image sequence.

Several tracking approaches exist, each with its advantages and limitations. Simple tracking methods, such as template matching, involve comparing a template image of the object to consecutive frames. This approach is computationally inexpensive but struggles with changes in object appearance, viewpoint, or illumination. More sophisticated methods utilize machine learning techniques, such as deep learning, to learn robust object representations. These deep learning-based trackers can handle significant variations in appearance and maintain tracking accuracy even under challenging conditions. Such methods can leverage the power of recurrent neural networks (RNNs) to model the temporal dependencies between frames, improving tracking robustness and accuracy.

Correlation filters are frequently employed for object tracking, offering a balance between computational efficiency and tracking accuracy. These filters learn a template that captures the appearance of the tracked object. They utilize the cross-correlation operation to identify the object's position in subsequent frames, efficiently searching for the best match. Multiple correlation filters can be combined to handle variations in object appearance, further enhancing robustness.

Another class of trackers employs Kalman filters or particle filters, Bayesian approaches that model the object's motion and update its estimated position based on observations. These methods excel in handling noisy data and uncertainties in object motion. Kalman filters, suitable for linear motion models, are effective for relatively smooth trajectories, whereas particle filters, applicable to nonlinear motion models, are better suited for more complex movements.

The evaluation of object tracking performance typically uses metrics such as precision, recall, and overlap ratio. Precision measures the proportion of correctly tracked frames, while recall measures the proportion of frames in which the object is actually present. The overlap ratio quantifies the degree of overlap between the predicted bounding box and the ground truth bounding box. These metrics provide a comprehensive assessment of the tracker's performance under varying conditions.

As with image segmentation, object tracking is an active area of research, with ongoing efforts focusing on improving robustness to occlusions, changes in illumination, and variations in object appearance. Dealing with challenging scenarios, like partial occlusions where only parts of the object are visible, remains a significant challenge, as does maintaining tracking accuracy across significant changes in viewpoint or object pose. The development of more robust and computationally efficient trackers that can operate in real-time remains crucial for a wide range of applications.

The future of both image segmentation and object tracking is closely intertwined with advancements in deep learning and the availability of large, annotated datasets. The development of more powerful and efficient deep learning architectures that can handle increasingly complex visual data is likely to play a central role. The combination of deep learning with other techniques, such as graph-based methods and Bayesian approaches, offers promising avenues for improved performance and robustness. Furthermore, incorporating domain-specific knowledge into the models, particularly in specialized applications, can lead to more accurate and meaningful segmentation and tracking results. These advancements will not only improve the accuracy and efficiency of these tasks but will also unlock new capabilities in diverse applications, driving innovation in fields such as healthcare, autonomous systems, and virtual and augmented reality. The ability to accurately segment images and track objects in real-time represents a significant step towards creating more intelligent and responsive systems that can interact effectively with the real world.

Applications of Computer Vision in Various Industries

The preceding discussion laid the groundwork for understanding the fundamental building blocks of computer vision: image segmentation and object tracking. Now, let's explore how these powerful techniques are transforming industries across the board. The applications are vast and varied, but a few key sectors illustrate the transformative potential of computer vision exceptionally well.

One area where computer vision has made a profound impact is healthcare. Medical image analysis, a cornerstone of modern diagnostics, relies heavily on computer vision algorithms. Radiologists, pathologists, and other medical professionals are increasingly using AI-powered tools to analyze medical images, such as X-rays, CT scans, MRIs, and ultrasounds. These tools can automate tasks like identifying tumors, detecting anomalies, and measuring organ sizes, significantly improving the speed and accuracy of diagnoses. For instance, computer vision algorithms are used to detect subtle signs of lung cancer in chest X-rays, often identifying lesions that might be missed by the human eye. This early detection can be crucial in improving patient outcomes. Beyond cancer detection, computer vision is proving invaluable in diagnosing cardiovascular diseases, neurological disorders, and other conditions through analysis of various medical images. The accuracy and efficiency offered by these tools significantly enhance the capabilities of medical professionals, enabling them to make more informed decisions and deliver better patient care. Moreover, the ability to process large volumes of medical images quickly allows for rapid analysis, leading to faster diagnosis and treatment. This is particularly important in situations where timely diagnosis is critical, such as stroke or trauma cases. The development of robust and reliable computer vision algorithms for medical image analysis remains a key focus of research, constantly striving for higher accuracy and efficiency. Ongoing research explores incorporating more complex features and integrating these tools seamlessly into clinical workflows, thereby maximizing their impact on patient care.

Another sector experiencing a revolution driven by computer vision is autonomous driving. The ability of self-driving vehicles to navigate complex environments safely and reliably depends heavily on computer vision. These vehicles use cameras and other sensors to perceive their surroundings, interpreting the visual information to make crucial driving decisions. Object detection, a critical aspect of this process, involves identifying and locating objects such as pedestrians, vehicles, and traffic signals in images captured by the vehicle's cameras. Lane recognition, another crucial component, utilizes computer vision to accurately identify and track lane markings, enabling the vehicle to stay within its lane and avoid collisions. The algorithms used in autonomous driving are incredibly sophisticated, capable of processing vast amounts of data in real-time to accurately perceive the dynamic and unpredictable nature of roadways. These algorithms must deal with varying weather conditions, lighting changes, and obstacles. The development and refinement of these vision systems are critical for the safety and reliability of autonomous vehicles. Researchers constantly work to improve the robustness and accuracy of object detection and lane recognition algorithms to handle increasingly complex scenarios, making self-driving cars safer and more reliable for widespread adoption. The progress made in this field highlights not just the technological advancements in computer vision, but also the advancements in other related fields such as sensor technology, data processing, and decision-making algorithms. The integration of these various components is crucial for creating truly autonomous vehicles that can operate safely and efficiently in diverse real-world environments.

Manufacturing is yet another area experiencing significant transformation due to computer vision. Quality control, a critical aspect of manufacturing, traditionally relies on manual inspection, which can be time-consuming, error-prone, and expensive.

Computer vision offers a powerful alternative, providing automated and precise inspection systems. These systems use cameras to capture images of products as they move along the assembly line, analyzing these images to identify defects such as scratches, cracks, or missing components. This automated inspection process greatly enhances efficiency, improves product quality, and reduces waste.

Computer vision systems can also be trained to identify subtle defects that might be missed by human inspectors, improving overall product quality and reducing the risk of defects reaching the consumer. Moreover, computer vision is not limited to the detection of obvious defects; it can also analyze subtle variations in dimensions, color, or texture, allowing for finer quality control. This precise control minimizes variability in the manufacturing process and enhances the consistency of final products. The integration of computer vision into manufacturing processes is crucial for streamlining operations, boosting productivity, and enhancing the quality and reliability of manufactured goods. The ongoing advancements in computer vision techniques promise even more precise and efficient quality control systems in the future.

Beyond these core applications, computer vision finds widespread use in numerous other sectors. In agriculture, computer vision assists in crop monitoring, precision spraying, and yield estimation, optimizing farming practices and improving crop yields. In retail, computer vision enables advanced analytics, customer behavior tracking, and inventory management. Security and surveillance benefit greatly from computer vision's ability to monitor activities, detect suspicious behavior, and enhance public safety. The integration of computer vision into robotics allows robots to better understand and interact with their environments, leading to more autonomous and efficient robotic systems. Even in areas like sports and entertainment, computer vision is finding creative applications–from automated replay systems in sports broadcasting to the creation of immersive virtual and augmented reality experiences.

The ongoing advancements in computer vision, driven by progress in deep learning and the availability of ever-larger datasets, are pushing the boundaries of what's possible. New algorithms are continually being developed, offering increased accuracy, speed, and robustness. The fusion of computer vision with other AI techniques, such as natural language processing and machine learning, is unlocking even more sophisticated applications. For example, the combination of computer vision with natural language processing allows for the development of systems that can both"see" and "understand" images, enabling a deeper level of analysis and interaction. Furthermore, the increasing availability of powerful and affordable hardware, such as GPUs and specialized AI processors, is making computer vision accessible to a wider range of users and industries. The future of computer vision promises an even greater transformative impact across virtually every sector of society, as the technology continues to improve and its applications expand. The ongoing research and development efforts are laying the groundwork for a world where computer vision plays an integral role in shaping our lives, revolutionizing industries, and solving some of the world's most challenging problems. The ability to "see" and interpret the visual world with increasing precision is not merely a technological advancement; it's a fundamental shift in how we interact with our environment and the information it contains.

Types of Robots and Their Capabilities

The seamless integration of artificial intelligence (AI) with robotics has ushered in a new era of automation and technological advancement. While computer vision empowers machines to "see," robotics provides the physical means to interact with and manipulate the world. This symbiotic relationship has resulted in a diverse range of robots, each designed for specific tasks and environments. Understanding these different types and their capabilities is crucial to grasping the full potential and implications of this rapidly evolving field.

One of the most common classifications of robots is based on their application and working environment. Industrial robots, for example, are the workhorses of manufacturing, performing repetitive, high-precision tasks with remarkable speed and consistency. These robots are typically large, stationary machines, often found on assembly lines where they weld, paint, assemble, and handle materials with unwavering accuracy. Their programming focuses on precise movements and repetitive actions, optimized for efficiency and throughput in a controlled industrial setting. The most common type within this category is the articulated robot, characterized by its multiple rotating joints, allowing it to reach and manipulate objects within a defined workspace. These are frequently employed in car manufacturing, electronics assembly, and other high-volume production environments. Cartesian robots, on the other hand, move along three linear axes (X, Y, and Z), providing precise movements in a straight line. These are ideal for applications requiring precise positioning, like pick-and-place operations or dispensing fluids with high accuracy. Cylindrical robots operate within a cylindrical coordinate system, with their arm rotating around a central axis, and this design is well-suited for applications requiring access to a larger workspace. Finally, SCARA (Selective Compliance Assembly Robot Arm) robots are designed for high-speed assembly operations, particularly for tasks requiring vertical movements and high precision. Their compliant nature makes them suitable for handling delicate components without causing damage.

In contrast to their industrial counterparts, collaborative robots, or "cobots," are designed to work safely alongside human workers. Unlike industrial robots that are typically caged for safety reasons, cobots are equipped with advanced safety features, such as force sensors and compliant actuators, that allow them to operate in close proximity to humans without posing a risk of injury. This collaborative nature significantly expands the range of applications where robots can be used, from small workshops to large manufacturing facilities. Cobots are particularly useful for tasks that are repetitive, physically demanding, or require a degree of dexterity, such as assembling small components, packaging products, or assisting with material handling. Their ease of programming and user-friendly interfaces make them accessible to a wider range of users, without requiring extensive robotics expertise. This accessibility contributes to their growing popularity in various industries, including manufacturing, healthcare, and logistics. The ability to reprogram cobots quickly for different tasks increases their versatility and value in dynamic production environments.

Beyond industrial and collaborative robots, there's a growing diversity of specialized robots designed for specific applications. Mobile robots, for instance, navigate freely within their environment, often using sensors and AI algorithms to avoid obstacles and reach their destinations autonomously. These robots are employed in a variety of settings, including warehouses, hospitals, and even homes. Autonomous guided vehicles (AGVs) are a prime example of this category, often used for material handling in factories and warehouses, transporting goods efficiently without human intervention. Delivery robots, becoming increasingly common in urban areas, represent another facet of mobile robotics, offering contactless delivery services. These robots navigate sidewalks and streets, using GPS, sensors, and AI to reach their designated addresses safely and effectively. Surgical robots represent a more specialized type, used in minimally invasive surgeries to enhance precision and reduce trauma to patients. These robots offer surgeons greater dexterity and control than traditional surgical techniques, allowing for more complex procedures with smaller incisions. The integration of AI in these surgical robots can further enhance accuracy and efficiency.

The field of robotics extends beyond these traditional categories, encompassing more experimental and specialized forms. Soft robotics utilizes flexible and compliant materials to create robots capable of adapting to unstructured environments and interacting safely with humans. These robots, often resembling biological organisms in their flexibility and resilience, are well-suited for tasks requiring dexterity and adaptability in complex, unpredictable scenarios. Aerial robots, commonly known as drones, represent another rapidly advancing area, capable of performing tasks in inaccessible or dangerous locations. Used for surveillance, aerial photography, package delivery, and even search and rescue operations, these autonomous flying robots are transforming numerous industries. Underwater robots, or remotely operated vehicles (ROVs) and autonomous underwater vehicles (AUVs), are employed for deep-sea exploration, underwater construction, and inspection of offshore structures. These robots operate in harsh environments, often equipped with specialized sensors and tools to perform their underwater tasks.

The capabilities of robots are continuously expanding, driven by advancements in AI, sensor technology, and materials science. AI plays a vital role in enhancing the perception, decision-making, and adaptability of robots. Advanced algorithms empower robots to interpret sensor data, navigate complex environments, and adapt to unexpected situations. Machine learning allows robots to learn from experience, improving their performance over time. Computer vision enables robots to "see" and understand their surroundings, while natural language processing enables them to interact with humans through voice commands. The development of more sophisticated sensors allows robots to gather richer information about their environment, improving their ability to navigate and perform tasks. Advancements in materials science allow the creation of lighter, stronger, and more durable robots, enabling their deployment in a wider range of environments.

The future of robotics promises even greater advancements, with robots playing increasingly crucial roles in various aspects of human life. We can anticipate robots taking on more complex and nuanced tasks, becoming more intuitive and responsive to human needs. Increased autonomy, driven by progress in AI, will allow robots to operate with minimal human intervention, expanding their applications in areas such as healthcare, logistics, and disaster relief. The integration of robots with other technologies, such as the Internet of Things (IoT) and cloud computing, will further enhance their capabilities and connectivity. The ongoing development of human-robot interaction (HRI) research focuses on creating more natural and intuitive ways for humans and robots to collaborate and communicate, improving the safety and efficiency of human-robot teams.

However, the rise of advanced robotics also raises important ethical and societal questions. Job displacement, due to automation, is a significant concern that requires careful consideration and proactive solutions. The potential for misuse of robotics, particularly in areas such as autonomous weapons systems, warrants close scrutiny and international cooperation to establish ethical guidelines and regulations. The issue of algorithmic bias in robot decision-making needs to be addressed to prevent discriminatory outcomes. Ensuring transparency and accountability in the development and deployment of robots are crucial to build public trust and confidence. Addressing these challenges requires a multi-faceted approach, involving researchers, policymakers, and industry leaders working collaboratively to navigate the ethical and societal implications of this transformative technology. The responsible development and deployment of robots are paramount to ensure that this powerful technology benefits all of humanity. The future of robotics holds immense promise, but realizing that promise requires thoughtful consideration of the ethical and societal implications alongside the technological advancements.

AIPowered Robotics Perception and Control

The preceding discussion outlined the diverse landscape of robotics, categorizing them by application and operational environment. However, the true power of modern robotics lies not simply in their physical form, but in their ability to perceive and interact with the world—a capability largely enabled by advancements in artificial intelligence. This section delves into the crucial role of AI in providing robots with the "senses" and "brains" necessary for effective operation. This involves a complex interplay of perception, decision-making, and control, all underpinned by sophisticated AI algorithms.

At the heart of AI-powered robotics is the ability to perceive the environment. This perception is not a passive observation, but an active process of information gathering, interpretation, and contextualization. Robots achieve this through a diverse array of sensors, each providing a unique perspective on their surroundings. Cameras provide visual information, interpreted through computer vision algorithms; lidar and radar systems offer distance measurements, creating a three-dimensional map of the space; sonar helps navigate in low-visibility conditions; and tactile sensors provide feedback on physical interactions. The challenge, however, lies not in acquiring this data, but in effectively processing and integrating it to build a coherent and accurate understanding of the environment.

Sensor fusion plays a critical role in this integration process. This technique combines data from multiple sensors to create a more comprehensive and robust representation of the environment than any single sensor could provide. For instance, combining data from a camera and a lidar system allows a robot to not only "see" objects but also to accurately estimate their distance and shape. This fusion is often achieved using probabilistic methods, such as Kalman filtering or particle filtering, which account for uncertainties inherent in sensor measurements and combine them in a statistically optimal way. These probabilistic approaches are robust to noise and uncertainties, ensuring reliable perception even in challenging environments. Furthermore, advancements in deep learning have enabled the development of sophisticated sensor fusion architectures capable of processing complex, multi-modal data efficiently and effectively. This allows robots to perceive intricate details and relationships in their surroundings, improving their decision-making capabilities.

Computer vision, the field of AI focused on enabling computers to "see," is central to robotic perception. Through the use of deep convolutional neural networks (CNNs), robots can learn to identify objects, recognize patterns, and understand scenes. Object detection algorithms enable robots to pinpoint the location and class of objects within an image or video stream, allowing them to identify obstacles, locate specific items, or interact with objects in a targeted manner. Scene understanding goes beyond simple object recognition; it involves interpreting the relationships between objects and understanding the context of the scene as a whole. This capability enables robots to navigate complex environments, understand human actions, and adapt their behavior based on the situation. For example, a robotic delivery vehicle might use scene understanding to navigate crowded sidewalks, distinguishing between pedestrians, vehicles, and obstacles while optimizing its path for safe and efficient delivery. This is a significant advancement over traditional robotic navigation techniques that often rely on pre-mapped environments and are less adaptable to dynamic situations.

Path planning is another crucial aspect of AI-enabled robotics, focusing on generating trajectories for robots to follow to achieve specific goals. Traditional path planning algorithms often rely on pre-defined maps and prioritize factors like minimizing distance or time. However, AI is enhancing path planning by enabling robots to handle more complex and dynamic environments. Machine learning techniques, such as reinforcement learning, allow robots to learn optimal paths through trial and error, adapting to unforeseen obstacles and changes in the environment. These algorithms can consider not only the physical constraints of the environment, but also factors like energy efficiency and safety. For example, a warehouse robot tasked with picking and placing items might use reinforcement learning to optimize its path through aisles, considering factors such as the weight of the items being carried, the location of other robots, and the risk of collisions. This allows for more efficient and reliable operation in busy and dynamic warehouse environments.

The control systems that govern robot movement and actions are equally critical to their performance. Traditional control methods often rely on pre-programmed trajectories and are not well-suited for adapting to dynamic environments. AI is revolutionizing robotics control through the use of adaptive control, model predictive control, and reinforcement learning. Adaptive control enables robots to adjust their behavior based on changes in the environment, such as unexpected forces or disturbances. Model predictive control anticipates future states of the environment and plans actions accordingly, allowing robots to react proactively to changes. Reinforcement learning can even learn complex control policies directly from sensor data, allowing robots to master highly intricate and dexterous movements. This is crucial for applications such as precise assembly tasks, surgical procedures, and even robotic manipulation in unstructured environments where precise, adaptive control is critical. Consider, for example, a surgical robot performing a minimally invasive procedure. The AI-driven control system must ensure precise movements, avoid unintended tissue damage, and adapt to changes in the patient's anatomy during the operation.

Furthermore, the synergy between AI and robotics extends to human-robot interaction (HRI). AI enables robots to understand and respond to human commands and intentions, fostering more seamless collaboration between humans and machines. Natural language processing (NLP) allows robots to interpret spoken or written instructions, while computer vision enables them to understand human gestures and facial expressions. This makes robots more intuitive and easier to use, broadening their potential applications. Consider the development of robotic companions designed to assist the elderly. These robots rely heavily on AI for natural language processing to understand commands and respond appropriately, computer vision to recognize emotions and interpret the needs of the user, and machine learning to continuously improve their ability to provide personalized care. The seamless integration of these AI capabilities is critical to their effectiveness and acceptability as helpful companions.

The development of AI-powered robotics, however, is not without challenges. One major hurdle is ensuring robustness and reliability in real-world environments, where unpredictable events and sensor noise can significantly impact performance. AI algorithms must be able to handle these uncertainties gracefully, ensuring that robots can function reliably even in challenging conditions. Developing algorithms that are both computationally efficient and robust to various environmental conditions remains an active area of research. Additionally, data requirements for training advanced AI models for robotic control and perception can be substantial.

Acquiring and annotating large datasets is costly and time-consuming, representing a significant barrier to entry for many researchers and developers. The efficient utilization of limited data through techniques like transfer learning and data augmentation is essential to overcome these challenges.

Another significant challenge is ensuring the safety and ethical implications of AI-powered robots are carefully considered. As robots become more autonomous and capable, it is crucial to develop safety mechanisms to prevent accidents and mitigate risks.

Moreover, the potential for bias in AI algorithms raises ethical concerns. Bias in training data can lead to robots exhibiting discriminatory behavior, and addressing this issue is paramount to ensuring fair and equitable use of robotic technology. Transparency in AI algorithms is also crucial to understanding how robots make decisions and to ensure accountability for their actions. The ongoing discussion surrounding AI ethics plays a critical role in shaping the development and deployment of AI-powered robotics, ensuring a responsible and beneficial integration into our society.

The future success of this field relies on a strong commitment to addressing these technical and ethical challenges proactively.

Robot Learning and Adaptation

The previous section detailed how AI provides robots with the capacity for perception and control. However, a truly intelligent robot must not only react to its environment but also learn from its experiences and adapt its behavior accordingly. This learning and adaptation process is crucial for enabling robots to operate
effectively in unpredictable and dynamic environments, surpassing the limitations of pre-programmed, rigid systems. This section delves into the fascinating field of robot learning, examining the techniques that allow robots to become increasingly autonomous and proficient over time.

At the forefront of robot learning is reinforcement learning (RL), a powerful machine learning paradigm that allows robots to learn optimal behaviors through trial and error. In RL, a robot interacts with its environment, receiving rewards for desirable actions and penalties for undesirable ones. Through this iterative process of exploration and exploitation, the robot learns a policy—a mapping from states to actions—that maximizes its cumulative reward over time. This learning process is often guided by sophisticated algorithms, such as Q-learning or policy gradients, which update the robot's policy based on the feedback it receives.

The application of RL in robotics is diverse and impactful. Consider the example of a robot learning to navigate a complex environment, such as a cluttered warehouse. The robot might receive a reward for successfully reaching a target location and a penalty for colliding with obstacles or straying off course. Through repeated interactions with the environment, the RL algorithm adjusts the robot's movement strategy, enabling it to find increasingly efficient and safe paths. Furthermore, RL can be used to learn complex manipulation tasks, such as grasping objects of varying shapes and sizes, or assembling intricate mechanical components. By receiving rewards for successful manipulations and penalties for failures, the robot can learn sophisticated motor skills through trial-and-error.

However, traditional RL approaches can be computationally expensive and require significant amounts of training data. This limitation has led to the development of more efficient RL techniques, such as proximal policy optimization (PPO) and trust region policy optimization (TRPO), which enhance the stability and convergence speed of the learning process. These improvements are crucial for deploying RL algorithms in real-world robotics applications, where training time and computational resources are often limited.

Beyond RL, imitation learning provides another powerful approach to robot learning. Instead of learning from rewards and penalties, imitation learning allows robots to learn from demonstrations provided by human experts or other robots. This approach can be particularly useful for tasks that are difficult or dangerous for robots to learn through trial and error. For instance, a surgeon might demonstrate a complex surgical procedure to a surgical robot, and the robot would then learn to replicate the procedure through imitation learning. This significantly accelerates the learning process and ensures that the robot learns optimal and safe behaviors from the outset.

Several techniques underpin imitation learning. Behavioral cloning is a common method where a robot directly imitates the actions of a demonstrator. However, this approach can struggle with situations not explicitly covered in the demonstrations. Inverse reinforcement learning (IRL) addresses this limitation by inferring the reward function that underlies the demonstrator's behavior. By learning this reward function, the robot can generalize its learned behavior to new, unseen situations. This allows the robot to adapt more effectively to variations in its environment and tasks.

The combination of RL and imitation learning represents a particularly powerful approach to robot learning. This hybrid approach leverages the strengths of both methods, allowing robots to learn from demonstrations while simultaneously refining their skills through trial and error. For example, a robot might initially learn to perform a manipulation task through imitation learning from a human expert. Then, the robot can refine its skills through RL, adapting to variations in the objects being manipulated and improving its dexterity and precision over time.

Another important aspect of robot learning is the ability to transfer knowledge between different tasks or robots. Transfer learning allows a robot to leverage its experience in one task to improve its performance in a related task. For instance, a robot that has learned to grasp and manipulate objects of one type might be able to quickly adapt to grasping and manipulating similar objects of a different type. This reduces the amount of training data required for each new task and accelerates the learning process.

However, robot learning is not without its challenges. One major hurdle is the problem of safety. As robots become more autonomous, ensuring their actions remain safe and predictable is paramount. This requires the development of robust learning algorithms that can handle unforeseen circumstances and prevent accidents. Moreover, addressing the ethical implications of robot learning is crucial. Bias in training data can lead to robots exhibiting unfair or discriminatory behavior. Therefore, careful consideration of these ethical concerns must inform the design and development of robot learning systems.

Furthermore, the computational cost of training advanced robot learning algorithms can be significant. This necessitates the development of efficient learning algorithms and hardware platforms capable of handling the computational demands of complex robot learning tasks. As AI hardware continues to advance, this constraint will likely be eased, allowing for the deployment of even more sophisticated robot learning algorithms.

The future of robot learning promises remarkable advancements. The integration of diverse learning paradigms, such as RL, imitation learning, and transfer learning, will allow robots to acquire complex skills and adapt to ever-changing environments. The development of more robust, efficient, and safe learning algorithms will pave the way for the widespread adoption of intelligent robots in various sectors, from manufacturing and logistics to healthcare and personal assistance. This integration will not only enhance the capabilities of robots but also create opportunities for human-robot collaboration, fostering a future where humans and machines work together seamlessly to address complex challenges and create new possibilities. As research continues to push the boundaries of robot learning, we can anticipate a future where robots are truly intelligent, adaptive, and capable of seamlessly integrating into our lives. The journey towards truly autonomous robots is ongoing, but the progress being made in robot learning offers a promising glimpse into a future where machines can learn, adapt, and collaborate with us in ways previously unimaginable.

Ethical Considerations in Robotics and AI

The preceding sections explored the remarkable advancements in robotics and AI, showcasing their potential to revolutionize various aspects of human life. However, the rapid progress in this field necessitates a careful examination of the ethical considerations that accompany such transformative technologies. Failing to address these concerns proactively could lead to unforeseen and potentially harmful consequences. The ethical landscape surrounding AI-powered robots is complex and multifaceted, encompassing issues of safety, liability, job displacement, autonomous weapons systems, and the overarching need for responsible AI development.

One of the most immediate and pressing ethical concerns is the safety of AI-powered robots. As robots become increasingly autonomous and capable of performing complex tasks, the potential for accidents or malfunctions increases. Consider a self-driving car involved in a collision. Determining liability becomes a complex legal and ethical problem. Is the manufacturer responsible for a software flaw? The owner for improper maintenance? Or is it simply an unavoidable accident? Similar questions arise in other contexts. A surgical robot causing harm during an operation, an industrial robot malfunctioning on a factory floor, or a domestic robot injuring a family member—each scenario presents unique challenges in assigning responsibility and establishing accountability. Current legal frameworks are often ill-equipped to handle these emerging complexities, necessitating new regulations and legal interpretations to ensure accountability and compensate victims fairly. The development of robust safety protocols and fail-safe mechanisms becomes paramount, along with rigorous testing and validation procedures to mitigate the risk of accidents.

Beyond individual accidents, the broader societal implications of increasingly autonomous robots must be carefully considered. One major concern is job displacement. As robots become more capable of performing tasks currently done by humans, the potential for widespread unemployment becomes a serious social and economic challenge. While some argue that AI and automation will create new job opportunities, there's concern that the transition might be uneven, leaving many workers behind and exacerbating existing inequalities. This necessitates proactive measures such as retraining and reskilling programs to help workers adapt to the changing job market, as well as the development of social safety nets to support those who are displaced. Furthermore, ensuring fair wages and working conditions for those whose jobs are not immediately replaced by automation is crucial. A just transition requires careful planning and collaboration between governments, businesses, and educational institutions.

The potential for autonomous weapons systems, often referred to as lethal autonomous weapons (LAWs), presents perhaps the most alarming ethical challenge. These systems, capable of selecting and engaging targets without human intervention, raise profound questions about accountability, proportionality, and the very nature of warfare. The lack of human control raises the specter of unintended escalation and the potential for errors with catastrophic consequences. The development and deployment of LAWS raise fundamental moral and ethical concerns, including the violation of international humanitarian law and the potential for undermining human dignity. A global consensus on the regulation and potential ban of these weapons is desperately needed to prevent a future arms race with potentially devastating outcomes. International cooperation and robust ethical guidelines are crucial for ensuring that AI is not used to create weapons that could threaten global security and human life.

The issue of bias in AI algorithms also presents a significant ethical challenge. AI systems are trained on vast amounts of data, and if this data reflects existing societal biases, the resulting AI system will likely perpetuate and even amplify those biases. This can lead to discriminatory outcomes in areas such as loan applications, hiring processes, and even criminal justice. For example, facial recognition systems have been shown to be less accurate in identifying individuals with darker skin tones, leading to potential misidentification and wrongful accusations. Mitigating bias in AI requires careful attention to data collection, algorithm design, and ongoing monitoring to ensure fairness and equity. Transparency in the development and deployment of AI systems is also critical to enabling scrutiny and accountability.

Furthermore, the concept of robot rights is emerging as an area of ethical debate. As robots become more sophisticated and exhibit increasingly complex behaviors, the question of whether they deserve some form of legal protection or rights arises. While this issue is still largely theoretical, it highlights the growing need to consider the ethical implications of creating machines that might exhibit characteristics we traditionally associate with sentience or consciousness. A nuanced approach is needed, one that balances the need for responsible development with the potential for unforeseen ethical implications as the technology advances.

The development of responsible AI requires a multi-pronged approach. This includes fostering ethical guidelines and standards for AI development, promoting transparency and accountability in AI systems, and investing in research on AI safety and robustness.

Collaboration between researchers, policymakers, and industry leaders is crucial to ensure that AI is developed and used in a way that aligns with human values and benefits society as a whole. The creation of independent oversight bodies could also help to ensure that AI development and deployment adhere to ethical principles.

Furthermore, public education and engagement are vital for fostering a broader understanding of the ethical implications of AI and fostering a more informed public discourse.

In conclusion, the ethical considerations surrounding AI-powered robots are profound and multifaceted. Addressing these challenges requires a proactive and collaborative approach involving researchers, policymakers, industry leaders, and the public.

Ignoring these ethical considerations could lead to unforeseen and potentially catastrophic consequences. The development of responsible and ethical AI is not just a technological challenge; it's a societal imperative that demands careful attention and proactive measures to ensure a future where AI benefits humanity as a whole. The future of AI depends not just on technical innovation, but also on our ability to develop ethical frameworks and regulations that guide the development and deployment of this transformative technology. This requires ongoing dialogue, collaboration, and a commitment to ensuring that AI remains a tool for human progress and not a source of unintended harm.

Future Trends in Robotics and AI

The convergence of advanced robotics and increasingly sophisticated AI algorithms is poised to reshape numerous sectors in the coming decades. We're moving beyond the era of robots performing simple, repetitive tasks in structured environments, like assembly lines. The future belongs to robots capable of operating in dynamic, unstructured settings – think robots navigating disaster zones, performing complex surgeries, or assisting the elderly in their homes. This necessitates breakthroughs in several key areas. One critical development is improved perception and manipulation capabilities. Current robots often struggle to accurately interpret their environment, especially in cluttered or unpredictable settings.

Advancements in computer vision, particularly the use of deep learning models trained on massive datasets of real-world images and videos, are rapidly enhancing robots' ability to "see" and understand their surroundings. Similarly, advancements in tactile sensing and dexterous manipulation are enabling robots to handle delicate objects and perform complex tasks with greater precision and control. The integration of advanced sensors, including force sensors, proximity sensors, and cameras, provides robots with a richer understanding of their physical interaction with the world.

Furthermore, the development of more robust and adaptable AI algorithms is paramount. Robots operating in unstructured environments need to be able to adapt to unexpected situations and learn from their experiences. Reinforcement learning, a technique where robots learn through trial and error by interacting with their environment, is showing great promise in this area. By rewarding desirable behaviors and penalizing undesirable ones, reinforcement learning algorithms can train robots to perform complex tasks without explicit programming. However, scaling reinforcement learning to complex real-world scenarios remains a challenge. The computational cost can be prohibitive, and ensuring the safety of the robot during the learning process is paramount. Safe reinforcement learning techniques are being actively developed, leveraging approaches such as simulations and constrained learning to ensure that robots learn safely and effectively. The integration of simulation environments, which allows robots to practice in a safe, virtual world before deploying them into real-world scenarios, significantly accelerates the training process and mitigates the risks associated with real-world experimentation.

The rise of human-robot collaboration (HRC) represents another transformative trend. The future of work is not about robots replacing humans, but rather robots working alongside humans, augmenting human capabilities and improving productivity. Collaborative robots, or "cobots," are designed to work safely and effectively with humans in shared workspaces. They are equipped with safety features to prevent accidents and are designed with intuitive interfaces that allow humans to easily interact with them. This collaborative approach leverages the strengths of both humans and robots – the creativity, adaptability, and complex decision-making abilities of humans combined with the precision, speed, and endurance of robots. Cobots are already finding applications in various industries, from manufacturing and logistics to healthcare and agriculture. In manufacturing, cobots can assist human workers with repetitive or physically demanding tasks, reducing the risk of injury and improving efficiency. In healthcare, cobots can assist surgeons with complex operations, providing greater precision and minimizing invasiveness. As cobots become more sophisticated and affordable, we can anticipate their adoption across a wider range of industries and applications. The design of intuitive and user-friendly interfaces is crucial to facilitating successful HRC; this requires addressing both technical and human factors, including the development of effective communication protocols and training programs.

Beyond industry, the impact of robotics and AI will extend to our homes and daily lives. Domestic robots are becoming increasingly sophisticated, offering assistance with tasks like cleaning, cooking, and providing companionship for the elderly. These robots rely heavily on AI for tasks such as navigation, object recognition, and natural language processing. Ethical considerations regarding data privacy and security are critical concerns in the development of such robots. Smart home technology integrates seamlessly with domestic robots, creating a more interconnected and automated living environment. However, concerns about data security, privacy violations, and potential biases embedded in algorithms must be addressed. The responsible development and deployment of domestic robots necessitate stringent ethical guidelines and regulatory frameworks to ensure that these technologies are used safely and ethically. The increasing sophistication of these robots necessitates a careful consideration of their potential impact on human relationships and social interactions.

The development of humanoid robots represents another significant area of progress. These robots are designed to resemble humans in appearance and movement, potentially leading to more natural and intuitive interactions. While still in their early stages of development, humanoid robots have the potential to revolutionize various sectors, from healthcare and education to customer service and entertainment. Challenges remain in replicating human dexterity, adaptability, and emotional intelligence, however. The creation of truly intelligent and autonomous humanoid robots is a complex task, requiring breakthroughs in various fields, including artificial intelligence, robotics, and materials science.

However, the rapid advancement of robotics and AI brings significant societal challenges. The displacement of human workers due to automation is a major concern, requiring proactive measures such as retraining and reskilling programs. Addressing potential biases in AI algorithms is crucial to prevent discriminatory outcomes. The ethical implications of autonomous robots, particularly in sensitive areas like healthcare and law enforcement, require careful consideration and appropriate regulatory frameworks. Robust safety measures are essential to mitigate the risk of accidents or malfunctions. These issues are not merely technical challenges; they are deeply social and political questions that necessitate collaboration between researchers, policymakers, and the public. Proactive planning and societal adaptation are critical to navigating the transformative impact of advanced robotics and AI. Public discourse, educational initiatives, and the development of responsible AI guidelines are crucial for ensuring a future where these powerful technologies benefit all of humanity.

Beyond the immediate impacts, the long-term implications of these technologies are even more profound. The potential for human augmentation through robotics and AI is a significant area of

exploration. Exoskeletons and other assistive devices could enhance human physical capabilities, while advanced AI systems could augment cognitive functions. This raises ethical considerations about fairness, accessibility, and the potential for exacerbating existing inequalities. The development of truly autonomous robots raises fundamental questions about the nature of intelligence, consciousness, and the potential for machines to exhibit behavior akin to human sentience. While these questions remain largely philosophical, their implications will need to be considered as the technology advances. Careful consideration of the ethical, social, and economic implications is crucial to shape a future where these advancements serve humanity. Transparent and accountable
development practices, along with robust regulatory frameworks, are essential to mitigating potential risks and maximizing the societal benefits of this technological revolution.

The future of robotics and AI is not predetermined. The path forward depends on the choices we make today. By fostering collaboration between researchers, policymakers, and the public, we can shape a future where these powerful technologies are harnessed for the betterment of society. This requires ongoing dialogue, a commitment to ethical principles, and a proactive approach to addressing the challenges and opportunities that lie ahead. The development of responsible AI and robotics is not just a technical endeavor; it is a societal imperative. By prioritizing ethical considerations, investing in education and training, and fostering international cooperation, we can ensure that these technologies serve as instruments of progress, rather than sources of unforeseen harm or inequality. The ultimate goal should be to create a future where robots and AI enhance human capabilities, improve lives, and contribute to a more just and equitable world. This requires a sustained commitment to responsible innovation and a proactive approach to managing the profound societal transformations that these technologies will undoubtedly bring about.

AIAssisted Diagnosis and Treatment Planning

The integration of artificial intelligence (AI) into healthcare is rapidly transforming how diseases are diagnosed and treatments are planned. This shift is driven by the ability of AI algorithms to analyze vast amounts of data with unprecedented speed and accuracy, empowering medical professionals to make more informed decisions and improve patient care. This section will explore the multifaceted applications of AI in assisting with diagnosis and treatment planning, focusing on key areas such as medical image analysis, genomic analysis, and the burgeoning field of personalized medicine.

One of the most significant impacts of AI in healthcare is its application to medical image analysis. Radiologists, pathologists, and other specialists routinely handle massive volumes of medical images – X-rays, CT scans, MRIs, and PET scans – searching for subtle anomalies that might indicate disease. Manually reviewing these images is a time-consuming and potentially error-prone process, even for highly trained professionals. AI algorithms, particularly those based on deep learning, offer a powerful solution. These algorithms are trained on massive datasets of medical images, learning to identify patterns and features associated with various diseases with remarkable accuracy. For example, AI systems have demonstrated impressive capabilities in detecting cancerous lesions in mammograms, identifying early signs of diabetic retinopathy in retinal images, and assisting in the diagnosis of cardiovascular diseases from echocardiograms.

The power of AI in medical image analysis extends beyond simple detection. AI algorithms can also quantify the size and extent of lesions, assess the severity of disease, and even predict the likelihood of disease progression or recurrence. This level of detail provides clinicians with more comprehensive information to guide treatment decisions. Furthermore, AI-powered image analysis tools can assist in standardizing diagnostic procedures, reducing inter-observer variability, and improving the overall consistency and reliability of diagnoses. While AI does not replace the expertise of human clinicians, it serves as a powerful augmentation, offering valuable assistance in making timely and accurate diagnoses.

Beyond medical imaging, AI is revolutionizing genomic analysis. The human genome contains a vast amount of information, and interpreting this information to understand an individual's predisposition to disease or to personalize treatment strategies is a complex task. AI algorithms are being used to analyze genomic data, identify genetic mutations associated with disease, and predict an individual's risk of developing certain conditions. This information is crucial in preventative medicine, allowing individuals to make informed lifestyle choices and seek early intervention if necessary. Moreover, AI can be instrumental in identifying potential drug targets and designing more effective therapies based on an individual's genetic profile. The ability to tailor treatments to an individual's genetic makeup is a cornerstone of personalized medicine.

Personalized medicine, often referred to as precision medicine, aims to provide tailored medical care based on an individual's unique characteristics, including genetics, lifestyle, and environmental factors. AI plays a vital role in making this approach a reality. By analyzing a patient's medical history, genomic data, lifestyle information, and other relevant factors, AI algorithms can predict the likelihood of disease progression, response to treatment, and the risk of adverse events. This predictive capability empowers clinicians to select the most effective treatment strategies, minimize side effects, and improve patient outcomes. For instance, in cancer treatment, AI can help determine the best chemotherapy regimen for a specific patient, based on their tumor's genetic profile and other clinical characteristics. This approach allows for more targeted treatment, maximizing efficacy and minimizing the toxic side effects associated with chemotherapy.

Furthermore, AI algorithms are being used to develop new drugs and therapies. The process of drug discovery and development is traditionally a lengthy and expensive undertaking. AI algorithms can accelerate this process by analyzing massive datasets of chemical compounds, identifying potential drug candidates, and predicting their efficacy and safety. Machine learning models can predict the binding affinity of drug molecules to their target proteins, identify potential drug-drug interactions, and predict the likelihood of adverse events. This ability to efficiently screen and analyze vast datasets allows researchers to prioritize promising drug candidates and significantly reduce the time and cost associated with drug development.

The successful implementation of AI in medical diagnosis and treatment planning requires addressing several challenges. One key challenge is the availability of high-quality data. AI algorithms are only as good as the data they are trained on. Large, well-annotated datasets of medical images, genomic data, and patient records are essential for training accurate and reliable AI models. Data privacy and security are also critical concerns. Protecting patient data and ensuring its confidentiality are paramount in the development and deployment of AI-powered healthcare solutions. Furthermore, algorithmic bias can lead to inaccurate or discriminatory outcomes. Careful consideration must be given to mitigate potential biases in AI algorithms to ensure fairness and equity in healthcare.

Another challenge lies in the integration of AI into existing healthcare workflows. Seamlessly integrating AI tools into electronic health records (EHRs) and clinical decision support systems is crucial for widespread adoption. User-friendly interfaces are also essential to ensure that clinicians can effectively use these tools. Education and training are necessary to equip healthcare professionals with the skills and knowledge to utilize AI effectively. Addressing these challenges requires collaborative efforts between AI researchers, healthcare providers, policymakers, and technology companies.

In conclusion, AI-assisted diagnosis and treatment planning represent a significant advancement in healthcare. By harnessing the power of AI algorithms to analyze vast amounts of data, medical professionals can make more informed decisions, improve diagnostic accuracy, personalize treatment strategies, and accelerate the development of new drugs and therapies. While challenges remain, the transformative potential of AI in healthcare is undeniable. The future of medicine will undoubtedly involve a closer collaboration between human clinicians and AI systems, working together to improve patient care and revolutionize the healthcare landscape. Continued investment in research, development, and responsible implementation will be crucial in realizing the full potential of AI to benefit humanity. The ethical considerations, data privacy concerns, and integration into existing healthcare systems are challenges that must be continuously addressed as the technology evolves and expands its capabilities within the healthcare domain. The focus should remain on patient safety, data security, and the equitable distribution of these groundbreaking advancements.

Drug Discovery and Development

The pharmaceutical industry faces a persistent challenge: the lengthy and costly process of drug discovery and development.

Traditional methods often involve years of research, extensive laboratory testing, and large-scale clinical trials, resulting in significant financial investment and a high rate of failure. However, the advent of artificial intelligence (AI) offers a transformative potential to streamline and accelerate this process, significantly reducing both time and cost while increasing the likelihood of success. AI's capacity to analyze vast datasets, identify patterns, and make predictions is revolutionizing how new drugs are conceived, tested, and brought to market.

One of the most significant applications of AI in drug discovery is in target identification and validation. The process of identifying a specific molecule or biological pathway that plays a crucial role in a disease is a critical first step. Traditional methods rely heavily on expert knowledge and laborious experimentation. AI, however, can analyze vast amounts of biological data – genomic sequences, protein structures, and clinical trial results – to identify potential drug targets with greater efficiency. Machine learning algorithms, particularly deep learning models, can uncover subtle relationships and patterns that may be missed by human researchers, leading to the identification of novel drug targets that would otherwise remain undiscovered. For example, AI algorithms can predict the likelihood that a particular protein is involved in a specific disease by analyzing its interactions with other proteins and its expression levels in diseased tissues. This predictive capability significantly reduces the time and resources required for target identification.

Once potential drug targets have been identified, the next challenge is to discover molecules that can effectively interact with these targets. This process traditionally involves screening vast libraries of chemical compounds, a labor-intensive and time-consuming task.

AI algorithms are significantly accelerating this process through virtual screening. AI models can predict the binding affinity of a molecule to its target protein, allowing researchers to prioritize compounds with a high probability of efficacy. This virtual screening approach significantly reduces the number of compounds that need to be synthesized and tested in the laboratory, leading to substantial cost savings and faster development times. Furthermore, AI can design novel molecules with enhanced properties, such as improved bioavailability, reduced toxicity, and increased efficacy. Generative models, a type of AI algorithm, are being used to create new chemical structures with desired properties, effectively expanding the chemical space explored for drug discovery.

Beyond target identification and molecule discovery, AI is playing a crucial role in predicting the efficacy and safety of drug candidates. Preclinical testing, which involves evaluating the drug's effectiveness and toxicity in cell cultures and animal models, is a crucial step before human clinical trials. AI algorithms can analyze data from preclinical studies to predict the likelihood that a drug will be effective in humans and to identify potential safety concerns. Machine learning models can integrate data from diverse sources – including chemical structures, biological activity data, and toxicology results – to predict the drug's pharmacokinetic and pharmacodynamic properties, offering insights into how the drug will be absorbed, distributed, metabolized, and excreted in the body. This predictive capability enables researchers to make more informed decisions about which drug candidates to advance to clinical trials, thereby minimizing the risk of failure and reducing the overall cost of drug development.

The design and execution of clinical trials are further optimized through the application of AI. Clinical trials are expensive and time-consuming, and their success is often hampered by factors like patient recruitment challenges and inefficient data management. AI can assist in several aspects of clinical trial design, including patient selection, trial stratification, and endpoint selection. AI algorithms can analyze patient data to identify individuals who are most likely to benefit from a particular treatment, leading to more efficient and effective trials. Furthermore, AI can optimize the trial design itself, leading to smaller, more focused trials that are faster and less expensive to conduct. AI can also analyze data generated during the clinical trial, identifying potential safety signals and enabling early detection of adverse events. This allows for more timely interventions, protecting patient safety and potentially preventing the premature termination of a promising trial.

However, the integration of AI in drug discovery and development is not without its challenges. One significant hurdle is the availability of high-quality data. AI algorithms require vast amounts of well-curated data to train effectively. The pharmaceutical industry is increasingly recognizing the importance of data sharing and collaboration to overcome this limitation. Data standardization and interoperability are also crucial for enabling seamless data integration and analysis. Another challenge is the "black box" nature of some AI algorithms, particularly deep learning models.

Understanding how these models arrive at their predictions can be difficult, which can hinder the interpretability and acceptance of AI-driven results by regulatory agencies and clinicians. Addressing this challenge necessitates developing more explainable AI (XAI) techniques that provide insight into the decision-making process of AI models. Furthermore, ethical considerations, such as bias in training data and data privacy concerns, must be carefully addressed to ensure the responsible development and deployment of AI in drug discovery and development.

Despite these challenges, the transformative potential of AI in this field is undeniable. AI is accelerating the pace of innovation, reducing the cost of drug development, and increasing the likelihood of discovering effective and safe new therapies. As AI algorithms become more sophisticated and as data availability improves, the impact of AI on drug discovery and development will only continue to grow. The future of pharmaceutical research will undoubtedly involve a closer collaboration between human scientists and AI systems, working together to accelerate the development of life-saving medicines and improve global health outcomes. The continued investment in research, development, and responsible implementation will be crucial in realizing the full potential of AI to benefit humanity. The ethical considerations, data privacy concerns, and responsible integration of AI into existing research practices must be addressed proactively as the technology advances, prioritizing patient safety and equitable access to these groundbreaking innovations.

Robotic Surgery and AIEnhanced Medical Procedures

The precision and dexterity of human hands, while remarkable, are inherently limited. In the intricate world of microsurgery, where the margin for error is minuscule, these limitations can have significant consequences. Robotic surgery, however, represents a transformative leap forward, offering surgeons unparalleled control and accuracy. These advancements are further enhanced through the integration of artificial intelligence (AI), creating a synergistic relationship that is revolutionizing surgical procedures and expanding the scope of minimally invasive techniques.

Robotic surgical systems consist of a surgeon's console, a robotic arm equipped with specialized instruments, and a high-definition 3D camera system. The surgeon controls the robotic arms from the console, manipulating the instruments with intuitive movements. The robotic arms translate these movements into precise actions within the patient's body, enabling smaller incisions, reduced trauma, and improved surgical outcomes. The 3D visualization provided by the camera system allows for a detailed view of the surgical field, facilitating greater accuracy and control. This technology has found widespread application in various surgical specialties, including cardiac surgery, urology, gynecology, and general surgery.

Beyond the mechanical precision afforded by robotic systems, the integration of AI elevates the capabilities of robotic surgery to a new level. AI algorithms can assist surgeons in several critical aspects of the procedure, enhancing accuracy, safety, and efficiency. One key application is image-guided surgery, where AI algorithms analyze medical images – such as CT scans, MRIs, and ultrasounds –to create a three-dimensional map of the patient's anatomy. This detailed map is overlaid onto the surgical field, guiding the surgeon's movements and minimizing the risk of damaging surrounding tissues. This is especially crucial in complex procedures where vital organs are in close proximity to the surgical site.

AI algorithms can also be trained to identify and highlight specific anatomical structures during surgery. For instance, in neurosurgery,

AI can automatically identify and delineate critical blood vessels, nerves, and tumors, ensuring their protection during the procedure. This reduces the likelihood of inadvertent damage and improves surgical precision. In minimally invasive procedures, where visualization is often challenging, AI can provide real-time guidance, assisting the surgeon in navigating intricate anatomical spaces. The system might even suggest the optimal path for the surgical instruments based on its analysis of the patient's anatomy and the surrounding tissues.

Furthermore, AI plays a crucial role in the development of new surgical techniques and the training of surgeons. Simulation platforms, powered by AI, offer surgeons a safe and controlled environment to practice complex procedures. These platforms provide realistic simulations of the surgical field, allowing surgeons to refine their skills and improve their dexterity before operating on actual patients. AI algorithms can also analyze surgical performance, providing surgeons with feedback on their technique and identifying areas for improvement. This leads to better training, faster learning, and ultimately, safer and more effective surgeries.

Another transformative aspect of AI in robotic surgery is the potential for remote surgery. While still in its early stages of development, remote surgery offers the promise of providing expert surgical care to patients in remote or underserved areas. AI-powered robotic systems enable surgeons to perform complex procedures remotely, guided by high-quality visual and haptic feedback. This technology could revolutionize healthcare access, particularly in areas with a shortage of skilled surgeons. Imagine a scenario where a specialist located in a major metropolitan area can perform a life-saving surgery on a patient in a rural community, bridging geographical barriers and overcoming limitations in access to care. While ethical considerations, such as regulatory hurdles and ensuring reliable communication networks, must be addressed, the potential benefits are undeniable.

However, the integration of AI into robotic surgery is not without its challenges. Data privacy and security are paramount, requiring robust systems to protect sensitive patient information. The potential for algorithmic bias must also be carefully addressed to ensure equitable access to this technology. Moreover, the "black box" nature of some AI algorithms can raise concerns about transparency and accountability. The development of explainable AI (XAI) is crucial to build trust and allow surgeons to understand the reasoning behind the AI's recommendations. Furthermore, the training of AI models requires large, high-quality datasets, which can be challenging to acquire and curate, especially for rare surgical procedures.

Despite these challenges, the synergy between robotic surgery and AI is undeniable. The combination promises a future where surgical procedures are safer, more precise, less invasive, and more accessible. AI algorithms are not intended to replace surgeons but rather to augment their capabilities, empowering them to make better decisions and achieve better outcomes. The ongoing research and development in this field are focused on enhancing the capabilities of robotic surgical systems, improving the accuracy and reliability of AI algorithms, and addressing the ethical and regulatory concerns associated with this technology. As AI technology continues to advance, we can expect even more significant breakthroughs in robotic surgery, ultimately leading to improved patient care and transforming the future of healthcare.

Beyond robotic surgery, AI is enhancing a broad range of medical procedures. In radiology, AI algorithms are used for image analysis, assisting radiologists in detecting subtle abnormalities in medical images such as X-rays, CT scans, and MRIs. These algorithms can highlight potential tumors, fractures, or other anomalies, aiding in earlier and more accurate diagnosis. AI-powered diagnostic tools can analyze medical images much faster than a human radiologist, potentially reducing diagnostic delays and improving patient outcomes. This is especially crucial in emergency situations where rapid diagnosis is critical. The algorithms can also flag images that require immediate attention, prioritizing cases that need urgent review by a specialist.

Similarly, in pathology, AI is being used to analyze microscopic images of tissue samples, assisting pathologists in diagnosing diseases such as cancer. AI algorithms can identify subtle cellular changes that may be difficult for human pathologists to detect, improving diagnostic accuracy. This technology has the potential to improve the speed and accuracy of cancer diagnosis, leading to earlier intervention and better treatment outcomes. By reducing the workload of pathologists and improving diagnostic precision, AI-powered tools can help address the growing shortage of skilled pathologists worldwide.

In cardiology, AI algorithms can analyze electrocardiograms (ECGs) and other cardiac data to detect arrhythmias and other heart conditions. This technology can help identify patients at risk of heart attacks or strokes, allowing for timely intervention. AI-powered devices can continuously monitor patients' heart rhythms, providing early warning signs of potential problems. This continuous monitoring improves the accuracy and timeliness of detection, leading to better patient outcomes.

AI is also transforming the field of ophthalmology. AI algorithms can analyze retinal images to detect early signs of diabetic retinopathy, glaucoma, and macular degeneration, improving the accuracy and speed of diagnosis. Early detection of these conditions is critical for preventing blindness, and AI-powered tools can assist ophthalmologists in providing timely and effective interventions. AI algorithms are being incorporated into diagnostic tools, enhancing their capabilities to detect subtle changes and reducing the possibility of missed diagnoses. The technology's role extends to automated image analysis, which can greatly enhance the efficiency of the diagnostic process.

The development and deployment of AI in healthcare procedures necessitate careful consideration of ethical implications. Data privacy and security are of paramount importance, and robust systems must be in place to protect patient information. Algorithmic bias is another major concern, as AI models trained on biased data can perpetuate and amplify existing healthcare disparities.

Transparency and accountability are crucial to building trust and ensuring that AI systems are used responsibly. Continuous monitoring and evaluation of AI systems are needed to identify and mitigate potential risks. The responsible development and implementation of AI in healthcare demand a multidisciplinary approach, involving experts from various fields to ensure that these powerful tools are used ethically and equitably. The aim is to harness the transformative potential of AI to improve healthcare for all, addressing systemic inequities and promoting health equity.

AIDriven Patient Monitoring and Management

The integration of AI extends far beyond the operating room and the diagnostic laboratory. A quieter, yet equally transformative revolution is underway in the realm of patient monitoring and chronic disease management. This involves a shift from reactive, episodic care to proactive, continuous health surveillance, leveraging the power of AI to anticipate and address health issues before they escalate into critical events. This paradigm shift is fueled by the proliferation of wearable sensors, the development of sophisticated remote patient monitoring (RPM) systems, and the application of increasingly powerful AI algorithms for early disease detection and personalized intervention.

Wearable technology has become ubiquitous, with smartwatches, fitness trackers, and other devices capable of continuously monitoring a range of physiological parameters, including heart rate, blood pressure, activity levels, sleep patterns, and even blood glucose levels. This continuous stream of data provides an unprecedented window into an individual's health status, far exceeding the snapshots provided by periodic physician visits. However, the sheer volume of data generated by these devices presents a significant analytical challenge. This is where AI comes into play.

AI algorithms can process and analyze this vast amount of physiological data, identifying subtle patterns and anomalies that might indicate an impending health problem. For example, an AI algorithm might detect a subtle but consistent increase in heart rate variability, indicative of an early stage of heart failure, or a persistent elevation in blood pressure, signaling a risk of hypertension. These early warnings allow for timely intervention, preventing the condition from progressing to a more severe state. The algorithm's capacity to identify trends over time, rather than focusing on isolated data points, is critical to effective disease prediction. It can learn individual baselines and flag deviations as potential warning signs, tailoring its alerts to the unique characteristics of each patient.

Remote patient monitoring (RPM) systems build upon this foundation, integrating wearable sensor data with other sources of information, such as electronic health records (EHRs), medication adherence data, and even self-reported symptoms. These systems provide a holistic view of the patient's health status, enabling clinicians to monitor patients remotely and intervene as needed.

The AI component of these systems plays a crucial role in automating data analysis, generating alerts, and providing clinicians with actionable insights. This can significantly reduce the burden on healthcare providers, allowing them to focus their time and resources on patients who require the most immediate attention.

AI-powered RPM systems are particularly valuable in managing chronic diseases such as diabetes, hypertension, and congestive heart failure. For patients with diabetes, for example, the system can monitor blood glucose levels continuously, alerting both the patient and the clinician to any significant fluctuations. This allows for timely adjustments to medication or lifestyle interventions, preventing potentially dangerous complications. For patients with hypertension, the system can monitor blood pressure remotely, identifying any significant increases that might require immediate medical attention. Similarly, for patients with congestive heart failure, the system can monitor weight, heart rate, and other parameters, detecting early signs of fluid retention or worsening heart function.

The use of AI in RPM systems extends beyond the detection of physiological anomalies. AI algorithms can also be used to predict future health events. For example, an AI algorithm might analyze a patient's historical data, combined with current sensor readings and other information, to predict the likelihood of a future hospitalization. This predictive capability enables proactive interventions, such as adjusting medication regimens or scheduling a timely clinic visit, potentially preventing a costly and potentially harmful hospitalization. The algorithms' predictive capacity is constantly refined as more data is collected, leading to increasingly accurate forecasts and more effective preventative measures.

Furthermore, AI can personalize care for each patient, adapting to their individual needs and preferences. AI algorithms can learn from a patient's response to different treatments, tailoring subsequent interventions to optimize outcomes. This personalized approach is crucial in managing chronic diseases, where patients may respond differently to the same treatment. The AI system's ability to learn from each patient's specific data and adjust treatment accordingly represents a powerful tool for precision medicine.

However, the implementation of AI-driven patient monitoring and management systems is not without its challenges. Data privacy and security are paramount concerns. The continuous collection and analysis of sensitive health data necessitate robust security measures to prevent unauthorized access and protect patient confidentiality. The ethical implications of using AI to predict and potentially intervene in a patient's life also demand careful consideration. Transparency and accountability are critical to building trust and ensuring that these systems are used responsibly.

It's crucial that patients understand how their data is being used and have the ability to control access to it.

Another challenge lies in the potential for algorithmic bias. If the AI algorithms are trained on data that reflects existing healthcare disparities, the resulting systems may perpetuate or even exacerbate these inequalities. This highlights the need for careful consideration of the data used to train AI models and for ongoing monitoring of the systems to ensure equitable outcomes for all patients.

Furthermore, the "black box" nature of some AI algorithms can make it difficult to understand how they arrive at their conclusions, raising concerns about transparency and accountability. The development of explainable AI (XAI) is essential to address these concerns and build trust in these powerful technologies.

The successful deployment of AI-driven patient monitoring and management systems also requires effective integration with existing healthcare infrastructure. This includes seamless interoperability with EHRs and other healthcare information systems, as well as the development of user-friendly interfaces for both patients and clinicians. The user experience is paramount to ensure widespread adoption. A system that is cumbersome or difficult to use will likely be ignored, negating its potential benefits.

Despite these challenges, the potential benefits of AI in patient monitoring and chronic disease management are immense. By enabling proactive, personalized, and continuous care, AI has the potential to significantly improve patient outcomes, reduce healthcare costs, and enhance the overall quality of life for millions of people worldwide. As AI technology continues to advance and as ethical concerns are appropriately addressed, we can expect to see even more widespread adoption of these powerful tools, transforming healthcare delivery and improving the health and well-being of populations globally. The future of healthcare is increasingly intertwined with AI, and the responsible development and implementation of this technology hold the key to unlocking a new era of preventative and personalized medicine.

Ethical Considerations and Challenges in AI Healthcare

The transformative potential of AI in healthcare is undeniable, yet its rapid advancement brings forth a complex web of ethical and legal challenges that demand careful consideration. The very foundation of AI's effectiveness in healthcare—the vast amounts of patient data it relies upon—presents a significant ethical dilemma.

The privacy and security of this sensitive information are paramount. Breaches of patient data, even unintentional ones, can lead to identity theft, financial losses, and significant emotional distress. Furthermore, the use of this data to train AI algorithms raises questions about informed consent. Patients often aren't fully aware of the extent to which their data is being used, let alone the specific algorithms employed to analyze it. This lack of transparency undermines trust and necessitates a robust framework for data governance, emphasizing the need for explicit consent and clear communication about data usage. Legislation such as HIPAA in the United States and GDPR in Europe provides a baseline, but continuous adaptation and refinement are crucial to keep pace with the evolving AI landscape.

Beyond data privacy, algorithmic bias emerges as a critical ethical concern. AI algorithms are trained on data, and if this data reflects existing societal biases—for example, racial or socioeconomic disparities in healthcare access and outcomes—the algorithms will inevitably perpetuate these biases. This can lead to discriminatory outcomes, where certain patient groups receive inferior or inadequate care. For instance, an AI system trained on data primarily from a specific demographic might misdiagnose or undertreat individuals from underrepresented groups, exacerbating existing health inequities. Addressing this requires careful attention to the diversity and representativeness of training datasets, rigorous testing for bias, and the development of fairness-aware algorithms that actively mitigate discriminatory outcomes. Ongoing monitoring and auditing of AI systems are crucial to detect and rectify any biases that may emerge, even after deployment.

The question of responsibility for medical decisions made by AI systems presents another significant hurdle. In instances where an

AI system provides an incorrect diagnosis or recommends an inappropriate treatment, who is accountable? Is it the developer of the AI system, the healthcare provider who relies on the system's recommendations, or the hospital where the system is implemented? Establishing clear lines of responsibility is essential for accountability and to foster trust in these systems. This necessitates a multi-faceted approach, encompassing stringent regulatory oversight, clear guidelines for the use and deployment of AI systems in healthcare, and the development of robust mechanisms for resolving disputes and assigning liability in case of errors. The legal framework needs to evolve to adapt to this novel situation, and collaboration between legal professionals, AI developers, and healthcare providers is crucial.

Another ethical dimension relates to the potential displacement of healthcare professionals. As AI systems automate certain tasks, concerns about job losses and the impact on the human element of care are valid. While AI can enhance efficiency and augment the capabilities of healthcare professionals, it shouldn't replace human interaction and empathy. The focus should be on augmenting human capabilities, not replacing them entirely. This necessitates investing in retraining and upskilling programs for healthcare professionals, ensuring a smooth transition and empowering them to work alongside AI systems effectively. A strategic approach that balances technological advancements with the preservation of human roles is necessary to maintain the integrity and human-centered nature of healthcare.

The issue of transparency in AI algorithms, often referred to as the "black box" problem, remains a substantial challenge. Many AI systems, particularly deep learning models, operate in ways that are difficult to understand, making it challenging to determine how they reach their conclusions. This lack of transparency can erode trust, particularly in high-stakes medical contexts. The development of explainable AI (XAI) is crucial to address this limitation. XAI aims to make the decision-making processes of AI systems more understandable and interpretable, providing insights into the reasoning behind their recommendations. This increased transparency enables healthcare professionals to better evaluate the AI's suggestions, identify potential errors, and build confidence in the system's reliability.

Furthermore, the potential for AI systems to be misused or weaponized is a critical ethical concern. These powerful systems could be used to manipulate data, create fake medical records, or even design targeted attacks against specific individuals or groups. This necessitates a proactive approach to cybersecurity and the development of safeguards to prevent misuse. Stricter regulations, security protocols, and ethical guidelines are essential to mitigate the risks associated with the malicious use of AI in healthcare. International cooperation and shared best practices are also crucial to address this global challenge effectively.

The increasing use of AI in diagnosing and treating mental health conditions presents unique ethical considerations. While AI offers the potential for early detection and personalized interventions, it is essential to address concerns about bias, privacy, and the therapeutic relationship between patients and clinicians. Ensuring that AI systems are culturally sensitive and do not perpetuate existing stigma surrounding mental health is paramount. The role of human oversight and the importance of maintaining the human-centered approach to mental health care must be carefully considered.

Finally, the equitable access to AI-driven healthcare solutions is another ethical imperative. The benefits of AI in healthcare should not be limited to those who can afford it. Addressing the digital divide and ensuring that AI technologies are accessible to all populations, regardless of socioeconomic status or geographic location, is crucial for equitable healthcare. This necessitates investment in infrastructure, education, and outreach programs to bridge the gap and promote the equitable distribution of AI-powered healthcare.

In conclusion, the ethical and legal landscape surrounding AI in healthcare is complex and rapidly evolving. Navigating this landscape effectively requires a multifaceted approach that integrates technological advancements with ethical considerations, robust legal frameworks, and a commitment to transparency, accountability, and equitable access for all. The collaboration of policymakers, AI developers, healthcare professionals, and ethicists is crucial to ensure that AI is used responsibly and beneficially to improve the health and well-being of populations worldwide. Only through careful consideration of these challenges can we harness the full potential of AI to create a more just, equitable, and effective healthcare system.

Algorithmic Trading and HighFrequency Trading

The application of artificial intelligence in finance is rapidly transforming the landscape of financial markets, particularly in the realm of trading. Algorithmic trading (AT), a broad term encompassing the use of computer programs to follow a defined set of instructions (an algorithm) to place a trade, has become ubiquitous. These algorithms analyze market data, identify trading opportunities, and execute trades at speeds and volumes far exceeding human capabilities. This automation brings efficiency and speed, but also introduces complexities and potential risks.

One of the most prominent subtypes of algorithmic trading is high-frequency trading (HFT). HFT employs sophisticated algorithms and powerful computing infrastructure to execute a vast number of trades in extremely short timeframes – often measured in milliseconds or even microseconds. HFT firms invest heavily in co-location facilities, placing their servers directly within or very near to stock exchanges' data centers to minimize latency and gain a crucial edge in speed. This speed advantage allows HFT algorithms to exploit tiny price discrepancies and profit from arbitrage opportunities – instances where the same asset is simultaneously priced differently in various markets. The sheer volume of trades executed by HFT firms significantly impacts market liquidity and price discovery. However, the opacity surrounding their algorithms and the speed at which they operate raise concerns about market manipulation and fairness.

The core of algorithmic trading lies in the sophistication of the algorithms themselves. These aren't simple "buy low, sell high" programs. Instead, they incorporate a range of advanced techniques drawn from fields like machine learning, statistical modeling, and optimization theory. For example, reinforcement learning algorithms, inspired by behavioral psychology, enable trading systems to learn optimal strategies through trial and error in simulated market environments. These algorithms adapt to changing market conditions and learn to exploit patterns and anomalies that might be invisible to human traders. Similarly, deep learning models, with their ability to analyze vast datasets and identify complex relationships, are used to predict market movements and inform trading decisions. Such models can ingest data from diverse sources, including news sentiment analysis, social media trends, economic indicators, and alternative data like satellite imagery or weather patterns impacting agricultural commodities.

The advantages of algorithmic trading are manifold. First and foremost, it offers speed and efficiency unmatched by human traders. Algorithms can process vast quantities of data in real-time, identifying and capitalizing on fleeting opportunities that would be missed by human intervention. This speed advantage is particularly crucial in volatile markets where rapid decision-making is paramount. Second, algorithmic trading reduces the impact of human emotions on trading decisions. Fear, greed, and other psychological biases can significantly impair investment choices.

Algorithms, devoid of such emotions, can execute trades objectively, based purely on pre-defined rules and data analysis. This objectivity minimizes impulsive decisions and contributes to consistent, risk-managed trading. Third, algorithmic trading allows for increased diversification and scalability. A single algorithm can manage multiple assets across diverse markets simultaneously, diversifying risk and maximizing returns. The same algorithm can be scaled up to manage exponentially larger trading volumes without a proportional increase in personnel or operational costs.

Despite the significant advantages, algorithmic trading also carries substantial risks. One major concern is the potential for algorithmic errors or malfunctions. A bug in an algorithm, a data input error, or even a network outage can lead to significant financial losses. This risk is amplified in HFT where even a tiny delay can be catastrophic. Robust testing, rigorous validation, and rigorous error handling protocols are crucial to mitigate these risks, but they can't eliminate them entirely. Another major risk is the potential for unintended consequences. Complex algorithms can behave unpredictably under certain conditions, producing outcomes that weren't anticipated by their creators. This is particularly concerning in tightly coupled, interconnected financial markets where a single unexpected event in one market can trigger cascading effects across others.

The complexity of many algorithms poses another challenge. The "black box" nature of some advanced machine learning models, where the decision-making process isn't easily transparent, makes it difficult to understand why a particular trade was executed or to identify the sources of errors. This lack of transparency can undermine trust and makes regulatory oversight significantly more challenging. Efforts are underway to develop "explainable AI" (XAI) techniques to address this opacity and enhance the transparency of algorithmic trading systems. However, finding a balance between model complexity and explainability remains a significant research challenge.

Furthermore, the use of AI in algorithmic trading raises significant ethical considerations. The potential for market manipulation through sophisticated algorithms is a substantial concern. Algorithms can be designed to collude with each other, creating artificial price movements or manipulating market liquidity to profit at the expense of other market participants. Regulators are grappling with the challenge of detecting and preventing such manipulative behavior, given the complexity and opacity of many trading algorithms. The concentration of market power in the hands of a few large HFT firms is another point of concern, as their speed advantage could potentially stifle competition and create an uneven playing field for smaller players.

The regulatory environment surrounding algorithmic trading is constantly evolving, as authorities struggle to keep pace with the rapid advancements in AI and the increasing sophistication of trading algorithms. Regulations designed to promote market fairness, transparency, and prevent manipulation are continually being updated and refined. A key challenge is balancing the need to regulate and prevent abuse with the desire to foster innovation and avoid stifling the development of potentially beneficial trading technologies. The lack of consistent global regulations across different jurisdictions also presents significant complexities. Finding a common ground and establishing internationally harmonized rules will be crucial to ensure fair and efficient global markets in the age of AI-driven trading.

The future of algorithmic and high-frequency trading hinges on several key factors. Further advancements in AI and machine learning will undoubtedly continue to drive the sophistication of trading algorithms. We can expect to see even more sophisticated models capable of processing exponentially larger datasets, making finer-grained predictions, and adapting more effectively to changing market conditions. This will likely lead to increased automation, higher trading speeds, and potentially even greater market efficiency. However, this also intensifies the need for robust regulation and safeguards to prevent abuse.

The development of more explainable and transparent AI models is crucial for building trust and ensuring accountability. The "black box" problem is a significant hurdle that needs to be overcome to foster widespread acceptance and responsible use of AI in financial markets. Advances in explainable AI and the development of techniques to audit and verify the behavior of algorithms will be pivotal in shaping the future of algorithmic trading. Finally, ongoing efforts to strengthen the regulatory framework, to ensure global coordination and standardization of rules, will be essential to mitigating risks and promoting fair and transparent markets. The interplay between technological innovation and regulatory oversight will define the evolution of algorithmic and high-frequency trading in the years to come. Striking the right balance is crucial to ensuring that AI benefits the entire financial ecosystem rather than concentrating power and exacerbating existing inequalities.

Fraud Detection and Risk Management

The integration of AI into fraud detection and risk management is revolutionizing the financial industry, offering unprecedented capabilities to identify and mitigate threats that were previously difficult, if not impossible, to detect. Traditional methods often relied on rule-based systems, which proved brittle and easily circumvented by sophisticated fraudsters. AI, particularly machine learning, offers a more adaptive and proactive approach. Instead of relying on pre-defined rules, machine learning algorithms learn from vast datasets of historical transactions, identifying patterns and anomalies indicative of fraudulent activity. This allows for the detection of previously unseen fraud patterns and the adaptation to evolving criminal tactics.

One of the most impactful applications of AI in fraud detection is in the realm of anomaly detection. Machine learning models, particularly unsupervised learning techniques like clustering and autoencoders, can identify transactions that deviate significantly from established norms. These deviations, which might go unnoticed by human analysts, can be early indicators of fraudulent activity. For example, an unexpected surge in transactions from an unusual geographic location, a sudden increase in transaction value, or a pattern of transactions that are unusually consistent can all trigger alerts. These alerts then trigger further investigation by human analysts, allowing for swift intervention and the prevention of significant financial losses.

The power of AI in fraud detection goes beyond simple anomaly detection. Sophisticated algorithms are being developed that can analyze transactional data in conjunction with other data sources, such as customer profiles, geolocation data, and even social media activity. This holistic approach allows for a more comprehensive risk assessment. For instance, a seemingly innocuous transaction might raise red flags when combined with other data points suggestive of identity theft or account takeover. For example, a sudden large withdrawal from an account might be flagged if it coincides with a reported data breach involving that account's credentials. Similarly, a series of seemingly small, individual transactions might be detected as potentially fraudulent when viewed in context with other activity indicative of money laundering schemes.

Credit risk assessment is another area where AI is making significant contributions. Traditional credit scoring models rely heavily on structured data, such as credit history and income. AI, however, allows for the integration of unstructured data, such as social media activity and online behavioral patterns, to provide a much richer picture of an individual's creditworthiness. This expanded data set enables more accurate risk assessments, potentially extending credit to deserving individuals who might be unfairly excluded under traditional systems. Conversely, it allows for a more precise identification of high-risk borrowers, reducing the likelihood of defaults.

Machine learning algorithms are also utilized to predict the likelihood of loan defaults. By analyzing historical loan data, including borrower demographics, credit history, and loan characteristics, these algorithms can identify patterns associated with defaults. These predictive models can then be used to dynamically adjust interest rates, set appropriate loan limits, and even make decisions on whether or not to approve a loan application. This proactive approach can significantly reduce the overall risk exposure for lenders, enhancing financial stability.

Beyond credit risk, AI is playing an increasingly important role in managing market risk. By analyzing vast amounts of market data, including historical price movements, economic indicators, and news sentiment, AI algorithms can identify patterns and predict potential market volatility. These predictions can be used to inform investment strategies, enabling investors to adjust their portfolios accordingly and mitigate potential losses. For example, an AI model might detect an impending market downturn based on subtle shifts in investor sentiment captured through the analysis of social media chatter. Such timely warnings allow investors to reposition their holdings, mitigating losses before a market crash materializes.

However, the application of AI in fraud detection and risk management also presents significant challenges. One of the biggest hurdles is the issue of data quality. AI algorithms are only as good as the data they are trained on. Inaccurate, incomplete, or biased data can lead to inaccurate predictions and potentially harmful outcomes. For instance, a model trained on biased data may inadvertently discriminate against specific demographics in the context of credit risk assessment. Addressing these biases and ensuring data quality is paramount for ensuring the fair and equitable application of AI.

Another challenge is the interpretability of AI models. Many sophisticated machine learning models, particularly deep learning models, operate as "black boxes," making it difficult to understand the reasons behind their predictions. This lack of transparency can make it difficult to identify errors and debug the model.

Furthermore, regulators may be hesitant to rely on models whose decision-making processes are opaque, potentially hindering the adoption of AI in regulated financial settings. The development of explainable AI (XAI) techniques is crucial for addressing this issue and promoting trust and transparency.

The ethical implications of using AI in finance also warrant careful consideration. The potential for algorithmic bias and discrimination must be carefully addressed. Transparency in the decision-making processes of AI systems is crucial to ensure fairness and accountability. Regulations and standards are needed to ensure that AI is used responsibly and does not exacerbate existing inequalities. There is a growing need for oversight bodies and industry-wide best practices to guide the development and deployment of AI in finance, ensuring fairness and ethical conduct.

Despite these challenges, the transformative potential of AI in fraud detection and risk management is undeniable. The ability to analyze vast amounts of data, identify complex patterns, and predict future trends offers the financial industry unparalleled opportunities to improve efficiency, reduce risks, and enhance customer experience.

However, responsible development and deployment of AI is essential. This includes careful consideration of data quality, model interpretability, and ethical implications. By addressing these challenges, the financial industry can harness the power of AI to build a more secure, efficient, and equitable financial system. The future of finance is undeniably intertwined with the responsible development and implementation of AI technologies; embracing both the opportunities and managing the risks effectively will be paramount in navigating this rapidly evolving landscape. Continued research and development in explainable AI, robust data governance, and ethical guidelines will shape the future of AI's role in safeguarding the financial industry. A collaborative approach involving financial institutions, regulators, and researchers is essential to navigating the complexities and realizing the full potential of AI in fraud detection and risk management, paving the way for a more secure and efficient financial ecosystem for all.

AIPowered Customer Service and Financial Advice

The increasing sophistication of AI is rapidly transforming the landscape of customer service and financial advice within the finance sector. Gone are the days of lengthy hold times and generic responses; AI-powered solutions are ushering in an era of personalized, efficient, and readily available support. This revolution is driven primarily by the development and deployment of sophisticated chatbots and virtual assistants, capable of handling a wide range of customer inquiries, offering tailored financial recommendations, and automating numerous customer service tasks.

These AI-powered assistants are not simply programmed to follow a rigid script. Instead, they leverage machine learning algorithms, particularly natural language processing (NLP) and deep learning, to understand and respond to human language with remarkable accuracy and nuance. They can interpret the intent behind a customer's query, even if it's phrased in an unconventional manner, and provide relevant and accurate information. This capacity for understanding context and intent is crucial for delivering truly personalized and helpful service.

For example, a customer might inquire about their account balance. A traditional automated system would provide only the numerical balance. An AI-powered assistant, however, could provide the balance along with contextual information such as recent transactions, upcoming payments, and any potential overdraft situations. It could also offer helpful suggestions, such as setting up automated savings plans or alerts for low balances, all tailored to the individual customer's specific needs and financial situation.

The benefits of AI-powered customer service extend beyond personalized responses. These systems can operate 24/7, providing immediate assistance regardless of time zone or staffing limitations. This is particularly beneficial for global financial institutions with customers spread across different regions. Furthermore, AI-powered systems can handle a far greater volume of inquiries than human agents, significantly reducing wait times and improving overall customer satisfaction. This scalability is critical as the demand for financial services continues to grow.

Beyond basic customer support, AI is playing an increasingly significant role in providing personalized financial advice. Robotic advisors (robo-advisors), powered by AI algorithms, are capable of analyzing an individual's financial situation, risk tolerance, and investment goals to create customized investment portfolios. These platforms typically employ algorithms that optimize portfolio allocation based on sophisticated mathematical models, often outperforming human advisors in certain market conditions. This democratization of financial advice makes professional investment management accessible to a broader range of individuals, regardless of their net worth.

However, the use of AI in financial advice is not without its challenges. One significant concern is the potential for bias in the algorithms themselves. If the data used to train these algorithms contains biases, for example, favoring certain demographics or investment strategies, the resulting advice might be skewed and unfair. This is a crucial issue that requires ongoing monitoring and rigorous testing to ensure fairness and equity. Transparency in the algorithmic decision-making process is paramount, allowing for scrutiny and ensuring accountability.

Another challenge is the limitation of AI in handling complex or nuanced financial situations. While AI can provide excellent support for routine tasks and basic financial planning, it may not be equipped to handle highly specialized or unusual circumstances that require human judgment and expertise. For instance, an AI-powered system may struggle to provide advice on complex tax strategies, estate planning, or highly specialized investment instruments. The human element remains vital, particularly in these more intricate scenarios.

The evolving landscape of regulatory compliance presents another hurdle. The use of AI in providing financial advice necessitates adherence to strict regulatory guidelines, ensuring transparency and accountability. Keeping pace with evolving regulations and implementing robust compliance measures is essential for the responsible adoption of AI in the financial services sector.

Furthermore, the issue of data privacy and security is paramount.
AI-powered systems require access to sensitive customer data,
raising concerns about data breaches and misuse. Robust security
measures are essential to safeguard customer information and
maintain trust. Compliance with data privacy regulations, such as
GDPR and CCPA, is crucial for maintaining customer confidence and
adhering to ethical standards.

Despite these challenges, the future of AI in customer service and
financial advice is bright. Continuous advancements in AI
technology, particularly in NLP and deep learning, are continually
expanding the capabilities of these systems. Researchers are actively
developing more sophisticated algorithms that are capable of
understanding and responding to more complex and nuanced
requests. Furthermore, efforts are underway to improve the
transparency and explainability of AI models, addressing concerns
about bias and lack of understanding.

The trend towards hybrid models, combining AI-powered systems
with human expertise, is emerging as a powerful solution. AI can
handle routine tasks and provide initial assistance, while human
advisors can address complex issues and provide personalized
guidance when needed. This collaborative approach leverages the
strengths of both AI and human intelligence, creating a more efficient,
effective, and trustworthy customer service and financial advice
experience.

The development of more sophisticated AI models capable of handling
complex financial scenarios and offering more nuanced advice is a key
area of focus. This involves advancements in
reinforcement learning and other machine learning techniques that
allow AI systems to learn from their interactions with customers and
improve their decision-making capabilities over time.

Furthermore, research into explainable AI (XAI) is critical. XAI aims to
make the decision-making processes of AI systems more
transparent and understandable, allowing for better scrutiny and
ensuring accountability. This increased transparency builds trust

and reduces the risk of bias.

Finally, continued collaboration between researchers, financial institutions, and regulators is essential for navigating the ethical and regulatory challenges associated with AI in finance. Developing robust standards and guidelines for the responsible development and deployment of AI is crucial for ensuring the fair, equitable, and secure use of AI in providing customer service and financial advice. This collaborative effort will shape the future of AI in the finance industry, fostering innovation while mitigating risks and ensuring a beneficial outcome for all stakeholders. The future of finance is increasingly reliant on harnessing the power of AI responsibly, balancing innovation with ethical considerations and regulatory compliance. This careful approach will ultimately shape a financial landscape that is more efficient, personalized, and accessible to all.

Regulatory and Ethical Implications of AI in Finance

The rapid integration of AI into the financial sector presents a compelling case study in the intersection of technological advancement and societal responsibility. While AI promises increased efficiency, personalized services, and potentially fairer access to financial resources, it also raises significant regulatory and ethical concerns that demand careful consideration and proactive solutions. The very power of AI—its ability to process vast datasets and make complex decisions autonomously—creates a need for robust oversight to prevent unintended consequences and ensure equitable outcomes.

One of the most pressing issues is the potential for bias in AI algorithms. Algorithms are trained on historical data, and if that data reflects existing societal biases—for example, in lending practices or investment strategies—the AI system will likely perpetuate and even amplify these biases. This could lead to discriminatory outcomes, disproportionately affecting certain demographic groups. For instance, an AI-powered loan application system trained on data showing historical lending disparities might unfairly deny loans to applicants from marginalized communities, regardless of their creditworthiness. The challenge lies not only in identifying and mitigating these biases but also in establishing mechanisms to ensure ongoing monitoring and adaptation of the algorithms as new data becomes available. This necessitates a shift towards explainable AI (XAI), which allows for greater transparency into the decision-making processes of AI systems, enabling identification of biases and potential points of failure. Without XAI, the "black box" nature of many AI algorithms makes it difficult to understand why a particular decision was made, hindering the ability to address algorithmic bias effectively.

Accountability is another critical area of concern. When an AI system makes a decision that results in financial harm—for instance, an incorrect fraud detection leading to an unwarranted account freeze or an algorithmic trading error causing significant losses—the question of responsibility becomes complex. Is the developer of the algorithm accountable? The financial institution deploying the system? Or is the AI system itself somehow culpable?

Establishing clear lines of accountability is essential for building trust and ensuring that those responsible are held answerable for the consequences of AI-driven decisions. This requires a nuanced legal framework that addresses the unique challenges posed by AI, possibly incorporating elements of strict liability or a hybrid approach combining negligence and strict liability depending on the nature of the harm caused.

The issue of transparency is inextricably linked to both bias and accountability. Financial institutions utilizing AI must be transparent about how their AI systems work, the data used to train them, and the potential limitations and risks associated with their deployment. This transparency is not only ethically desirable but also legally necessary in many jurisdictions, particularly with respect to data privacy regulations such as GDPR and CCPA. These regulations mandate transparency about data collection and usage, and the use of AI in finance necessitates compliance with these stringent rules. Transparency also fosters trust with customers, who need to understand how their data is being used and the basis for AI-driven decisions impacting their finances. This includes providing clear and accessible explanations of algorithmic decisions, especially when those decisions have significant consequences for individuals.

Furthermore, the regulatory landscape surrounding AI in finance is still evolving, presenting both challenges and opportunities. Existing regulations often lag behind the rapid pace of technological advancement, creating a need for proactive regulatory frameworks that are flexible and adaptable to emerging AI technologies. These frameworks should prioritize consumer protection, ensuring that AI-driven financial products and services are fair, transparent, and do not discriminate. International collaboration is essential in developing consistent standards and guidelines for AI in finance, preventing regulatory arbitrage and ensuring a level playing field for financial institutions across different jurisdictions. Regulatory sandboxes, where new AI-based financial technologies can be tested and evaluated in a controlled environment, offer a valuable mechanism for promoting innovation while managing risks.

The ethical considerations extend beyond bias, accountability, and transparency. The use of AI in finance raises questions about data privacy and security. AI systems often rely on vast amounts of sensitive personal data, making them attractive targets for cyberattacks. Robust security measures are crucial to protect this data from unauthorized access and misuse. Financial institutions must invest in robust cybersecurity infrastructure and employ best practices to safeguard customer information. This includes implementing data encryption, access controls, and regular security audits. Furthermore, the ethical implications of using AI for surveillance and profiling require careful consideration. While AI can enhance fraud detection and prevent financial crime, it must be used responsibly and ethically, avoiding the potential for undue surveillance or discriminatory practices.

The future of AI in finance hinges on addressing these regulatory and ethical challenges effectively. This will require a multi-faceted approach involving collaboration between policymakers, regulators, financial institutions, technology developers, and researchers. Developing a robust ethical framework for AI in finance requires a continuous dialogue among all stakeholders, fostering a culture of responsible innovation. Ethical guidelines should be integrated into the development lifecycle of AI systems, starting from the initial design phase and continuing through deployment and ongoing monitoring. Regular ethical reviews and audits can help ensure that AI systems are aligned with ethical principles and societal values.

The integration of AI into finance offers tremendous potential benefits, but it also presents significant risks. By proactively addressing the regulatory and ethical challenges, we can harness the transformative power of AI while mitigating its potential harms.

A collaborative and forward-thinking approach will be crucial in ensuring that AI in finance serves the interests of all stakeholders, promoting a more efficient, inclusive, and equitable financial system. The success of this integration depends on our collective ability to balance innovation with responsibility, ensuring that technological advancements serve humanity's best interests. The journey ahead will require continuous adaptation, robust oversight, and a deep commitment to ethical principles, ensuring that AI in finance fosters a future where technological progress is aligned with human well-being and societal justice.

Future Trends in AI and the Financial Industry

The convergence of artificial intelligence and finance is not a static phenomenon; it's a dynamic interplay constantly reshaped by technological innovation and evolving market forces. Looking ahead, several key trends will define the future of AI in finance, profoundly altering how financial services are delivered, managed, and regulated.

One of the most transformative trends is the increasing integration of blockchain technology and its related concept, decentralized finance (DeFi). Blockchain's inherent security, transparency, and immutability offer significant advantages in financial transactions. Its distributed ledger technology can streamline processes like cross-border payments, reducing costs and delays associated with traditional banking systems. Furthermore, smart contracts, self-executing contracts with the terms of the agreement directly written into code, can automate complex financial operations, eliminating the need for intermediaries and reducing the risk of fraud. This potential for automation extends to areas such as escrow services, loan origination, and even insurance claims processing. The efficiency gains are substantial, promising faster settlement times, lower transaction fees, and increased transparency for all parties involved.

DeFi, built upon blockchain technology, represents a radical departure from traditional centralized finance. DeFi platforms offer decentralized lending and borrowing services, decentralized exchanges (DEXs) for trading cryptocurrencies and other assets, and various other financial products without the need for traditional intermediaries like banks or brokers. This decentralization fosters greater financial inclusion by removing barriers to entry for individuals and businesses who may not have access to traditional financial services. The potential for disrupting traditional financial systems is enormous, but it also presents significant regulatory challenges. The anonymity associated with some DeFi platforms poses risks related to money laundering and illicit activities, requiring careful regulatory oversight to balance innovation with the need to maintain financial stability and integrity.

The rise of AI-powered robo-advisors is another significant trend shaping the future of the financial industry. Robo-advisors utilize AI algorithms to provide automated, personalized financial advice and portfolio management services at a fraction of the cost of traditional human advisors. These algorithms analyze an individual's financial situation, risk tolerance, and investment goals to create a customized investment strategy. While robo-advisors are not yet a replacement for human advisors, particularly for high-net-worth individuals requiring complex financial planning, their accessibility and cost-effectiveness are democratizing access to sophisticated financial advice for a broader range of people. As AI algorithms continue to improve, robo-advisors are likely to become increasingly sophisticated, capable of handling more complex financial decisions and offering a wider range of services. The development of hybrid models combining the strengths of AI and human expertise is also a promising area of growth, leveraging the speed and efficiency of AI with the nuanced judgment and empathy of human advisors.

Beyond robo-advisors, AI is revolutionizing other aspects of financial services. AI-powered fraud detection systems are becoming increasingly sophisticated in identifying and preventing fraudulent transactions, significantly reducing financial losses for both institutions and individuals. Machine learning algorithms can analyze massive datasets of transaction history, identifying patterns and anomalies indicative of fraudulent activity that may be missed by human analysts. These systems can adapt and learn from new data, improving their accuracy and efficiency over time. This is particularly crucial in the face of increasingly sophisticated cyberattacks and evolving fraud techniques. Similarly, AI is enhancing cybersecurity by improving threat detection and response capabilities. AI-powered systems can analyze network traffic and system logs in real-time, identifying potential threats and vulnerabilities before they can be exploited.

The increasing use of AI in risk management is another transformative trend. AI algorithms can analyze vast amounts of economic and market data to identify and assess various risks, from credit risk and market risk to operational risk. This allows financial institutions to make more informed decisions, optimize their portfolios, and manage their overall risk profiles more effectively.

Sophisticated AI models can predict potential market downturns, enabling institutions to adjust their investment strategies proactively and mitigate potential losses. Moreover, AI's ability to process and analyze unstructured data—such as news articles, social media posts, and economic reports—offers valuable insights that can inform risk assessments and improve decision-making.

However, the integration of AI in finance is not without its challenges. Concerns about algorithmic bias, data privacy, and the lack of transparency in AI decision-making processes require careful consideration and proactive solutions. The potential for AI systems to perpetuate existing societal biases—for example, in credit scoring or loan approvals—is a serious ethical concern. Ensuring fairness and preventing discrimination requires careful design, rigorous testing, and ongoing monitoring of AI systems. Similarly, data privacy is paramount, particularly given the sensitive nature of financial information. Robust security measures are crucial to prevent data breaches and protect customer information. The development of explainable AI (XAI) is also essential, providing greater transparency into how AI systems make decisions and enabling the identification and mitigation of potential biases.

The regulatory landscape surrounding AI in finance is still evolving, presenting both challenges and opportunities. Regulators are grappling with the need to balance the promotion of innovation with the need to protect consumers and maintain financial stability. The development of clear and consistent regulatory frameworks is crucial to ensure responsible AI adoption and prevent unintended consequences. International collaboration is essential in establishing global standards and guidelines for AI in finance, fostering a level playing field for financial institutions and promoting trust in the AI-powered financial system.

The future of AI in finance is likely to be characterized by a continued increase in the adoption of AI-powered solutions across various aspects of the industry. This will lead to increased efficiency, improved risk management, and enhanced customer experiences. However, addressing the ethical and regulatory challenges associated with AI is crucial to ensure the responsible and sustainable development of the AI-powered financial system.

Collaboration between policymakers, regulators, financial institutions, and technology developers is essential to create a framework that balances innovation with ethical considerations and safeguards the interests of all stakeholders. The path forward necessitates continuous adaptation, robust oversight, and a commitment to ethical principles to ensure that AI in finance contributes to a more efficient, inclusive, and equitable financial system for all. The journey towards this future will demand a constant dialogue, a commitment to transparency, and a resolute focus on fostering trust in an increasingly AI-driven world.

Personalized Learning and Adaptive Education Technologies

The transformative potential of AI extends far beyond the realms of finance and healthcare; its impact on education promises a revolution in how we learn and teach. Personalized learning, powered by AI, is poised to redefine the educational landscape, moving away from the one-size-fits-all approach that has long characterized traditional classrooms. This shift is driven by the increasing availability of powerful algorithms capable of analyzing vast amounts of student data to identify individual learning styles, strengths, and weaknesses. This data-driven insight allows for the creation of customized learning paths, tailored to the unique needs of each student, maximizing their potential and fostering a deeper understanding of the subject matter.

Adaptive learning platforms represent a key manifestation of this AI-driven personalization. These platforms utilize sophisticated algorithms to dynamically adjust the difficulty and content of learning materials based on a student's performance. Instead of a fixed curriculum, the platform continuously assesses the student's progress, identifying areas where they excel and areas where they struggle. This allows the system to adapt in real-time, providing more challenging material when a student demonstrates mastery and offering additional support and practice when difficulties arise.

This adaptive approach ensures that students are constantly challenged but never overwhelmed, leading to increased engagement and improved learning outcomes. Several commercially available platforms exemplify this concept, employing various AI techniques to achieve personalized learning experiences. For instance, some platforms use Bayesian networks to model student knowledge and predict their future performance, dynamically adjusting the learning path based on these predictions. Others employ reinforcement learning algorithms to optimize the sequence of learning activities, maximizing the student's learning efficiency. The sophistication of these algorithms continues to evolve, leading to increasingly personalized and effective learning experiences.

Intelligent tutoring systems (ITS) represent another significant application of AI in personalized learning. These systems function as virtual tutors, providing individualized guidance and support to students as they work through learning materials. Unlike static tutorials or textbooks, ITS can adapt their instruction based on the student's responses, providing feedback, hints, and explanations tailored to their specific needs. They can identify misconceptions, address common errors, and offer customized practice exercises designed to strengthen the student's understanding. The ability of ITS to provide personalized feedback is particularly valuable, as it allows students to receive immediate and targeted assistance, preventing them from developing ingrained misconceptions or falling behind. Many ITS incorporate natural language processing (NLP) capabilities, allowing them to engage in conversational interactions with students, answering questions, clarifying concepts, and providing encouragement. This interactive approach fosters a more engaging and supportive learning environment, encouraging students to actively participate and seek help when needed. The use of natural language generation (NLG) further enhances the conversational capabilities of these systems, allowing them to generate coherent and informative responses to complex student queries.

The effectiveness of adaptive learning platforms and ITS is demonstrably improved by incorporating data from multiple sources. Integrating performance data from various assessment tools, alongside data on student engagement, learning styles, and even emotional responses, provides a much richer and more nuanced picture of the student's learning journey. This comprehensive data allows for a more accurate assessment of individual learning needs and facilitates the development of highly targeted learning interventions. For example, integrating data from eye-tracking technology can reveal areas of difficulty or confusion in learning materials, allowing the system to adapt the presentation or provide additional explanations. Similarly, integrating data from physiological sensors, such as heart rate monitors, can indicate levels of stress or anxiety, allowing the system to adjust the pacing or complexity of the learning materials to maintain optimal engagement. The use of sentiment analysis of student written responses and chat logs allows the system to better understand the student's emotional state and provide targeted support. The ethical implications of collecting and using such extensive student data require careful consideration, emphasizing the necessity for transparency, privacy safeguards, and informed consent.

Beyond individual student learning, AI is transforming the way educators teach and assess students. AI-powered tools can automate time-consuming tasks such as grading, providing teachers with more time to focus on individual student needs and curriculum development. Automated essay grading systems, for example, can rapidly and efficiently evaluate student writing, identifying grammatical errors, stylistic issues, and content gaps. While not yet a perfect replacement for human grading, these tools can significantly reduce the workload for teachers, allowing them to provide more meaningful and individualized feedback to students on their writing. Similarly, AI-powered tools can assist in creating and personalizing assessments, ensuring that the tests accurately measure student understanding and cater to their specific learning styles. By analyzing student performance data, these tools can identify gaps in knowledge and adjust assessments accordingly, ensuring that students are challenged appropriately.

However, the widespread adoption of AI in education is not without its challenges. Concerns about data privacy, algorithmic bias, and the potential for increased educational inequality require careful consideration. The collection and use of student data must be transparent and ethical, ensuring that students' privacy is protected and their data is used responsibly. Algorithmic bias, where AI systems perpetuate or amplify existing societal biases, is a serious concern. AI algorithms trained on biased data can lead to unfair or discriminatory outcomes for certain student groups, exacerbating existing inequalities. Rigorous testing and ongoing monitoring of AI systems are necessary to identify and mitigate these biases.

Ensuring equitable access to AI-powered educational tools is also critical. The cost of developing and implementing these technologies can be substantial, potentially widening the gap between well-funded and under-resourced schools. Addressing this challenge requires policies that promote equitable access and affordable solutions for all students.

The future of AI in education is likely to be characterized by a continued integration of AI-powered tools across all aspects of the learning process. This will lead to more personalized, engaging, and effective learning experiences for students, as well as more efficient and effective teaching practices for educators. However, addressing the ethical and societal challenges associated with AI in education is crucial to ensure that this transformative technology is used responsibly and equitably. This necessitates a collaborative effort involving educators, policymakers, technology developers, and researchers to create a framework that balances innovation with ethical considerations and safeguards the interests of all stakeholders. Open dialogue, continuous monitoring, and a commitment to transparency are essential to building trust and ensuring that AI in education contributes to a more equitable and effective educational system for all learners. Furthermore, the integration of AI should not be seen as a replacement for human interaction and the essential role of teachers in the learning process.

The most effective use of AI in education will likely involve a collaborative model, leveraging the strengths of both AI and human educators to create a truly personalized and enriching learning experience. The path forward demands a constant evaluation of both the benefits and risks associated with this rapidly evolving technology, ensuring its responsible and ethical application within the educational ecosystem.

Automated Grading and Assessment

Automated grading and assessment represent a significant application of AI in education, promising to revolutionize how educators evaluate student work. The sheer volume of assignments faced by educators, particularly in large lecture courses, often makes timely and thorough feedback a significant challenge. AI offers a powerful tool to alleviate this bottleneck, allowing educators to dedicate more time to individual student interactions and curriculum development. This automation, however, is not without its complexities and ethical considerations, demanding careful implementation and ongoing evaluation.

One of the most advanced areas of automated assessment is essay grading. Early systems primarily focused on identifying grammatical errors and stylistic issues, offering a rudimentary assessment of writing quality. However, recent advancements in natural language processing (NLP) have enabled a much more sophisticated approach. Modern AI-powered essay graders utilize deep learning models, often based on recurrent neural networks (RNNs) or transformers, to analyze the semantic meaning and coherence of student writing. These models are trained on large corpora of essays, graded by human experts, allowing them to learn to identify key characteristics of well-written essays, such as clarity, organization, argumentation, and use of evidence. Beyond simply assigning a numerical score, these systems can provide detailed feedback on specific aspects of the writing, highlighting areas for improvement and suggesting specific revisions. For example, an AI grader might point out weak transitions between paragraphs, suggest stronger evidence to support a claim, or identify instances of unclear language. This detailed feedback can be far more valuable to a student than a simple grade, guiding them toward improved writing skills.

The effectiveness of AI essay graders is continuously improving, with ongoing research focused on refining the models and addressing their limitations. One significant challenge is the subjective nature of essay grading. Human graders may differ in their assessment of an essay, depending on their individual preferences and biases. AI graders are not immune to this issue; their assessments are heavily influenced by the data they are trained on. Addressing this requires careful curation of the training data, ensuring a diverse representation of writing styles and perspectives to minimize bias. Techniques like adversarial training can also help to improve the robustness of the models to different writing styles and reduce the impact of potential biases.

Furthermore, the integration of multiple AI models, each with different strengths and weaknesses, can lead to more reliable and comprehensive assessments.

Beyond essays, AI is being applied to automate the grading of a wide range of assignments, including coding assignments, multiple-choice tests, and even more complex problem-solving tasks.

Automated grading of coding assignments, for instance, presents unique challenges, as the correctness of a program often depends on subtle details of implementation and efficiency. AI-powered systems can be trained to assess the correctness and efficiency of code by testing it against a range of inputs and comparing the outputs to expected results. Moreover, advanced systems can even analyze the code's structure and style, providing feedback on coding practices and suggesting improvements. For example, the system might flag inefficient algorithms or highlight areas where code could be made more readable and maintainable.

Multiple-choice tests, traditionally easy to grade automatically, can benefit from AI through adaptive testing. Adaptive testing systems use AI algorithms to adjust the difficulty of the test questions based on the student's performance in real-time. This ensures that students are challenged appropriately, neither bored by easy questions nor overwhelmed by overly difficult ones. The system's ability to tailor the test to each student's proficiency level results in more accurate and reliable assessment of their understanding. Moreover, adaptive testing can also significantly reduce the length of the test, as it only requires students to answer the minimum number of questions needed to accurately assess their knowledge.

For more complex problem-solving tasks, AI can provide more nuanced feedback than simple correctness assessments. For example, in a mathematics problem, the system can identify the steps where the student made a mistake, providing targeted explanations to help them understand their error. This type of feedback is invaluable for learning, as it focuses on the underlying conceptual issues rather than simply stating whether the final answer is correct or incorrect. Similar approaches can be employed in other disciplines, such as physics or chemistry, where problem-solving involves multiple steps and intermediate calculations.

The development of AI-powered grading systems also necessitates careful consideration of pedagogical implications. While automation can save teachers valuable time, it's crucial to ensure that the automated feedback complements, rather than replaces, the human element of teaching. The goal is to create a collaborative system where AI enhances the educator's ability to provide effective feedback and personalized support. The use of AI should not lead to a reduction in the quality or depth of feedback students receive.

Ideally, automated systems should free up teachers to focus on higher-level tasks such as providing in-depth feedback on critical thinking and creativity, aspects that are often challenging for AI systems to evaluate objectively.

Equally important are the ethical considerations surrounding the use of AI in grading. Bias in the training data can lead to unfair or inaccurate assessments of students from certain demographics. It's vital to ensure that the data used to train AI grading systems is diverse and representative, minimizing the risk of bias.

Transparency in the algorithms used for grading is also critical; educators and students should understand how the systems work and the basis for their assessments. Furthermore, the use of AI in grading should not create a sense of depersonalization in the learning experience. The human element of teaching—the personal connection between teachers and students—remains essential for fostering a positive learning environment. Striking a balance between utilizing the efficiency of AI and preserving the human element of education is key to successful implementation.

The future of AI-driven automated grading promises continued improvements in accuracy, efficiency, and pedagogical effectiveness. The integration of more sophisticated NLP models, advancements in computer vision for evaluating visual assignments, and better understanding of human learning processes will contribute to more insightful and personalized feedback. However, ongoing research, careful implementation, and a constant evaluation of ethical implications remain paramount. The focus should always remain on leveraging AI to enhance, not replace, the core values of effective education—a human-centered approach that fosters critical thinking, creativity, and personalized learning experiences for all students. The successful integration of AI in automated assessment requires a collaborative effort involving educators, researchers, policymakers, and AI developers, ensuring that this technology enhances the learning process and creates a more equitable and effective educational system.

AIPowered Tools for Educators

Beyond automated assessment, AI offers a powerful arsenal of tools designed to significantly enhance the educator's role, moving beyond simply grading assignments to proactively supporting student learning and well-being. These tools are transforming how educators manage administrative tasks, personalize learning experiences, and identify students who require additional support.

The effective integration of these AI-powered tools promises to create a more efficient and effective educational system, empowering educators to focus on the core aspects of teaching: fostering critical thinking, nurturing creativity, and building meaningful relationships with students.

One crucial area where AI is making a substantial impact is student data management. Educators are often overwhelmed by the sheer volume of data they need to manage: grades, attendance records, student performance on assessments, and individual learning styles. AI-powered systems can streamline this process considerably. These systems can automatically collect and organize data from various sources, including learning management systems (LMS), assessment platforms, and even student engagement trackers within online learning environments. This automation eliminates tedious manual data entry, freeing up educators' time for more valuable tasks. Furthermore, AI can analyze this aggregated data to identify trends and patterns that might otherwise go unnoticed. For example, an AI system might detect a decline in a student's performance across multiple subjects, signaling a potential issue requiring intervention. This early warning system allows educators to proactively address challenges before they escalate, providing timely support and preventing students from falling significantly behind.

The ability to personalize learning is another key benefit of AI in education. Traditional teaching methods often struggle to cater to the diverse learning styles and paces of individual students. AI-powered systems offer the potential to personalize learning experiences on an unprecedented scale. Intelligent tutoring systems (ITS), for example, use AI algorithms to adapt the learning content and pace to each student's needs. These systems can analyze a student's performance on previous tasks, identifying areas of strength and weakness. Based on this analysis, the system can then tailor the learning materials, providing additional support in areas where the student is struggling and challenging them with more advanced content where they are proficient. This personalized approach not only enhances learning efficiency but also boosts student motivation by ensuring that each student is challenged appropriately and feels supported in their learning journey.

Beyond adapting the content, AI can also personalize the feedback students receive. While automated grading systems offer a valuable initial assessment, AI can also enhance the quality and specificity of feedback by providing individualized explanations and suggestions. Imagine an AI system that analyzes a student's essay and not only identifies grammatical errors but also pinpoints the underlying reasons for these errors, such as confusion about specific grammatical rules. The system could then provide tailored explanations and exercises to help the student master these rules, moving beyond simple correction to focused instruction. This type of personalized feedback is far more effective than generic comments, leading to significant improvements in student writing and comprehension. Similarly, in mathematical problem-solving, AI systems can identify the exact point where a student deviated from the correct solution path, providing targeted explanations and hints to guide the student towards the correct answer.

The potential of AI to identify at-risk students is particularly significant. Early intervention is crucial in preventing students from falling behind, and AI can significantly improve the effectiveness of early identification strategies. By analyzing student performance data, attendance records, and even engagement patterns in online learning environments, AI systems can identify students who are at risk of disengagement or academic failure. These systems can detect subtle indicators that might be missed by educators overwhelmed with other responsibilities. For instance, a consistent pattern of late submissions, low engagement in online discussions, or a decline in participation in class could indicate a potential problem. By alerting educators to these early warning signs, AI can empower them to provide timely interventions, such as offering additional support, connecting students with relevant resources, or addressing underlying personal or academic challenges.

The integration of AI in education also extends to administrative tasks, significantly reducing the burden on educators. AI-powered systems can automate a wide range of administrative duties, such as scheduling classes, managing student records, communicating with parents, and handling routine inquiries. This automation allows educators to dedicate more time to teaching and interacting with students, improving the overall quality of instruction. AI-powered chatbots, for example, can provide immediate answers to frequently asked questions, freeing up educators to focus on more complex issues. These chatbots can answer questions about deadlines, course materials, and administrative procedures, providing students with readily available support.

Furthermore, AI tools can help educators improve their teaching practices. AI-powered analytics can provide educators with insights into the effectiveness of their teaching methods. By analyzing student performance data, AI systems can identify areas where students are struggling and suggest adjustments to the curriculum or teaching approach. This data-driven approach to teaching can lead to significant improvements in student learning outcomes. Moreover, AI can help educators create more engaging and effective lesson plans. AI-powered tools can generate interactive simulations, games, and other learning materials tailored to specific topics and student needs. These interactive learning experiences can improve student engagement and enhance learning outcomes.

However, the implementation of AI in education is not without its challenges. One key concern is data privacy. AI systems collect and process large amounts of student data, raising concerns about the potential for misuse or unauthorized access. It's crucial to implement robust security measures to protect student data and ensure compliance with privacy regulations. Moreover, there are ethical considerations surrounding the use of AI in education. For example, the use of AI systems for grading could inadvertently perpetuate existing biases present in the training data. It's crucial to develop and implement AI systems that are fair, equitable, and unbiased. Additionally, the potential for AI to displace human educators is a concern that needs careful consideration. It's important to recognize that AI should be used as a tool to support and enhance the role of human educators, not to replace them. The integration of AI should be carefully planned and implemented to ensure that it complements and enhances human expertise, not diminishing the essential human element of teaching.

The future of AI in education is bright, promising a transformative shift in how we teach and learn. AI-powered tools have the potential to create a more personalized, engaging, and effective learning experience for all students, empowering educators to focus on what truly matters: building strong relationships with their students and fostering a love of learning. The key lies in carefully navigating the ethical and practical challenges, embracing collaboration between educators, researchers, and AI developers to ensure that AI is used responsibly and ethically to improve the lives of students and educators alike. This requires ongoing dialogue, transparent development, and a commitment to ensuring that AI serves as a powerful tool for good within the educational landscape.

The ultimate goal is not the replacement of educators but their empowerment, leveraging the capabilities of AI to enhance their capacity to inspire, guide, and support each student on their individual journey of learning and growth.

Accessibility and Inclusivity in AI Education

The transformative potential of AI in education hinges not only on its technical capabilities but also on its ability to foster accessibility and inclusivity. A truly equitable educational system powered by AI must cater to the diverse needs of all learners, dismantling barriers that prevent students from fully participating and achieving their potential. This requires a multifaceted approach encompassing technological design, pedagogical strategies, and policy considerations.

One crucial aspect is designing AI-powered learning tools that are inherently accessible. This goes beyond simply making the interface compatible with assistive technologies like screen readers and text-to-speech software. It necessitates a deeper consideration of how learners with diverse needs interact with the technology. For example, AI-powered tutoring systems should be adaptable to various learning styles and preferences. Students with dyslexia may benefit from different font sizes, colors, and spacing adjustments, while students with auditory processing difficulties might need visual aids and transcripts accompanying audio content.

Furthermore, the language used in the AI system should be clear, concise, and free of jargon, catering to students with varying language proficiency levels. The user interface itself should be intuitive and easy to navigate, minimizing cognitive load and frustration, particularly for students with cognitive disabilities.

Moreover, the development and implementation of AI-powered educational tools must explicitly address the digital divide. Access to reliable internet connectivity and appropriate devices remains a significant barrier to equitable access to technology, disproportionately affecting students from low-income backgrounds and underserved communities. Efforts to bridge this digital divide are essential for ensuring that the benefits of AI in education reach all students. This could involve initiatives to provide affordable internet access, distributing devices to students in need, and creating robust offline versions of AI-powered learning tools.

Investing in robust infrastructure and deploying strategies to enhance digital literacy within these communities are also vital steps to guarantee equitable access. Without such measures, the promise of AI-enhanced education risks exacerbating existing inequalities.

Beyond technological accessibility, inclusive pedagogy is crucial for leveraging AI effectively. Educators need training and support to understand how to integrate AI tools into their teaching practices in a way that caters to diverse learning styles and needs. This involves adopting a pedagogical approach that embraces differentiated instruction, recognizing that students learn at different paces and through different modalities. AI can be a valuable tool in supporting this approach, providing educators with data-driven insights into individual student learning patterns and needs. Educators can then leverage this information to tailor their instruction, providing differentiated assignments, personalized feedback, and targeted interventions. This necessitates a shift away from a "one-size-fits-all" approach towards a more individualized and responsive learning environment.

The ethical considerations surrounding the use of AI in education are paramount in ensuring inclusivity. AI algorithms are trained on data, and if that data reflects existing societal biases, the algorithms themselves will perpetuate and potentially amplify those biases. For example, an AI-powered assessment tool trained on data that overrepresents certain demographics could unfairly disadvantage students from other backgrounds. Therefore, ensuring fairness and equity in AI systems requires careful attention to data collection, algorithm design, and ongoing monitoring for bias. Transparency in the algorithms used and the data they are trained on is essential to build trust and address concerns about potential biases.

Furthermore, rigorous evaluation of AI systems for fairness and equity is necessary to prevent unintended discriminatory outcomes.

Collaboration between educators, AI developers, and accessibility specialists is essential to overcome the challenges of ensuring inclusive AI in education. A collaborative approach fosters the development of tools that are not only technically accessible but also pedagogically sound and ethically responsible. This collaborative model necessitates open communication and shared decision-making throughout the development lifecycle. Educators can provide valuable insights into the practical needs and challenges faced by students with different learning needs, while AI developers can leverage their technical expertise to design solutions that address these needs effectively. Accessibility specialists can ensure that the tools meet established accessibility standards and guidelines.

Addressing the issue of bias in AI systems requires a multifaceted approach involving data augmentation, algorithm modification, and post-processing techniques. Data augmentation involves supplementing the training data with examples that represent the full diversity of the student population, thereby reducing the overrepresentation of certain groups. Algorithm modification involves adjusting the algorithms themselves to mitigate bias, for instance, by incorporating fairness constraints or using bias-aware evaluation metrics. Post-processing techniques involve adjusting the output of the AI system after it has produced results to minimize bias. This might involve calibrating scores to account for demographic disparities or weighting different assessment components differently. Ongoing monitoring and evaluation are essential to ensure that these techniques are effective in minimizing bias over time.

Policymakers also play a crucial role in ensuring accessible and inclusive AI in education. They can create policies that mandate accessibility standards for AI-powered education technologies, allocate resources to support the development and implementation of inclusive technologies, and provide funding for professional development for educators to effectively integrate AI tools into their teaching practices. Moreover, policies could incentivize the development of AI systems that prioritize fairness and equity, potentially through grant programs or tax breaks for companies that demonstrate a commitment to inclusive AI. Legislation could also protect student data privacy and ensure compliance with accessibility standards.

In conclusion, creating an accessible and inclusive AI-powered educational system requires a collaborative effort from diverse stakeholders, including educators, AI developers, accessibility specialists, and policymakers. By addressing the technical, pedagogical, and ethical challenges, we can harness the transformative power of AI to create a more equitable and effective educational experience for all students, empowering them to reach their full potential regardless of their learning differences or socioeconomic backgrounds. The future of AI in education is dependent on this commitment to accessibility and inclusivity, ensuring that this powerful technology serves as a tool for progress and positive change in education.

Challenges and Ethical Considerations in AI Education

The integration of AI into education, while promising significant advancements, presents a complex array of challenges and ethical considerations that demand careful attention. These concerns extend beyond the purely technical realm, encompassing crucial aspects of data privacy, algorithmic fairness, and the evolving role of educators in an AI-enhanced learning environment. Failing to address these issues head-on risks exacerbating existing inequalities and undermining the very potential of AI to revolutionize education for the better.

One of the most pressing concerns is the issue of data privacy. AI systems in education often rely on vast amounts of student data, including learning patterns, performance metrics, and even personal information. This data, if not handled responsibly, can be vulnerable to breaches, misuse, and unauthorized access. The potential consequences are severe, ranging from identity theft and reputational damage to the erosion of trust in educational institutions. Robust data security measures, including encryption, access control, and regular audits, are paramount. Furthermore, transparent data governance policies, clearly outlining how student data is collected, used, and protected, are essential to build trust and ensure compliance with relevant regulations like FERPA (Family Educational Rights and Privacy Act) in the United States and GDPR (General Data Protection Regulation) in Europe. The challenge lies in balancing the need for data to improve AI systems with the imperative to protect the privacy and confidentiality of student information. This necessitates a proactive approach to data minimization, using only the data necessary for specific purposes and avoiding the collection of unnecessary or sensitive information.

Algorithmic bias presents another significant challenge. AI algorithms are trained on data, and if this data reflects existing societal biases, the algorithms themselves will perpetuate and even amplify these biases. For instance, an AI-powered assessment tool trained on data that predominantly represents students from privileged backgrounds might unfairly disadvantage students from underrepresented groups. This can lead to discriminatory outcomes, undermining the very principles of equitable education. Mitigating algorithmic bias requires a multifaceted approach. Firstly, careful attention must be paid to the diversity and representativeness of the training data. Efforts should be made to ensure that the data reflects the full range of student demographics and learning styles.

Secondly, the algorithms themselves need to be designed with fairness in mind, incorporating techniques that explicitly address bias and promote equitable outcomes. This might involve incorporating fairness constraints into the algorithm design or using bias-aware evaluation metrics. Finally, continuous monitoring and evaluation are critical to detect and address any biases that may emerge even after deployment. Transparency in algorithm design and data usage is crucial to build trust and enable external scrutiny. Regular audits and independent evaluations can help identify and rectify potential biases, ensuring fairness and equity in AI-powered educational systems.

The impact of AI on the role of teachers is another critical ethical consideration. While AI can automate certain tasks, such as grading and providing personalized feedback, it cannot replace the human element of teaching. The fear that AI will lead to widespread teacher displacement is a valid concern, and the transition should be managed carefully to ensure that teachers are not rendered obsolete. Instead, AI should be viewed as a tool to augment, not replace, teachers, empowering them to focus on higher-order tasks like fostering critical thinking, creativity, and social-emotional learning. This requires significant investment in professional development for teachers, equipping them with the skills and knowledge to effectively integrate AI into their teaching practices. Teachers need to be trained not just on how to use AI tools but also on how to understand and interpret the data generated by these tools, making informed decisions about how to tailor instruction to meet individual student needs. Moreover, ongoing support and mentorship are crucial to help teachers navigate the challenges and opportunities presented by AI in education.

The ethical considerations surrounding AI in education extend beyond the individual student level to broader societal impacts. Concerns about the potential for AI to exacerbate existing inequalities in access to quality education need careful consideration. The digital divide, characterized by unequal access to technology and internet connectivity, remains a significant barrier to equitable access to AI-powered educational resources. Students from low-income backgrounds and underserved communities are disproportionately affected by this divide, potentially widening the achievement gap. Addressing this requires a concerted effort to ensure equitable access to technology and digital literacy training for all students. This might involve initiatives to provide affordable internet access, distribute devices to students in need, and create robust offline versions of AI-powered learning tools. The ethical responsibility lies in ensuring that AI in education is a force for good, promoting inclusivity and closing the achievement gap rather than exacerbating it.

Furthermore, the use of AI in education raises concerns about the potential for surveillance and control. AI systems can collect extensive data about students' learning behaviors and preferences, raising concerns about the potential for misuse of this information. Ethical frameworks must be established to protect student autonomy and prevent the excessive monitoring of students. These frameworks should emphasize transparency, informed consent, and clear guidelines on data usage, ensuring that student data is not used in ways that could be detrimental to their well-being or privacy. The balance between leveraging data to enhance learning and protecting student privacy and autonomy must be carefully struck, prioritizing ethical considerations and safeguarding the rights of students.

Finally, the development and implementation of AI in education necessitate a collaborative approach involving educators, AI developers, policymakers, and other stakeholders. This collaboration is crucial to address the challenges and ethical concerns associated with AI in education and ensure that its potential benefits are realized equitably. Open communication and shared decision-making are essential to develop and deploy AI systems that are not only technically sound but also pedagogically appropriate and ethically responsible. Policymakers play a vital role in establishing ethical guidelines, regulations, and funding mechanisms to support the responsible development and implementation of AI in education. This includes ensuring data privacy protections, promoting algorithmic fairness, and providing resources for teacher training and support.

In conclusion, the integration of AI into education offers tremendous potential, but its successful implementation requires a careful consideration of the numerous challenges and ethical considerations involved. By proactively addressing issues of data privacy, algorithmic bias, teacher roles, equitable access, surveillance, and collaboration, we can harness the power of AI to create a more effective, inclusive, and equitable educational system for all learners. The journey toward responsible AI in education demands a continuous commitment to ethical principles, rigorous evaluation, and open dialogue among stakeholders. Only through this collaborative and ethically informed approach can we ensure that AI serves as a powerful catalyst for progress and positive change in the field of education.

Robotics and Automation in Manufacturing Processes

The integration of artificial intelligence into manufacturing processes is revolutionizing the industry, leading to unprecedented levels of efficiency, precision, and productivity. A key component of this transformation is the rise of robotics and automation, impacting every stage of the manufacturing lifecycle, from raw material handling to finished goods delivery. This isn't merely about replacing human workers; it's about augmenting human capabilities and creating entirely new possibilities for production.

One of the most visible applications of robotics in manufacturing is on assembly lines. Traditional assembly lines, while efficient in their own right, often rely on repetitive, manual tasks that can be prone to human error. Robots, on the other hand, can perform these tasks with tireless consistency and accuracy. They can handle delicate components, work in hazardous environments, and maintain a steady pace throughout the entire production run, minimizing downtime and maximizing output. Furthermore, advanced robotics systems, equipped with sophisticated sensors and AI-powered vision systems, can adapt to variations in components and adjust their movements accordingly, handling a wider range of products with minimal reprogramming. This flexibility is crucial in modern manufacturing where product customization and rapid prototyping are increasingly important.

Beyond assembly lines, robots are playing a crucial role in material handling. The movement of materials throughout a manufacturing facility is a complex and labor-intensive process. Robots can automate this process, efficiently transporting raw materials, work-in-progress, and finished goods between different stages of production. This includes tasks such as palletizing, stacking, and transporting items in warehouses and factories. Autonomous guided vehicles (AGVs), equipped with AI-powered navigation systems, can navigate complex factory layouts, avoiding obstacles and optimizing their routes for maximum efficiency. This not only speeds up the material flow but also reduces the risk of damage and delays caused by human error. The use of AI in AGV navigation is particularly beneficial in dynamic environments, where the layout of the factory floor may change frequently. These systems can learn and adapt to these changes, ensuring continuous operation even with modifications to the production line.

Quality control is another area significantly impacted by robotics and automation. Traditional quality control methods often involve manual inspection by human workers, a process that can be time-consuming, subjective, and prone to fatigue. Robots, equipped with advanced sensor technologies, can perform precise and objective quality inspections at a much higher rate and with greater accuracy.

AI-powered vision systems can detect even minute defects that might be missed by the human eye, ensuring consistently high product quality. This is particularly important in industries with stringent quality requirements, such as aerospace, automotive, and pharmaceuticals. The data collected by these robotic inspection systems can also be used to identify patterns and trends in defects, providing valuable insights for process optimization and preventing future quality issues. The use of machine learning in quality control analysis can further enhance this capability, leading to predictive maintenance and proactive quality improvements.

The impact of robotics and automation extends beyond individual tasks, reshaping the overall organizational structure and workforce dynamics within manufacturing companies. While some fear job displacement, the reality is more nuanced. While certain routine, repetitive tasks are indeed automated, this creates opportunities for workers to focus on more complex, higher-value activities such as programming, maintenance, and process optimization. The transition towards Industry 4.0 necessitates a shift in skills and training. Manufacturers are increasingly investing in workforce development programs to equip their employees with the skills needed to work alongside robots and AI systems. This includes training in areas such as robotics programming, data analysis, and cybersecurity. The result is a more skilled and adaptable workforce, capable of managing and maintaining increasingly sophisticated production systems.

The introduction of robotics and automation is also driving innovation in manufacturing processes. The ability to collect and analyze data from robotic systems provides manufacturers with unprecedented insight into their operations. This data-driven approach allows for optimization of processes, reduction of waste, and improvement of overall efficiency. The use of AI in predictive maintenance is a prime example. By analyzing data from sensors on robots and other equipment, AI systems can predict potential equipment failures before they occur, allowing for preventative maintenance and minimizing downtime. This predictive capability reduces maintenance costs, improves production uptime, and enhances overall operational efficiency. Moreover, the integration of AI and robotic systems allows for real-time adjustments to production based on changing market demands and unforeseen circumstances, enhancing flexibility and responsiveness.

However, the implementation of robotics and automation in manufacturing isn't without its challenges. The initial investment costs can be substantial, requiring significant capital expenditure for robot procurement, integration, and training. The need for skilled labor to program, maintain, and operate these systems represents another hurdle. Finding and retaining qualified personnel with expertise in robotics and AI is a growing concern for many manufacturers. Furthermore, the integration of new robotic systems into existing production lines can be a complex and time-consuming process, potentially disrupting existing workflows and requiring substantial adjustments to the manufacturing process. Overcoming these challenges requires careful planning, strategic investment, and a commitment to ongoing workforce development.

Another consideration is the ethical implications of widespread automation. The potential for job displacement remains a significant concern, requiring proactive measures to mitigate the impact on the workforce. This includes government policies supporting retraining and reskilling programs, as well as initiatives by manufacturers to upskill their existing employees. Moreover, the increasing reliance on automation raises questions about workforce safety and the potential for unforeseen errors in robotic systems.

Robust safety protocols and rigorous testing procedures are essential to mitigate these risks. Furthermore, ensuring the ethical and responsible development and deployment of AI in manufacturing requires careful consideration of bias in algorithms and the potential for misuse of data collected from robotic systems.

Addressing these ethical concerns is vital to ensure that the benefits of automation are shared equitably and contribute to a just and sustainable future for manufacturing.

The future of robotics and automation in manufacturing is bright, promising further advancements in efficiency, productivity, and product quality. As AI technology continues to evolve, we can expect even more sophisticated robotic systems capable of performing increasingly complex tasks. Collaborative robots, or "cobots," designed to work safely alongside human workers, are already becoming more prevalent, fostering a collaborative relationship between humans and machines. The integration of AI into supply chain management is also leading to greater optimization and efficiency in material procurement and logistics. The ability to predict demand, optimize inventory levels, and manage logistics more effectively is transforming the entire manufacturing value chain.

The journey towards a fully automated and AI-powered manufacturing landscape requires a collaborative approach involving manufacturers, researchers, policymakers, and educators. Manufacturers must invest in the necessary infrastructure and workforce development to integrate new technologies effectively. Researchers must focus on developing more robust, reliable, and adaptable AI systems. Policymakers must create a supportive regulatory environment that encourages innovation while addressing the ethical and societal implications of widespread automation. Finally, educators must play a key role in preparing the next generation of skilled workers for the jobs of the future in the rapidly evolving field of manufacturing. Only through this coordinated effort can we fully unlock the potential of robotics and AI to transform manufacturing and build a more prosperous and sustainable future for all.

Predictive Maintenance and Optimization of Manufacturing Systems

Predictive maintenance represents a significant leap forward in manufacturing efficiency. Traditional reactive maintenance, where repairs are only undertaken after equipment failure, leads to costly downtime, production losses, and unexpected expenses. AI offers a powerful alternative, enabling manufacturers to move from reactive to proactive maintenance strategies. This shift is driven by the ability of AI algorithms to analyze vast amounts of sensor data from machines, identifying patterns and anomalies that indicate potential failures before they occur.

The process begins with the deployment of sensors throughout the manufacturing facility. These sensors collect a wide range of data, including vibration levels, temperature, pressure, current draw, and acoustic emissions. This data, often streaming in real-time, provides a detailed picture of the health and performance of each machine.

The data is then fed into AI models, typically machine learning algorithms, which are trained to recognize patterns associated with impending equipment failures. These models are trained on historical data from the machines, including data from past failures and maintenance events. By analyzing this data, the AI system learns to identify subtle deviations from normal operating parameters that might indicate an impending malfunction.

The sophistication of these AI-powered predictive maintenance systems varies greatly depending on the specific application and the complexity of the equipment being monitored. Simple systems might use rule-based algorithms to identify thresholds for specific sensor readings, triggering an alert if a value exceeds a predetermined limit. More advanced systems leverage machine learning techniques such as deep learning and neural networks, enabling the analysis of complex, high-dimensional data sets and the detection of subtle patterns that are invisible to human operators. These advanced systems are capable of analyzing data from multiple sensors simultaneously, considering the interdependencies between different machine components and environmental factors. This holistic approach allows for a more accurate prediction of potential failures and a more precise assessment of the remaining useful life of equipment.

One key advantage of AI-powered predictive maintenance is its ability to handle the variability inherent in manufacturing environments. Factors such as temperature fluctuations, variations in raw materials, and operator behavior can all influence the performance of equipment. AI algorithms can learn to adapt to these variations, improving the accuracy of their predictions over time. Furthermore, AI systems can continuously learn and improve their predictive capabilities as they are exposed to more data. This continuous learning process allows for the refinement of predictive models, leading to increasingly accurate predictions and more effective maintenance strategies.

The implementation of AI-powered predictive maintenance typically involves several key steps. First, the selection of appropriate sensors and data acquisition systems is crucial. The types of sensors chosen depend on the specific equipment being monitored and the types of failures that are most likely to occur.

Second, data preprocessing and cleaning are essential steps to ensure the accuracy and reliability of the data used to train the AI models. This involves handling missing data, removing outliers, and transforming the data into a format suitable for analysis by the chosen algorithm. Third, the selection and training of the AI model is a critical aspect of the process. Different machine learning algorithms have different strengths and weaknesses, and the choice of algorithm depends on the specific characteristics of the data and the desired level of prediction accuracy. Finally, the integration of the AI system into the existing manufacturing management system is essential to ensure that maintenance actions are scheduled and executed efficiently.

The benefits of AI-powered predictive maintenance extend beyond the reduction of unplanned downtime and the associated costs. It also allows for optimized scheduling of maintenance activities. By predicting failures in advance, manufacturers can schedule maintenance during periods of low production or planned downtime, minimizing disruption to production. This proactive approach also allows for more efficient use of maintenance personnel, as maintenance tasks can be planned and prioritized based on the predicted severity and urgency of potential failures. Furthermore, AI-powered predictive maintenance can help manufacturers reduce their overall maintenance costs by preventing catastrophic failures that can result in extensive repairs and replacement of expensive equipment.

Beyond predictive maintenance, AI is also transforming how manufacturers optimize their production lines. AI algorithms can analyze data from various sources, including production line sensors, quality control systems, and historical production data, to identify bottlenecks, inefficiencies, and areas for improvement. This data-driven approach allows for the optimization of various aspects of the production process, leading to significant improvements in efficiency and reduced waste. For instance, AI can be used to optimize the scheduling of production tasks, ensuring that materials and resources are used efficiently and minimizing idle time. This optimization can lead to increased throughput and reduced production costs.

AI can also be used to improve the quality of products by identifying and correcting defects in real time. AI-powered vision systems can inspect products as they are produced, detecting even minute defects that might be missed by human inspectors. This enables manufacturers to identify and correct defects early in the production process, preventing the production of defective products and reducing waste. This real-time quality control capability also reduces the need for extensive post-production inspection, freeing up resources and reducing costs. Furthermore, AI can be used to analyze quality data to identify patterns and trends in defects, enabling manufacturers to address the root causes of quality problems and implement preventative measures.

The optimization of production lines through AI extends to the management of energy consumption. AI algorithms can analyze data from energy meters and production equipment to identify areas where energy can be saved. This can involve optimizing production schedules to minimize energy consumption during off-peak hours, identifying and repairing energy-inefficient equipment, or adjusting production parameters to reduce energy usage. The reduction in energy consumption can lead to significant cost savings and a reduced environmental footprint.

The implementation of AI for production line optimization often involves the use of digital twins. A digital twin is a virtual representation of a physical production line or piece of equipment. AI algorithms can be used to simulate the behavior of the digital twin, allowing manufacturers to test different scenarios and optimize the production process without disrupting the physical production line. This virtual testing capability allows for the rapid identification of optimal production parameters and the efficient deployment of changes to the physical production line. This iterative process of simulation and optimization allows manufacturers to continuously refine their production processes, leading to ongoing improvements in efficiency and productivity.

However, the successful implementation of AI in predictive maintenance and production line optimization requires careful consideration of several factors. Data quality is crucial, as the accuracy of AI predictions depends on the reliability and completeness of the data being analyzed. The integration of AI systems into existing manufacturing infrastructure can also be challenging, requiring significant investments in hardware, software, and skilled personnel. Furthermore, the ethical implications of using AI in manufacturing must be carefully considered. Concerns about data privacy, algorithmic bias, and job displacement need to be addressed to ensure the responsible and ethical implementation of AI in the manufacturing industry. Despite these challenges, the potential benefits of AI in predictive maintenance and production line optimization are significant, promising a future where manufacturing processes are more efficient, reliable, and sustainable. The ongoing development and refinement of AI technologies will undoubtedly further enhance these capabilities, driving further improvements in manufacturing productivity and competitiveness.

Quality Control and Defect Detection

The integration of AI into manufacturing extends far beyond predictive maintenance and production line optimization; it's revolutionizing quality control and defect detection. Traditional methods of quality control often rely heavily on manual inspection, a process that is inherently slow, prone to human error, and ultimately, expensive. Human inspectors, while capable of identifying obvious defects, often miss subtle flaws that can significantly impact product quality and lead to costly recalls or customer dissatisfaction. AI, specifically computer vision powered by deep learning algorithms, offers a transformative solution, enabling automated, high-throughput quality control with unprecedented accuracy and efficiency.

Computer vision systems used in automated quality control typically involve sophisticated cameras and imaging sensors that capture detailed images of products as they move along the assembly line. These images are then fed into AI algorithms, often convolutional neural networks (CNNs), which are specifically designed to process visual data. These CNNs are trained on massive datasets of images, some depicting perfect products and others showcasing various types of defects. Through this training process, the AI system learns to identify complex patterns and subtle variations that indicate defects, even those imperceptible to the human eye.

The training process itself is a crucial element of the effectiveness of these AI-powered quality control systems. The quality and quantity of the training data directly influence the accuracy and reliability of the AI's defect detection capabilities. High-quality datasets require meticulous preparation, including proper image annotation and the inclusion of a diverse range of defect types and variations. The annotation process involves carefully labeling each image with precise information about the location and type of any defects present. This meticulous labeling is essential for the AI system to learn to accurately associate specific visual patterns with particular defect types. Furthermore, the training data should be representative of the real-world variations in product appearance that might occur due to factors like lighting conditions, surface texture, and minor manufacturing variations. A poorly trained AI system, one trained on limited or biased data, can result in high rates of false positives or false negatives, rendering the system ineffective and potentially even harmful.

Once trained, these AI systems can analyze thousands of product images per hour, significantly surpassing the capacity of human inspectors. This high-throughput capability reduces inspection bottlenecks, accelerates the manufacturing process, and enables real-time quality control. This means that defects can be identified and addressed immediately, preventing defective products from reaching the end of the production line. The immediate feedback provided by the AI system enables faster corrective actions, minimizing waste and optimizing production efficiency.

Furthermore, the data collected by these AI systems provides valuable insights into the causes of defects, enabling manufacturers to identify and address the root causes of quality problems in their production processes. This proactive approach to quality control leads to continuous improvement and the creation of more robust and reliable manufacturing processes.

The application of AI in quality control extends beyond simple visual inspection. AI can also be used to analyze data from other sources, such as sensor data from manufacturing equipment, to identify potential sources of defects before they even manifest in the final product. This predictive capability allows for preventative measures to be implemented, reducing the likelihood of defects occurring in the first place. For example, if an AI system detects an anomalous pattern in sensor data from a welding machine, indicating a potential problem with the welding process, manufacturers can adjust the machine settings or perform preventative maintenance to prevent defects from forming in the welded components. This combination of real-time defect detection and predictive analysis offers a comprehensive approach to quality control, ensuring higher product quality and greater operational efficiency.

The benefits of AI-powered quality control are numerous and far-reaching. The increased accuracy and speed of defect detection lead to a significant reduction in the number of defective products produced, reducing waste and saving costs. The improved efficiency of the inspection process frees up human inspectors to focus on more complex tasks, utilizing their expertise more effectively. The real-time feedback provided by AI systems enables faster responses to quality issues, leading to a more agile and responsive manufacturing process. Furthermore, the data collected by these systems provides valuable insights into the root causes of defects, enabling continuous improvement and optimization of manufacturing processes. This data-driven approach to quality control enhances the overall quality and consistency of products, enhancing customer satisfaction and brand reputation.

The sophistication of AI-powered quality control systems varies depending on the complexity of the products being inspected and the types of defects that need to be detected. Simple systems might be designed to detect obvious defects, such as scratches or missing parts. More advanced systems can identify more subtle defects, such as microscopic cracks or variations in color or texture. The selection of appropriate AI algorithms and hardware is crucial to achieve the desired level of accuracy and efficiency. For instance, the choice between different types of CNNs, such as ResNet or Inception, depends on the specific characteristics of the data and the desired level of performance. The choice of hardware, such as the type of cameras and imaging sensors used, also plays a significant role in determining the system's overall performance and cost.

Implementing AI-powered quality control systems requires careful planning and execution. The initial investment in hardware, software, and training data can be substantial, but the long-term benefits often outweigh the initial costs. The integration of AI systems into existing manufacturing infrastructure can also present challenges, requiring careful consideration of data flow, security, and compatibility with existing systems. The training of personnel to operate and maintain these systems is equally critical to ensure the system's successful and effective operation.

However, despite the challenges, the advantages of AI-powered quality control are compelling. The improved accuracy, efficiency, and cost-effectiveness of these systems make them an increasingly attractive option for manufacturers across various industries. The continuous development and refinement of AI technologies will further enhance the capabilities of these systems, leading to even higher levels of accuracy, speed, and flexibility. As AI algorithms become more sophisticated and readily available, the implementation of AI-powered quality control systems will become more widespread, transforming the manufacturing landscape and ushering in a new era of precision, efficiency, and sustainability.

This continuous advancement in AI will invariably lead to more robust and adaptable manufacturing processes, fostering greater competitiveness and enhanced product quality in the global market.

The future of manufacturing is undoubtedly intertwined with the ongoing evolution of AI technologies, promising a future where production is not only efficient but also flawlessly precise. The integration of AI, therefore, signifies not just an upgrade, but a fundamental paradigm shift in the manufacturing process, one that promises to redefine quality control standards for years to come.

Supply Chain Management and Logistics

The transformative impact of AI extends beyond the factory floor, significantly reshaping supply chain management and logistics. Traditional approaches to supply chain optimization often struggle with the inherent complexities of predicting demand, managing inventory, and coordinating the intricate web of transportation and distribution. These challenges lead to inefficiencies, increased costs, and potential disruptions throughout the entire supply chain.

However, AI offers a powerful toolkit for addressing these issues, promising enhanced efficiency, reduced costs, and improved resilience.

One of the most significant contributions of AI lies in its ability to accurately forecast demand. Traditional forecasting methods often rely on historical data and simple statistical models, which can struggle to account for the dynamic and often unpredictable nature of market demand. AI, particularly machine learning algorithms, can analyze vast amounts of data from diverse sources—including sales data, social media trends, economic indicators, and even weather patterns—to generate significantly more accurate and nuanced demand predictions. These algorithms can identify complex patterns and correlations that would be invisible to human analysts, enabling businesses to anticipate changes in demand more effectively. This improved forecasting accuracy allows for better inventory management, reducing the risk of stockouts or overstocking, both of which represent significant costs for businesses.

The application of AI in inventory management goes beyond just demand forecasting. AI-powered systems can optimize inventory levels across the entire supply chain, from raw materials to finished goods. These systems can consider various factors, such as lead times, storage costs, and transportation costs, to determine the optimal inventory levels at each stage of the supply chain. This optimization minimizes inventory holding costs while ensuring sufficient stock to meet customer demand. Furthermore, AI can enhance inventory visibility, providing real-time tracking of inventory levels across the entire supply chain. This enhanced visibility empowers businesses to make more informed decisions about inventory replenishment, reducing the risk of stockouts and ensuring timely delivery to customers.

AI is also revolutionizing logistics operations, from transportation planning to route optimization. Traditional transportation planning methods often rely on manual processes and static routing algorithms, which can be inefficient and costly. AI-powered systems can analyze real-time traffic data, weather conditions, and other relevant factors to dynamically optimize transportation routes, minimizing delivery times and fuel consumption. These systems can also optimize the scheduling of transportation assets, such as trucks and ships, maximizing utilization and reducing idle time.

Furthermore, AI can improve the efficiency of warehouse operations, optimizing the placement of inventory, streamlining picking and packing processes, and improving the accuracy of order fulfillment.

The use of AI in supply chain management is not limited to individual optimization tasks. AI-powered systems can integrate and coordinate various aspects of the supply chain, creating a more holistic and efficient operation. These systems can analyze data from across the entire supply chain, identifying bottlenecks, inefficiencies, and potential disruptions. This holistic view allows for proactive intervention, mitigating risks and ensuring the smooth flow of goods. For instance, an AI system might detect a potential delay in the shipment of raw materials due to unforeseen circumstances. It can then proactively adjust the production schedule, minimizing the impact on the overall supply chain.

The integration of AI in supply chain management also presents opportunities for enhanced collaboration and transparency. AI-powered platforms can facilitate better communication and data sharing between different stakeholders in the supply chain, such as suppliers, manufacturers, distributors, and retailers. This improved collaboration leads to better coordination, reduced lead times, and enhanced responsiveness to changing market conditions. The increased transparency afforded by AI systems can also build trust and foster stronger relationships between different partners in the supply chain.

However, the implementation of AI in supply chain management is not without its challenges. The integration of AI systems requires significant investment in infrastructure, software, and data. The quality of the data used to train AI algorithms is critical, and obtaining high-quality data can be expensive and time-consuming. Furthermore, the successful implementation of AI requires a skilled workforce capable of operating and maintaining these complex systems. Addressing data security and privacy concerns is also essential, particularly given the sensitive nature of the data involved in supply chain management.

Despite these challenges, the benefits of AI in supply chain management are undeniable. The improved accuracy of demand forecasting, the optimization of inventory levels, and the streamlining of logistics operations lead to significant cost reductions and enhanced efficiency. The increased resilience and responsiveness of AI-powered supply chains enable businesses to adapt more effectively to changing market conditions and unforeseen disruptions. The enhanced collaboration and transparency fostered by AI systems strengthen relationships between stakeholders, leading to a more robust and efficient supply chain ecosystem.

The ongoing advancements in AI technology, such as the development of more sophisticated algorithms and the increasing availability of affordable computing power, are further accelerating the adoption of AI in supply chain management. As AI systems become more powerful and accessible, they will play an even more crucial role in shaping the future of supply chain operations.

Businesses that embrace AI-powered solutions will be better positioned to compete in a rapidly evolving global market, characterized by increasing demand for efficiency, resilience, and sustainability.

The future of supply chain management is intrinsically linked to the continued evolution of AI. The ability of AI to analyze vast amounts of data, identify complex patterns, and optimize complex processes will continue to transform how goods are produced, moved, and delivered. This transformation will not only enhance efficiency and reduce costs but also create opportunities for greater collaboration, transparency, and resilience across the entire supply chain ecosystem. The adoption of AI in supply chain management is not simply a matter of technological upgrade; it's a fundamental shift towards a data-driven, intelligent, and adaptive approach to managing the flow of goods in a globally interconnected world. This intelligent integration promises not only to streamline operations but also to foster greater sustainability and responsiveness to the ever-changing dynamics of global commerce. The seamless integration of AI into supply chain management is no longer a futuristic vision; it's rapidly becoming the new standard for competitive success. The companies that proactively embrace this transformation will be the ones best positioned to thrive in the years to come. The future is intelligent, and that intelligence is powered by AI.

Challenges and Ethical Considerations in AI Manufacturing

The integration of AI into manufacturing, while promising unprecedented levels of efficiency and productivity, presents a complex array of challenges and ethical considerations that demand careful attention. One of the most pressing concerns revolves around the impact on employment. The automation potential of AI-powered robots and systems raises legitimate fears about job displacement across various manufacturing roles, from assembly line workers to quality control inspectors. While some argue that AI will create new jobs in areas like AI development, maintenance, and oversight, the transition period could be disruptive, potentially leading to significant unemployment and social unrest if not managed proactively. This necessitates a proactive approach to workforce development, focusing on reskilling and upskilling programs designed to equip displaced workers with the competencies required for the emerging roles in AI-driven manufacturing environments. These initiatives must be comprehensive, encompassing not only technical training but also softer skills such as problem-solving, critical thinking, and adaptability, crucial for navigating the evolving landscape of AI-integrated workplaces. Furthermore, governments and industries must collaborate to create supportive safety nets, providing financial assistance and job placement services to those impacted by automation.

Beyond job displacement, the ethical implications of AI in manufacturing extend to the very nature of the AI systems themselves. The increasing autonomy of robots and automated systems raises critical questions about accountability and responsibility. When an AI-powered system makes a decision that leads to an accident or defect, determining liability becomes a complex legal and ethical puzzle. Is the manufacturer responsible? The AI developer? The operator of the system? Establishing clear lines of responsibility is essential to ensure accountability and prevent future incidents. This requires developing robust regulatory frameworks that address the unique legal and ethical challenges posed by autonomous AI systems in manufacturing settings.

Furthermore, the potential for bias in AI algorithms poses a significant risk. AI systems are trained on data, and if that data reflects existing societal biases, the AI system will likely perpetuate and even amplify those biases in its decision-making processes. This can lead to discriminatory outcomes, such as unfair allocation of tasks or unequal treatment of workers. Mitigating bias requires careful attention to data curation and algorithm design, ensuring that training data is representative and free from biases that could lead to unfair or discriminatory outcomes. Transparency in AI algorithms is also crucial, allowing for scrutiny and identification of potential biases.

The safety of AI systems in manufacturing environments is paramount. Malfunctioning or compromised AI systems could lead to accidents, injuries, or even catastrophic failures. Robust safety protocols and testing procedures are essential to ensure the reliability and safety of these systems. This includes rigorous testing and validation of AI algorithms before deployment, as well as ongoing monitoring and maintenance of these systems throughout their operational lifespan. Furthermore, incorporating human oversight into the decision-making processes of AI systems can serve as a vital safeguard, providing a layer of human judgment to prevent unintended consequences. The design of human-AI collaborative systems, where humans and AI work together to make decisions, can leverage the strengths of both while mitigating the risks associated with fully autonomous systems. This collaborative approach requires careful consideration of human-computer interaction design to ensure seamless and effective collaboration between human workers and AI systems.

Data privacy and security are also critical considerations. AI systems in manufacturing often collect and process large amounts of sensitive data, including employee information, production data, and intellectual property. Protecting this data from unauthorized access, use, or disclosure is crucial. Robust cybersecurity measures are essential to prevent data breaches and ensure the confidentiality, integrity, and availability of sensitive data.

Implementing strict data governance policies and complying with relevant data privacy regulations are paramount. Regular security audits and vulnerability assessments are necessary to identify and address potential security weaknesses. The ethical implications of data collection and usage must be considered throughout the entire lifecycle of the AI system, ensuring that data is collected and used responsibly and ethically. Transparency with employees about data collection practices is also vital to build trust and ensure compliance with ethical standards.

The responsible development and deployment of AI in manufacturing necessitate a multi-faceted approach encompassing technological advancements, robust regulatory frameworks, and ethical guidelines. Collaboration between stakeholders, including manufacturers, AI developers, policymakers, and workers, is vital to navigate the challenges and harness the opportunities presented by AI in manufacturing. Open dialogue and continuous monitoring of the ethical implications are critical to ensuring that AI is used in a way that benefits society as a whole. This collaborative effort should focus on creating a future where AI enhances productivity and efficiency while protecting workers' rights, upholding safety standards, and respecting ethical principles. The focus should not be on replacing human workers but rather on augmenting their capabilities, allowing them to perform their tasks more efficiently and safely. This requires a paradigm shift in how we view work in the age of AI, moving away from a solely production-focused approach to one that prioritizes human well-being and ethical considerations.

Furthermore, the long-term societal impact of AI in manufacturing requires careful consideration. The potential for increased inequality, both in terms of income distribution and access to opportunities, necessitates proactive measures to mitigate these risks. Investing in education and training programs that equip workers with the skills needed to thrive in an AI-driven economy is crucial to ensuring a just and equitable transition. Moreover, the ethical implications extend beyond the workplace, impacting the entire supply chain and the global economy. Sustainable practices and responsible sourcing of materials are critical considerations, ensuring that AI-driven manufacturing does not contribute to environmental degradation or social injustices elsewhere in the world.

The challenges and ethical considerations surrounding AI in

manufacturing are not insurmountable. With careful planning, proactive measures, and ongoing dialogue, we can harness the transformative power of AI while mitigating the potential risks. A future where AI empowers human workers, improves safety, and promotes sustainable manufacturing practices is attainable, but it requires a concerted effort from all stakeholders to navigate the complex landscape of technological advancement and ethical responsibility. The journey towards a responsible and ethical AI-driven manufacturing future demands a constant commitment to adaptation, collaboration, and a shared vision of a society that benefits from this technological revolution. By proactively addressing these challenges, we can ensure that the integration of AI into manufacturing leads to a more productive, equitable, and sustainable future for all. The continuous evolution of AI demands a continuous evolution of our ethical frameworks and regulatory responses, ensuring that this powerful technology serves humanity's best interests.

Autonomous Vehicles Technology and Development

The transition from human-driven vehicles to autonomous vehicles represents a monumental leap in transportation technology, fueled by advancements in artificial intelligence. This shift hinges on a complex interplay of sophisticated technologies working in concert to emulate, and in many ways surpass, human driving capabilities. Understanding these technologies is crucial to grasping the potential and limitations of self-driving cars.

At the heart of autonomous driving lies the intricate system of sensor fusion. Modern autonomous vehicles are equipped with a diverse array of sensors, each providing a unique perspective on the vehicle's surroundings. These sensors include LiDAR (Light Detection and Ranging), which uses lasers to create a 3D point cloud map of the environment; radar, which employs radio waves to detect objects and their velocities; cameras, which capture visual information similar to human eyesight; and ultrasonic sensors, providing short-range proximity detection. The challenge lies not just in collecting data from these disparate sources, but in intelligently fusing this data to create a comprehensive and accurate understanding of the vehicle's environment. This requires sophisticated algorithms that can reconcile conflicting data points, filter out noise, and create a unified representation of the surroundings, compensating for the individual limitations of each sensor modality. For example, LiDAR excels at providing precise distance measurements but struggles in adverse weather conditions like heavy rain or fog, while radar is less susceptible to these conditions but provides less detailed information. Effective sensor fusion algorithms are crucial in mitigating these limitations and creating a robust perception system.

This fused sensor data feeds into the vehicle's perception system, a crucial component responsible for interpreting the environment and identifying relevant objects and events. This involves object detection and classification, determining the type, location, and movement of objects such as vehicles, pedestrians, cyclists, and traffic signals. Advanced machine learning techniques, particularly deep learning, are employed to train these perception systems on massive datasets of real-world driving scenarios. Convolutional neural networks (CNNs), a type of deep learning architecture particularly well-suited for image processing, are commonly used for object detection in camera data. Similarly, recurrent neural networks (RNNs) can be utilized to model the temporal dynamics of objects and predict their future trajectories. The accuracy and reliability of the perception system are paramount to the safety and efficacy of the autonomous vehicle, as incorrect interpretations can lead to dangerous situations. Ongoing research focuses on improving the robustness of these perception systems in challenging conditions, such as low light, poor weather, and crowded urban environments. The development of more sophisticated algorithms that can handle ambiguity and uncertainty is a key area of ongoing research.

Once the environment has been perceived, the vehicle's path planning system determines the optimal route to reach the destination. This involves considering various factors, such as traffic conditions, road geometry, speed limits, and the locations and movements of other vehicles and pedestrians. Path planning algorithms typically employ graph search techniques, such as A search, to find efficient and safe routes. These algorithms must account for dynamic changes in the environment, adapting the planned path in real-time to avoid collisions and maintain a smooth and efficient trajectory. The complexity of path planning increases significantly in challenging environments with dense traffic or unpredictable pedestrian behavior. Advanced algorithms employing techniques like model predictive control (MPC) are being developed to handle these complex scenarios. MPC algorithms predict the future state of the environment and optimize the vehicle's trajectory accordingly, enabling more proactive and responsive path planning.

Finally, the control algorithms execute the planned path by manipulating the vehicle's steering, acceleration, and braking systems. These algorithms must precisely control the vehicle's actions based on the planned trajectory and the real-time sensor inputs, ensuring accurate following of the path and maintaining stability and safety. Control systems often involve advanced control techniques such as PID controllers, which maintain stability and precision in the vehicle's movement. The control algorithms must be robust enough to handle unexpected events, such as sudden braking by another vehicle or an unexpected obstacle appearing in the path. This requires integrating the perception and path planning systems seamlessly with the control system to ensure appropriate responses to dynamic situations. Sophisticated control algorithms are crucial in enabling the autonomous vehicle to navigate complex maneuvers such as lane changes, turns, and merging onto highways smoothly and safely.

The levels of autonomy in autonomous vehicles are typically categorized according to the SAE (Society of Automotive Engineers) levels. Level 0 represents no automation, with the driver in complete control. Level 1 involves driver assistance features, such as adaptive cruise control and lane keeping assist. Level 2 combines these features, allowing for partial automation, but still requiring driver supervision. Level 3 introduces conditional automation, where the vehicle can handle most driving tasks under specific conditions, but the driver needs to be ready to take over. Level 4 signifies high automation, where the vehicle can operate autonomously in defined areas without human intervention. Finally, Level 5 represents full automation, where the vehicle can operate autonomously in all conditions, effectively eliminating the need for a human driver. Achieving Level 5 autonomy remains a significant challenge, as it requires robust systems capable of handling unforeseen events and extremely complex situations. The development of truly autonomous vehicles necessitates breakthroughs in various areas, including sensor technology, artificial intelligence, and robust control systems. Furthermore, establishing trust and acceptance among the public remains a critical hurdle to widespread adoption.

The development of autonomous vehicles presents numerous challenges beyond the technological hurdles. Ensuring safety remains paramount, requiring rigorous testing and validation of the autonomous systems in a wide range of scenarios. The ethical implications of autonomous driving, such as decision-making in unavoidable accident scenarios, need careful consideration and the development of robust ethical frameworks. The legal framework surrounding autonomous vehicles is still evolving, requiring clear definitions of liability and responsibility in the event of accidents.

The integration of autonomous vehicles into existing transportation infrastructure requires careful planning and coordination, addressing issues such as traffic management, communication networks, and infrastructure upgrades. Furthermore, the economic impact of widespread autonomous vehicle adoption needs to be considered, including its effects on employment in the transportation sector and its potential to reshape urban planning and infrastructure development. Addressing these challenges requires collaborative efforts from researchers, engineers, policymakers, and the public to ensure the safe, ethical, and responsible deployment of autonomous vehicles. The journey towards fully autonomous vehicles is a marathon, not a sprint, demanding continuous improvement and innovation across multiple disciplines. The path forward necessitates not only technological advancements but also a careful consideration of the societal, ethical, and economic ramifications of this transformative technology. Only through careful planning and proactive adaptation can we harness the full potential of autonomous vehicles while mitigating the associated risks and challenges.

Traffic Management and Optimization

The promise of autonomous vehicles hinges not only on their individual capabilities but also on their seamless integration into the existing transportation ecosystem. This integration requires a fundamental rethinking of how we manage and optimize traffic flow, a challenge that AI is uniquely positioned to address. The current paradigm of traffic management, often relying on static signal timing and reactive interventions, is demonstrably inadequate for the complexities of modern urban environments. AI offers a powerful alternative, promising a more dynamic, efficient, and responsive approach to traffic control.

Intelligent Transportation Systems (ITS) represent the vanguard of this AI-driven transformation. These systems leverage a multitude of data sources, including real-time traffic sensor data from cameras, radar, and GPS-equipped vehicles, to gain a comprehensive understanding of traffic conditions across a city or region. This data is then processed using sophisticated AI algorithms to identify patterns, predict future traffic flow, and optimize signal timing in real-time. This contrasts sharply with traditional traffic management systems which rely on pre-programmed signal timings based on historical averages, often failing to adapt effectively to unexpected events such as accidents or special events.

Adaptive Traffic Control Systems (ATCS) exemplify the power of AI in optimizing traffic flow. These systems continuously monitor traffic conditions and adjust signal timings dynamically to minimize congestion and delay. Sophisticated algorithms, such as reinforcement learning, are employed to learn optimal signal control strategies based on real-time feedback from the traffic network. Reinforcement learning algorithms allow the ATCS to adapt to varying traffic patterns and optimize for multiple objectives, such as minimizing total travel time, reducing vehicle stops, and improving fuel efficiency. For example, an ATCS might prioritize traffic flow on a particular arterial during peak hours, while giving preference to cross-traffic during off-peak periods.

Furthermore, AI can predict potential congestion points based on historical data and current conditions, proactively adjusting signal timings to prevent bottlenecks from forming.

Beyond reactive adjustments, AI enables proactive traffic management by anticipating and mitigating potential congestion hotspots. This predictive capability relies on machine learning models trained on massive datasets of historical traffic data, weather patterns, and even social media trends that can indicate potential congestion events. For example, a machine learning model might predict increased traffic volume on a specific highway during a major sporting event based on past attendance figures and real-time social media activity. This prediction would allow traffic managers to preemptively adjust signal timings or suggest alternative routes to drivers, mitigating potential congestion before it occurs. This predictive power extends beyond simple volume prediction; AI can also anticipate the impact of unforeseen events such as accidents or road closures. By analyzing traffic patterns and historical data, AI algorithms can estimate the extent of disruption and suggest appropriate rerouting strategies.

The use of AI extends beyond centralized traffic management systems; it also enables intelligent routing and navigation systems for individual drivers. Navigation apps already leverage real-time traffic data to suggest optimal routes, but AI can further enhance these capabilities by learning individual driver preferences and incorporating dynamic factors such as road conditions, weather, and construction zones. This personalized approach ensures that drivers are routed to the most efficient path based on their specific needs and the current traffic conditions. Moreover, AI can provide more accurate estimations of travel times, reducing uncertainty and enabling better trip planning. AI-powered navigation systems can also adapt to unexpected events, rerouting drivers around accidents or road closures in real-time.

The integration of AI in traffic management is not without its challenges. Data privacy concerns must be addressed, ensuring that the vast amounts of traffic data collected are handled responsibly and ethically. The development and implementation of robust and transparent algorithms are crucial to prevent bias and ensure fair and equitable traffic management. The computational resources required to process real-time traffic data from a large network can be substantial, requiring sophisticated infrastructure and efficient algorithms. Furthermore, ensuring the security and reliability of AI-powered traffic management systems is paramount to prevent disruptions and maintain public trust.

The effectiveness of AI-powered traffic management is also contingent upon the quality and availability of data. The deployment of a comprehensive network of sensors and data collection infrastructure is essential to provide the necessary real-time data for AI algorithms to operate effectively. This requires significant investment in infrastructure development and data standardization. Furthermore, the accuracy of AI predictions depends on the quality of the training data used, highlighting the importance of data quality control and ongoing model refinement.

Looking to the future, the integration of autonomous vehicles will profoundly impact traffic management. Autonomous vehicles are expected to communicate with each other and with traffic management systems, sharing real-time information on their location, speed, and intended trajectory. This enhanced level of information sharing will allow for even more precise and efficient traffic optimization, potentially leading to significant reductions in congestion and improved safety. However, the seamless integration of autonomous vehicles into existing traffic management systems will require significant technological advancements and a coordinated effort between various stakeholders, including vehicle manufacturers, transportation authorities, and software developers.

The development of standardized communication protocols and data sharing mechanisms is crucial to ensuring interoperability between autonomous vehicles and traffic management systems.

In conclusion, the application of AI to traffic management offers a transformative potential for enhancing urban mobility. From adaptive traffic control systems to predictive traffic modeling and personalized navigation, AI-powered solutions are poised to revolutionize how we manage and optimize traffic flow in urban environments. However, the successful implementation of these technologies requires addressing crucial challenges related to data privacy, algorithm transparency, infrastructure development, and the integration of autonomous vehicles. Overcoming these hurdles is vital to harnessing the full potential of AI to create safer, more efficient, and more sustainable transportation systems for the future. The next generation of smart cities will be defined not only by their technological advancements but by their ability to leverage AI to solve the complex challenges of urban mobility, making cities more livable, productive, and enjoyable for all their inhabitants.

This requires a long-term vision and a concerted effort from researchers, policymakers, and technology developers to ensure that AI-powered traffic management systems are not only efficient but also ethical, fair, and sustainable. The ongoing evolution of AI in this field promises a future where traffic congestion is a problem of the past, replaced by a smooth and efficient flow of vehicles, significantly improving the quality of life in urban areas worldwide.

Air Traffic Control and Drone Management

The revolution in ground transportation powered by AI is poised to be mirrored, and perhaps even surpassed, in the skies. Air traffic control, a system managing millions of flights annually with remarkable safety, is ripe for disruption and enhancement through AI-driven solutions. The sheer volume of data generated by air traffic—flight plans, weather patterns, aircraft positions, and communication logs—presents a significant challenge for human controllers. AI offers a path toward more efficient and safer management of this complexity. Current systems often rely on human expertise and established procedures, leading to potential inefficiencies and delays, especially in high-traffic areas or during unexpected events. AI algorithms, capable of processing vast datasets in real-time, can assist in predicting potential conflicts, optimizing flight routes, and improving overall airspace efficiency.

One of the most promising applications of AI in air traffic control is conflict detection and resolution. Traditional methods often rely on human controllers identifying potential conflicts visually on radar screens, a process that becomes increasingly challenging with the increasing number of flights. AI-powered systems can analyze flight data, weather forecasts, and other relevant information to predict potential conflicts with far greater accuracy and speed than a human controller. These systems can then suggest corrective actions, such as adjusting flight altitudes or speeds, to prevent collisions. This proactive approach enhances safety and efficiency by preventing near-miss incidents and minimizing disruptions to the flight schedule. Furthermore, AI can learn from past near-miss incidents and incorporate this knowledge into its algorithms to enhance its predictive capabilities, constantly refining its ability to identify and mitigate potential risks. This continuous learning aspect is crucial for improving the system's overall performance and reliability over time.

Beyond conflict detection, AI is being explored for optimizing air traffic flow. Currently, air traffic management often follows predetermined routes and procedures, which may not be optimal in all conditions. AI algorithms can analyze real-time data, such as wind patterns and air traffic density, to dynamically adjust flight paths and optimize overall airspace utilization. This dynamic routing can lead to shorter flight times, reduced fuel consumption, and lower carbon emissions. The algorithms can also consider various factors simultaneously, such as minimizing delays, optimizing fuel efficiency, and reducing environmental impact, leading to a more holistic and sustainable approach to air traffic management. This is particularly relevant in the context of increasing air travel demand and the growing need for sustainable aviation practices. Imagine a system that seamlessly adapts to unexpected weather patterns, rerouting flights to minimize delays and ensure safe landings, all without the need for extensive human intervention.

The integration of AI into air traffic control is not without its challenges. One significant concern is the need for robust and reliable systems. The consequences of an AI system malfunctioning are potentially catastrophic, necessitating stringent safety protocols and rigorous testing. Furthermore, the complexity of AI algorithms can make it difficult to understand their decision-making processes, posing a challenge for transparency and accountability. Explainable AI (XAI) techniques are being developed to address this issue, enabling controllers to understand the reasoning behind the AI's recommendations. This is vital for building trust and ensuring that human controllers retain ultimate oversight and control. The development of robust validation and verification methods is crucial to ensure the reliability and safety of these AI-powered systems before their widespread deployment.

The integration of AI in air traffic control also raises questions about the role of human air traffic controllers. While AI can significantly augment their capabilities, it is unlikely to completely replace them. The human element remains crucial for handling unexpected situations, resolving complex conflicts that require nuanced judgment, and making critical decisions in emergency scenarios. The future of air traffic control is likely to involve a collaborative partnership between human controllers and AI systems, where AI assists controllers with routine tasks, allowing them to focus on more complex and critical aspects of their job. This collaborative approach enhances both safety and efficiency while preserving human oversight and control.

The rise of drones presents a new layer of complexity for air traffic management. The increasing number of drones operating in airspace requires a new paradigm for managing and controlling drone traffic, ensuring safe separation from manned aircraft and avoiding potential conflicts. AI is uniquely positioned to address this challenge. AI-powered systems can track and manage drone flights in real-time, monitor their trajectories, and detect potential conflicts with other aircraft or obstacles. These systems can also manage airspace allocation, ensuring that drones operate within designated zones and do not interfere with other air traffic.

Furthermore, AI can automate drone communication and coordination, streamlining the management process and reducing the workload on human operators.

The development of autonomous drone systems further amplifies the need for sophisticated AI-powered management tools.

Autonomous drones, capable of operating without human intervention, require even more robust and reliable AI systems to ensure their safe operation. These systems must be able to anticipate potential hazards, navigate around obstacles, and react to unexpected events, all without human intervention. The development of such systems involves a combination of computer vision, machine learning, and sensor fusion, enabling autonomous drones to perceive their environment and make informed decisions. This is a rapidly evolving field with significant challenges related to safety, security, and regulatory compliance.

The effective management of drone traffic also necessitates a robust communication infrastructure that allows drones to communicate with each other and with air traffic control systems. This requires the development of standardized communication protocols and data sharing mechanisms, ensuring interoperability between different drone models and systems. The development of secure communication channels is crucial to prevent malicious attacks and ensure the safety and security of drone operations. Furthermore, a robust system for identifying and tracking individual drones is vital for managing their flights and preventing potential conflicts. The integration of AI-powered surveillance systems can assist in identifying and tracking drones, even in complex and crowded environments.

The implications of AI-powered drone management extend beyond safety and efficiency. Drones have the potential to revolutionize various industries, from delivery and inspection to agriculture and surveillance. However, the widespread adoption of drones necessitates a robust and reliable management system that ensures their safe and responsible operation. AI-powered systems can help to unlock the full potential of drones while mitigating potential risks. This integration requires close collaboration between technology developers, regulators, and policymakers to establish a regulatory framework that balances innovation with safety and security.

In conclusion, the application of AI to air traffic control and drone management is transforming the aviation landscape. From enhancing safety and efficiency in air traffic management to facilitating the safe and responsible integration of drones into airspace, AI is poised to revolutionize how we navigate the skies.

However, the successful implementation of these technologies requires careful consideration of the challenges related to safety, security, reliability, and ethical implications. Addressing these issues is crucial for harnessing the full potential of AI to create a safer, more efficient, and more sustainable aviation system for the future. The collaborative effort of researchers, policymakers, and industry stakeholders will be instrumental in shaping the future of air travel and ensuring the safe and responsible integration of AI in this crucial sector. The coming decades will witness a dramatic shift in how we manage air traffic, driven by the ever-increasing capabilities of AI and the growing demands of an increasingly connected and technologically advanced world.

Public Transportation and Mobility Services

The transformation of transportation extends beyond the skies and encompasses the ground as well. Public transportation systems, often burdened by inefficiencies and unpredictable demand, are witnessing a significant overhaul thanks to the integration of artificial intelligence. AI is no longer a futuristic concept; it's actively shaping how cities move their populations, impacting everything from bus scheduling to the optimization of entire transit networks.

One of the most immediate applications of AI in public transport is the optimization of bus routes and schedules. Traditional methods often rely on fixed schedules and routes, which may not be optimal given fluctuating passenger demand throughout the day and across different days of the week. AI algorithms, powered by machine learning, can analyze vast datasets encompassing historical ridership patterns, real-time traffic conditions, and even weather forecasts to dynamically adjust bus routes and schedules. This dynamic optimization can lead to significant improvements in efficiency, reducing wait times for passengers and improving overall service reliability. For example, imagine a system that automatically adjusts bus frequencies during rush hour to accommodate increased passenger demand, or reroutes buses in real-time to avoid traffic congestion. This level of adaptive scheduling simply wasn't possible before the advent of powerful AI algorithms and real-time data integration.

The use of predictive analytics is another critical aspect of AI's impact on public transport. By analyzing historical data and identifying patterns, AI algorithms can accurately predict passenger demand at different times and locations. This predictive capability enables transport operators to allocate resources more efficiently, deploying additional buses or trains during peak hours to alleviate overcrowding and reduce wait times. Conversely, in periods of low demand, resources can be reallocated to other routes or temporarily taken out of service, optimizing operational costs and improving overall efficiency. This predictive power allows for proactive adjustments, rather than reactive responses to unpredictable surges in demand. The ability to anticipate and adapt to changing patterns translates to better passenger experiences and more efficient use of public funds.

Beyond buses, AI is transforming rail operations. Train scheduling, historically a complex and often manually intensive process, is being streamlined through AI-powered optimization algorithms. These algorithms can analyze numerous factors—track occupancy, train capacity, maintenance schedules, and even potential delays—to create optimized schedules that maximize efficiency and minimize delays. The integration of real-time data from various sources, such as train positioning systems and passenger counters, further enhances the accuracy and effectiveness of AI-driven scheduling. This leads to more punctual train arrivals and departures, reducing passenger frustration and increasing overall ridership. Moreover, predictive maintenance, powered by AI, is minimizing the likelihood of unexpected disruptions. By analyzing sensor data from trains and tracks, algorithms can identify potential mechanical issues before they lead to breakdowns, reducing downtime and improving overall system reliability.

The integration of AI is also impacting the passenger experience directly. Many transit agencies are employing AI-powered mobile applications that provide real-time information about bus and train arrivals, route planning assistance, and even potential delays. These apps leverage GPS tracking data and other sources to provide accurate and up-to-the-minute information, enabling passengers to make informed decisions and plan their journeys more effectively.

Furthermore, some systems use AI-powered chatbots to answer passenger queries, providing immediate support and addressing concerns without the need for human intervention. This not only enhances passenger convenience but also frees up human staff to focus on more complex tasks.

The rise of ride-sharing services has introduced a new dimension to the urban transportation landscape, and AI plays a vital role in optimizing their operations. Companies like Uber and Lyft rely heavily on AI algorithms to match riders with drivers, predict surge pricing based on demand, and optimize the routing of vehicles to minimize travel times. These algorithms are constantly learning and adapting to changes in traffic patterns, weather conditions, and passenger preferences, improving the efficiency and effectiveness of these services. Moreover, AI is being used to detect and prevent fraudulent activities, ensuring the safety and security of both riders and drivers. The sophisticated matching algorithms take into account various factors, including rider location, driver availability, and estimated travel times, to ensure efficient and convenient rides.

The algorithms also learn from past ride data to improve their accuracy and efficiency over time, constantly refining their ability to optimize the matching process.

The integration of ride-sharing services with public transportation presents an exciting opportunity for improved urban mobility. AI-powered systems can facilitate seamless transfers between ride-sharing services and public transit, providing integrated journey planning and enhancing the overall user experience. Imagine an app that suggests the most efficient route, combining ride-sharing with public transport to minimize travel time and cost. This integrated approach can encourage more people to use public transport, reducing traffic congestion and promoting sustainable transportation options. Furthermore, AI-powered systems can optimize the allocation of resources within ride-sharing networks, ensuring that vehicles are deployed effectively to meet demand while minimizing environmental impact.

However, the widespread adoption of AI in public transportation also presents several challenges. Data privacy is a major concern, as the collection and use of passenger data requires careful consideration of ethical implications and adherence to privacy regulations. Ensuring the security of AI systems is also crucial, as any vulnerabilities could lead to disruptions in service or even security breaches. Transparency and explainability are also important factors, as it's essential for passengers and stakeholders to understand how AI-powered systems make decisions. The "black box" nature of some AI algorithms needs to be addressed to build trust and ensure accountability. Furthermore, the cost of implementing and maintaining AI systems can be substantial, requiring significant investment from transport agencies and service providers.

The equitable access to AI-powered transportation services is another critical issue. The benefits of AI-driven optimization should be available to all members of society, irrespective of their socioeconomic status or location. This requires careful planning and implementation to ensure that AI systems are not biased against certain groups or communities. The digital divide also presents a challenge, as not all individuals have access to the technology required to utilize AI-powered transportation apps and services. Addressing these issues requires a holistic approach that considers the needs of all members of society.

In conclusion, AI is revolutionizing public transportation and mobility services, offering significant improvements in efficiency, reliability, and passenger experience. From optimizing bus routes and train schedules to predicting passenger demand and enhancing ride-sharing services, AI is transforming how cities move their populations. However, the successful implementation of AI in this sector requires careful consideration of ethical, security, and accessibility challenges. Addressing these concerns is crucial to harness the full potential of AI to create more efficient, sustainable, and equitable transportation systems for the future. The ongoing collaboration between technology developers, policymakers, and transportation agencies will be essential in shaping the future of urban mobility and ensuring that AI is used responsibly and ethically to benefit all members of society. The future of urban transportation will likely be characterized by a seamless integration of various modes of transport, all optimized by intelligent systems that prioritize efficiency, sustainability, and equitable access for all.

Ethical and Safety Considerations in AI Transportation

The integration of AI into transportation promises a future of seamless mobility, but this progress is inextricably linked to a complex web of ethical and safety considerations. Autonomous vehicles, in particular, present unprecedented challenges, demanding a careful examination of liability, data privacy, and the development of robust safety protocols. The very nature of these systems, relying on intricate algorithms and sensor data to navigate and make decisions, raises questions that traditional legal and regulatory frameworks are ill-equipped to handle.

One of the most pressing concerns revolves around liability in the event of an accident. In a human-driven vehicle, assigning responsibility is relatively straightforward. However, when an autonomous vehicle is involved, the lines of accountability blur. Is the manufacturer liable for a defect in the software or hardware? Is the owner responsible for the vehicle's actions? Or does the burden fall on the developers of the AI algorithms themselves? These questions are not merely philosophical; they have significant legal and financial implications. The lack of clear legal frameworks currently leaves this area shrouded in uncertainty, potentially hindering the widespread adoption of autonomous vehicles. The need for international standardization and harmonization of liability laws is paramount to create a stable and predictable environment for the industry to flourish. Furthermore, robust testing and certification procedures are essential, ensuring that autonomous vehicles meet stringent safety standards before being deployed to the public. This requires a collaborative effort between regulatory bodies, manufacturers, and AI researchers to define clear metrics for safety and performance.

Beyond the issue of liability, data privacy represents another significant ethical challenge. Autonomous vehicles generate vast quantities of data, including location information, driving patterns, and even passenger interactions within the vehicle. This data presents a lucrative opportunity for various entities, from advertisers to insurance companies, raising concerns about potential misuse and exploitation. Ensuring the privacy and security of this data is crucial, requiring robust data encryption and anonymization techniques. Furthermore, transparency is essential. Individuals should have the right to access and control their own data, understanding how it is being collected, used, and protected. The development of clear data privacy regulations tailored specifically to the context of autonomous vehicles is crucial to build public trust and promote responsible innovation. These regulations must strike a balance between protecting individual privacy and enabling the development and deployment of beneficial AI-powered transportation systems. This delicate balance will require ongoing dialogue and collaboration among policymakers, technology developers, and civil liberties advocates.

The safety of AI-powered transportation systems is paramount.

While autonomous vehicles have the potential to significantly reduce accidents caused by human error, the inherent complexity of these systems introduces new risks that must be carefully mitigated. The reliability of sensor technology is critical. Autonomous vehicles rely heavily on sensors to perceive their surroundings, and any failure or malfunction can have catastrophic consequences.

Redundant systems and robust error-handling mechanisms are necessary to ensure that the vehicle can safely navigate unexpected situations. The robustness of AI algorithms is equally important. The algorithms must be able to adapt to a wide range of conditions and handle unexpected events without compromising safety.

Rigorous testing and validation are needed to verify the ability of the system to respond safely under all conceivable scenarios.

Moreover, the ethical programming of these algorithms is a major consideration. Decisions regarding emergency braking, for instance, must be carefully considered to minimize harm to all stakeholders.

Such considerations require more than just technical expertise, necessitating the input of ethicists, philosophers, and social scientists in the design process.

The potential for algorithmic bias in autonomous vehicles is another critical safety concern. If the algorithms used to train the AI systems are biased, the resulting systems may exhibit discriminatory behavior, disproportionately impacting certain demographics. For example, a system trained primarily on data from one geographic region or demographic group may perform poorly or even unsafely when deployed in other settings. Mitigating algorithmic bias requires careful data curation, ensuring that the training data is diverse and representative of the wider population. Regular audits and testing are crucial to identify and address any biases that may emerge. Furthermore, the development of transparent and explainable AI algorithms is crucial for accountability and for building trust in these systems. The black-box nature of some AI algorithms can make it difficult to understand how decisions are made, hindering the ability to identify and correct biases or errors. The drive towards explainable AI is a critical step towards building safer and more trustworthy autonomous vehicles.

Furthermore, cybersecurity presents a significant threat to the safety and security of AI-powered transportation systems.

Autonomous vehicles are connected systems, reliant on various communication networks for data exchange and control. This connectivity introduces vulnerabilities to cyberattacks, with potentially devastating consequences. The potential for hackers to take control of a vehicle remotely or to manipulate its sensor data is a serious concern. Robust cybersecurity protocols are essential to protect these systems from malicious attacks. Regular security audits and penetration testing are necessary to identify and address vulnerabilities. Moreover, the development of secure communication protocols and encryption techniques is crucial to safeguard data and prevent unauthorized access. Collaboration between technology developers, cybersecurity experts, and regulatory bodies is vital to develop and implement effective cybersecurity measures for autonomous vehicles and other AI-powered transportation systems. This collaboration should focus on fostering a culture of security throughout the development lifecycle of these systems, from design to deployment and maintenance.

The ethical and safety considerations surrounding AI in transportation are not merely technical challenges; they are deeply intertwined with broader societal issues. The equitable distribution of the benefits of this technology, for example, is a paramount concern. The deployment of autonomous vehicles should not exacerbate existing inequalities, but rather contribute to a more just and equitable society. This requires careful consideration of the impact on employment, particularly within the transportation sector. Retraining programs and social safety nets may be necessary to help workers transition to new roles in the changing landscape.

Furthermore, ensuring equitable access to these technologies is crucial, avoiding a situation where the benefits are concentrated in specific geographic areas or socioeconomic groups. Addressing these societal implications requires a holistic approach involving policymakers, industry leaders, and community stakeholders. This approach must ensure that the benefits of AI-powered transportation are shared broadly, promoting inclusivity and avoiding the exacerbation of social inequalities.

In conclusion, the integration of AI into transportation offers enormous potential to revolutionize mobility, improving efficiency, safety, and accessibility. However, realizing this potential requires a proactive and comprehensive approach to address the complex ethical and safety considerations discussed above. The development of robust legal frameworks, stringent safety protocols, transparent data privacy policies, and effective cybersecurity measures is essential. Furthermore, a societal dialogue addressing broader ethical implications, including issues of algorithmic bias, equitable access, and job displacement, is crucial. Only through a collaborative effort involving policymakers, industry leaders, researchers, and the public can we ensure that the transformative potential of AI in transportation is harnessed responsibly and ethically, benefiting all members of society. The future of transportation hinges not only on technological advancements but also on our ability to navigate the complex ethical and societal challenges that accompany them.

Climate Change Modeling and Prediction

The escalating climate crisis demands increasingly sophisticated predictive tools, and artificial intelligence (AI) is emerging as a powerful ally in this fight. Traditional climate models, while valuable, struggle to fully capture the intricate complexities of the Earth's climate system. The sheer volume of data involved – from atmospheric temperatures and ocean currents to ice sheet dynamics and land use changes – is overwhelming for conventional computational methods. AI, particularly machine learning, offers a transformative approach to analyzing this data deluge and extracting meaningful insights with unprecedented accuracy.

Machine learning algorithms excel at identifying patterns and relationships within massive datasets that might be imperceptible to human analysts. These algorithms can sift through terabytes of climate data, encompassing historical observations, satellite imagery, and outputs from existing climate models, to uncover subtle correlations and predict future trends with greater precision.

This capability is crucial for refining existing climate models and generating more accurate projections of future climate scenarios. For instance, AI can be used to improve the representation of cloud formation and feedback mechanisms in climate models, which are critical factors influencing global temperature. Clouds, notoriously complex to simulate accurately, exert a significant influence on the Earth's radiative balance, and AI's ability to identify subtle patterns in cloud behavior can significantly enhance the accuracy of climate predictions.

One particularly promising application of AI is in downscaling global climate models. Global climate models (GCMs) provide valuable insights into large-scale climate patterns, but they often lack the spatial resolution needed to capture regional variations in climate change impacts. AI techniques can be used to "downscale"the output of GCMs, generating higher-resolution climate projections for specific regions. This allows for more accurate assessments of the impacts of climate change on local communities and ecosystems, informing targeted adaptation strategies and disaster preparedness plans. For example, AI-powered downscaling can provide more accurate predictions of extreme weather events like floods, droughts, and heatwaves at a local level, enabling communities to develop more effective mitigation and response strategies.

Furthermore, AI is playing a crucial role in integrating diverse sources of climate data. Climate data is collected from a variety of sources, including weather stations, satellites, ocean buoys, and even citizen science initiatives. These datasets often vary in quality, resolution, and format, making it challenging to integrate them into a coherent analysis. AI can help overcome this challenge by developing algorithms that can automatically process, harmonize, and integrate data from heterogeneous sources. This allows for a more comprehensive understanding of the Earth's climate system, improving the accuracy and reliability of climate models. Moreover, AI can be used to fill in gaps in existing climate data, using machine learning techniques to reconstruct missing data points based on available information. This is particularly valuable in regions with limited historical climate data, where accurate climate projections are crucial for informing adaptation strategies.

Beyond improving climate models, AI is also being employed to predict the impacts of climate change on various environmental systems. For instance, AI can be used to predict the future distribution of species based on changes in climate and habitat, allowing for the development of effective conservation strategies. It can also be used to predict the impact of climate change on agricultural yields, informing the development of climate-resilient agricultural practices. AI is even being used to model the complex interactions between climate change and human health, enabling public health officials to anticipate and mitigate the potential risks of heat stress, infectious diseases, and other climate-related health threats.

However, the application of AI to climate modeling and prediction is not without its challenges. One significant challenge is the issue of data bias. Climate data can be biased, reflecting historical biases in data collection methods or geographical limitations. This bias can propagate through AI models, leading to inaccurate or misleading predictions. Addressing data bias requires careful data cleaning, preprocessing, and validation techniques. Researchers are exploring various methods to mitigate the impact of bias in climate data, including techniques like data augmentation and adversarial training.

Another challenge is the "black box" nature of some AI algorithms. While machine learning algorithms can generate impressive predictions, it can be difficult to understand how they arrive at these predictions. This lack of transparency can make it challenging to assess the reliability and trustworthiness of AI-based climate predictions. The development of explainable AI (XAI) techniques is crucial to address this challenge, making AI-based climate models more transparent and understandable. Explainable AI aims to create AI systems that can not only provide accurate predictions but also explain the reasoning behind those predictions, increasing confidence in their reliability and allowing for better scrutiny.

Furthermore, the computational resources required for training and deploying sophisticated AI-based climate models can be substantial. High-performance computing infrastructure is necessary to handle the vast datasets and complex computations involved. As AI models become more sophisticated, the computational demands will likely increase, requiring ongoing investment in advanced computing technologies. Access to these resources is crucial to ensuring that AI-based climate modeling is widely accessible to researchers and policymakers around the world. Collaboration and resource-sharing among institutions are paramount to overcome this challenge.

The ethical implications of using AI for climate modeling and prediction should also be carefully considered. The predictions generated by AI models can have significant societal and economic implications, influencing policy decisions and resource allocation. It is crucial to ensure that AI-based climate models are used responsibly and ethically, avoiding biases and promoting transparency. The development of clear guidelines and best practices for the responsible use of AI in climate modeling is essential to build trust and confidence in the results.

In conclusion, AI is poised to revolutionize our understanding of climate change and our ability to predict its impacts. By leveraging the power of machine learning to analyze massive datasets and identify complex patterns, AI can significantly improve the accuracy and sophistication of climate models. This will enable more effective adaptation and mitigation strategies, helping us to address the urgent challenges posed by climate change. However, it is crucial to address the challenges associated with data bias, model transparency, computational resources, and ethical considerations to ensure the responsible and effective use of AI in this critical domain. The future of climate modeling and prediction hinges not only on technological advancements but also on our ability to navigate the complex ethical and societal implications of this transformative technology. The collaborative effort of climate scientists, AI researchers, policymakers, and the broader community will be critical in harnessing the full potential of AI to combat the climate crisis.

Environmental Monitoring and Conservation

The integration of artificial intelligence (AI) into environmental monitoring and conservation represents a paradigm shift in our approach to safeguarding the planet. Traditional methods, often reliant on manual data collection and analysis, are inherently limited in scope and speed, struggling to keep pace with the rapid pace of environmental change. AI, however, offers a powerful suite of tools capable of processing vast quantities of data from diverse sources, identifying subtle patterns, and predicting future trends with unprecedented accuracy. This section explores how AI is revolutionizing environmental monitoring and conservation, enhancing our ability to detect pollution, manage resources effectively, and protect endangered species.

One of the most significant applications of AI in environmental monitoring is the deployment of extensive sensor networks. These networks, often comprised of thousands of individual sensors strategically positioned across landscapes, collect real-time data on a wide range of environmental parameters. This data includes, but is not limited to, air and water quality, soil conditions, temperature, humidity, and noise levels. The sheer volume of data generated by these networks would be practically impossible to analyze manually. AI, however, enables efficient and effective data processing, pattern recognition, and anomaly detection. Machine learning algorithms can be trained to identify deviations from established baselines, indicating potential environmental hazards such as pollution spills, deforestation, or illegal wildlife activity. For example, a network of sensors monitoring water quality in a river system can alert authorities to a sudden increase in pollutants, allowing for rapid response and remediation efforts. Similarly, sensors deployed in forests can detect illegal logging activities based on changes in acoustic patterns or tree cover density. Furthermore, AI can be used to optimize the placement and deployment of these sensor networks, maximizing their effectiveness while minimizing resource consumption. This optimization can consider factors such as terrain, accessibility, and the likelihood of encountering specific environmental events, ensuring that monitoring efforts are targeted and efficient.

Satellite imagery provides another crucial data source for AI-powered environmental monitoring. Satellites equipped with high-resolution sensors continuously capture images of the Earth's surface, providing a vast repository of information on land use changes, deforestation rates, glacial melt, and other environmental phenomena. AI algorithms, particularly deep learning models like convolutional neural networks (CNNs), are exceptionally adept at analyzing satellite imagery. CNNs can be trained to identify specific features within images, such as the extent of deforestation, the presence of pollutants in water bodies, or the distribution of endangered species. This capability enables efficient and large-scale environmental monitoring across vast geographical areas, providing valuable insights that would be unattainable through traditional methods. For instance, AI can be used to monitor the health of coral reefs, identifying areas experiencing coral bleaching due to rising ocean temperatures. Similarly, AI algorithms can track the expansion of urban areas into natural habitats, providing data crucial for urban planning and conservation efforts. The increasing availability of high-resolution satellite imagery, coupled with the advancements in AI algorithms, allows for more accurate and timely assessments of environmental change, informing effective management strategies.

Beyond sensor networks and satellite imagery, AI is also being integrated with other data sources to create a comprehensive understanding of environmental systems. This includes incorporating data from weather stations, climate models, and even citizen science initiatives. AI's ability to fuse these diverse data streams allows for more accurate and holistic environmental assessments. For instance, AI can integrate data from weather stations with satellite imagery to predict the likelihood of wildfires, enabling early warning systems and improved fire management strategies. Similarly, integrating data from citizen science initiatives, such as wildlife sightings or water quality observations, with other data sources can enhance our understanding of environmental trends and inform conservation efforts.

The application of AI in resource management is another area of significant promise. AI algorithms can optimize the allocation of resources such as water, energy, and land, improving efficiency and sustainability. For instance, AI can be used to optimize irrigation systems in agriculture, minimizing water waste and maximizing crop yields. This involves analyzing factors such as soil moisture levels, weather patterns, and crop growth stages to determine the optimal amount and timing of irrigation. Similarly, AI can optimize energy grids, balancing energy supply and demand to minimize waste and reduce reliance on fossil fuels. This optimization can take into account factors such as renewable energy sources, energy storage capacity, and real-time energy consumption patterns. In land management, AI can help optimize land use patterns, balancing the needs of human development with environmental protection. This includes using AI to identify areas suitable for urban development while minimizing the impact on natural habitats and biodiversity.

Perhaps one of the most compelling applications of AI in environmental conservation is its ability to protect endangered species. Traditional methods of tracking and monitoring endangered species are often labor-intensive and limited in scope. AI, however, offers innovative solutions, particularly through the use of image recognition and acoustic analysis. AI algorithms can analyze images from camera traps, identifying and classifying individual animals, providing insights into population dynamics, distribution, and behavior. This can assist in the development of targeted conservation strategies, focusing efforts on areas where endangered species are most vulnerable. Furthermore, AI can analyze acoustic data from environmental sensors, identifying the calls and vocalizations of endangered species. This acoustic monitoring can provide valuable information on species distribution, abundance, and overall health, enabling efficient and targeted conservation efforts. The continuous advancements in AI capabilities, coupled with the deployment of more sophisticated sensor networks, will enhance the scope and effectiveness of such wildlife monitoring programs. In addition to real-time monitoring, AI can be employed to analyze historical data, creating predictive models that can anticipate future threats to endangered species and inform proactive conservation interventions.

However, the adoption of AI in environmental monitoring and

conservation is not without its challenges. Data bias, a common problem in machine learning, can affect the accuracy and reliability of AI-based environmental models. Bias can stem from limitations in data collection methods, geographical representation, or inherent biases within the data itself. Mitigation strategies involve careful data curation, validation, and the development of algorithms robust to bias. Moreover, the computational resources required to train and deploy sophisticated AI models can be substantial, posing a barrier to broader adoption, particularly in resource-constrained settings. Overcoming this challenge requires investment in high-performance computing infrastructure and the development of more computationally efficient algorithms. Additionally, the "black box" nature of some AI algorithms can pose a challenge, making it
difficult to understand the rationale behind predictions. The development of explainable AI (XAI) techniques is crucial to addressing this issue, ensuring transparency and building trust in AI-based environmental monitoring and conservation efforts.

Ethical considerations, such as data privacy and responsible use of AI technologies, must also be carefully considered to ensure that these technologies are deployed responsibly and ethically.

In summary, AI is rapidly transforming environmental monitoring and conservation, enhancing our ability to track environmental changes, manage resources effectively, and protect endangered species. From the deployment of extensive sensor networks to the analysis of satellite imagery and acoustic data, AI provides powerful tools for understanding and safeguarding our planet. While challenges remain, the potential of AI to contribute to a more sustainable future is undeniable. Addressing data bias, computational resource limitations, and promoting transparency through XAI will be critical to realizing the full potential of AI in environmental protection and ensuring its responsible and ethical application. The collaborative efforts of environmental scientists, AI researchers, policymakers, and the global community are essential to harness the power of AI for a healthier and more sustainable planet.

Renewable Energy Optimization

The integration of AI into renewable energy systems marks a pivotal moment in the transition towards a sustainable energy future. The intermittent and unpredictable nature of renewable sources like solar and wind power presents significant challenges to grid stability and efficient energy distribution. Traditional methods of forecasting and managing these energy sources often lack the precision and responsiveness needed to meet the fluctuating demands of modern energy grids. AI, however, offers a powerful set of tools to address these challenges, enabling more accurate predictions, optimized grid management, and enhanced overall efficiency.

One of the most significant applications of AI in renewable energy is the forecasting of energy production. Accurate predictions are crucial for grid operators to balance energy supply and demand, ensuring grid stability and minimizing reliance on fossil fuel backups. Traditional forecasting methods often rely on historical weather data and simple statistical models, which can be inadequate in capturing the complex dynamics of renewable energy generation. AI, particularly machine learning algorithms, offers a significant improvement in predictive accuracy. These algorithms can analyze vast quantities of data from various sources, including weather forecasts, historical energy production data, satellite imagery, and even real-time sensor readings from renewable energy installations. By identifying complex patterns and correlations within this data, AI models can provide significantly more accurate forecasts of solar and wind energy output, often with lead times ranging from minutes to days. This enhanced predictability allows grid operators to make more informed decisions about energy dispatch, storage, and potential reliance on conventional power plants, thereby reducing the overall reliance on fossil fuels and improving grid stability.

For example, sophisticated machine learning models, such as recurrent neural networks (RNNs) and long short-term memory (LSTM) networks, are particularly well-suited for time series forecasting, making them ideal for predicting the fluctuating output of renewable energy sources. These models can learn the temporal dependencies in the data, capturing seasonal variations, weather patterns, and other factors influencing energy production.

Furthermore, advanced AI techniques, such as ensemble methods, which combine predictions from multiple models, can further enhance forecast accuracy and robustness. By integrating multiple data sources and employing sophisticated algorithms, AI-powered forecasting systems can achieve accuracy levels significantly exceeding those of traditional methods, providing grid operators with the information they need to make optimal decisions regarding energy management.

Beyond forecasting, AI plays a crucial role in optimizing the management of energy grids themselves. The integration of large-scale renewable energy sources into existing grids presents unique challenges due to the intermittent nature of these sources. AI-powered grid management systems can dynamically adapt to changes in energy supply and demand, ensuring grid stability and minimizing disruptions. These systems leverage AI algorithms to optimize power flow, voltage regulation, and frequency control, ensuring a reliable and efficient energy supply. They can analyze real-time data from across the grid, identifying potential bottlenecks, predicting future demands, and proactively adjusting grid operations to maintain stability. For example, AI can optimize the routing of electricity from renewable energy sources to different parts of the grid, minimizing transmission losses and maximizing efficiency.

Furthermore, AI plays an increasingly important role in optimizing energy storage systems. Renewable energy sources are often intermittent, necessitating efficient energy storage solutions to manage fluctuations in energy supply and demand. AI algorithms can optimize the charging and discharging of energy storage systems, maximizing their effectiveness and extending their lifespan. These algorithms can analyze real-time data from renewable energy sources, energy consumption patterns, and energy storage levels to determine the optimal charging and discharging schedules. This optimization can ensure that energy storage systems are used efficiently, minimizing energy waste and maximizing their contribution to grid stability. The deployment of advanced battery storage systems, coupled with AI-powered management systems, is crucial for integrating a larger share of intermittent renewable energy into existing grids.

AI also significantly contributes to enhancing the efficiency of renewable energy systems themselves. For instance, AI can be used to optimize the design and placement of solar panels and wind turbines, maximizing their energy output. AI algorithms can analyze factors such as sunlight exposure, wind patterns, and terrain characteristics to determine the optimal locations and orientations for these installations. This optimization can significantly enhance the overall efficiency of renewable energy projects, reducing costs and maximizing energy yield. Similarly, AI can be used to optimize the operation and maintenance of renewable energy systems. AI-powered predictive maintenance systems can analyze sensor data from wind turbines and solar panels to predict potential equipment failures. This allows for proactive maintenance interventions, minimizing downtime and reducing the costs associated with unexpected repairs. Predictive maintenance is particularly crucial for offshore wind farms, where maintenance can be expensive and time-consuming.

However, the integration of AI into renewable energy systems is not without its challenges. The complexity of AI algorithms and the need for extensive data sets can pose significant barriers to adoption. Developing and deploying sophisticated AI models requires significant computational resources and expertise.

Moreover, data security and privacy issues need to be carefully addressed, as AI algorithms often rely on vast amounts of data from various sources. Ensuring the ethical and responsible use of AI in renewable energy is also critical. Bias in training data can lead to inaccurate predictions and unfair outcomes, necessitating the use of robust and unbiased datasets. Addressing these challenges requires collaboration between AI researchers, energy professionals, policymakers, and the broader community. Investing in research and development, establishing clear regulatory frameworks, and promoting responsible AI practices will be crucial for realizing the full potential of AI in the renewable energy sector.

Looking ahead, the integration of AI into renewable energy systems will continue to expand, driving innovation and accelerating the transition towards a sustainable energy future. As AI algorithms become more sophisticated and data availability increases, we can expect even more significant improvements in forecasting accuracy, grid management efficiency, and overall renewable energy system performance. The development of explainable AI (XAI) techniques will enhance transparency and build trust in AI-based energy systems, facilitating broader adoption and fostering collaboration among stakeholders. The integration of AI with other emerging technologies, such as blockchain and the Internet of Things (IoT), will further enhance the efficiency and security of renewable energy grids. The collective efforts of researchers, engineers, policymakers, and the global community will be instrumental in harnessing the power of AI to create a more sustainable and resilient energy future. The potential for AI to revolutionize the renewable energy sector is vast, paving the way for a cleaner, more efficient, and sustainable energy future for all. The continuous development and refinement of AI algorithms, coupled with increasing data availability and advanced computing power, will be critical in further optimizing renewable energy systems and addressing the challenges of energy transition. The combination of AI and renewable energy represents a powerful force for positive change, promising a future powered by clean, sustainable, and efficient energy sources.

Precision Agriculture and Sustainable Farming

Precision agriculture, fueled by the advancements in artificial intelligence, is transforming the way we cultivate our planet's resources. Gone are the days of blanket approaches to farming; AI empowers a new era of targeted interventions, maximizing efficiency while minimizing environmental impact. This shift towards sustainable farming practices is not merely an improvement in yield; it's a critical step towards ensuring food security in a world facing growing climate challenges and dwindling resources.

One of the most visible applications of AI in this domain is the widespread adoption of drones. These unmanned aerial vehicles, equipped with high-resolution cameras and multispectral sensors, provide farmers with an unprecedented level of insight into their fields. They can capture detailed imagery of crop health, identifying areas of stress, disease, or nutrient deficiency with remarkable precision. This data, processed using sophisticated computer vision algorithms and machine learning models, generates detailed maps highlighting specific areas requiring attention. This targeted approach eliminates the need for broad-spectrum treatments, reducing the overuse of pesticides, fertilizers, and water, thus mitigating environmental damage. For instance, a drone might identify a localized infestation of pests, enabling farmers to apply targeted pesticide treatments only to the affected areas, instead of spraying the entire field. This not only minimizes pesticide use, protecting beneficial insects and reducing water pollution, but also significantly reduces costs associated with unnecessary chemical applications.

Beyond visual data, drones can also collect data on soil conditions, moisture levels, and even microclimates within a field. This multi-faceted data collection allows farmers to develop a far more nuanced understanding of their land than ever before. This intricate knowledge base informs more precise irrigation strategies, optimizing water usage and preventing wasteful overuse. In arid regions where water is a precious resource, this precision can be the difference between a successful harvest and crop failure.

Furthermore, the data collected by drones can be integrated with weather forecasts and soil analysis to predict future needs, allowing farmers to proactively adjust their farming practices. This predictive capability minimizes risks associated with unpredictable weather patterns and ensures that resources are allocated effectively throughout the growing season.

Sensors play a crucial, complementary role in the AI-driven agricultural revolution. These devices, deployed throughout the field, continuously monitor various environmental factors and crop parameters. From soil moisture sensors embedded in the ground to sensors on individual plants measuring leaf temperature and chlorophyll levels, the data gathered provides a real-time picture of crop health and environmental conditions. This continuous stream of data, far more granular than periodic manual observations, is then fed into AI models for analysis and prediction. Machine learning algorithms, trained on vast datasets of sensor readings and corresponding crop yields, can identify patterns and correlations that might be missed by human observation. For example, a machine learning model could detect subtle changes in leaf temperature that indicate early signs of disease or stress, allowing for timely interventions and preventing significant yield losses.

The integration of AI in irrigation systems is a prime example of how this technology translates into tangible, sustainable gains. Traditional irrigation methods often involve flooding entire fields, leading to significant water wastage and nutrient runoff. Smart irrigation systems, guided by AI algorithms, utilize sensor data and weather forecasts to precisely control the amount and timing of irrigation. This tailored approach ensures that plants receive the precise amount of water they need, minimizing waste and preventing waterlogging, which can damage roots and reduce yields. This precision not only conserves precious water resources but also reduces the environmental impact of agriculture. Reduced water usage translates to less energy consumed for pumping and distributing water, further contributing to environmental sustainability.

Another critical area where AI significantly contributes to sustainable farming is in the optimization of fertilizer application.

Excessive fertilizer use leads to nutrient runoff, contaminating waterways and harming aquatic ecosystems. AI-powered systems, leveraging data from sensors, drones, and soil analysis, can determine the precise nutrient requirements of each section of the field. This targeted application of fertilizers minimizes overuse, reducing environmental pollution and maximizing nutrient uptake by plants. This approach, known as variable rate fertilization, ensures that plants receive the optimal balance of nutrients, improving yields while minimizing the environmental impact.

Furthermore, AI can also optimize the timing of fertilizer application, maximizing nutrient uptake and minimizing losses due to leaching or volatilization.

Beyond these individual applications, the integration of AI into farm management systems offers a holistic approach to sustainable agriculture. By combining data from various sources, including drones, sensors, weather forecasts, and historical yield data, AI can provide farmers with a comprehensive overview of their operations. This data-driven insight enables farmers to make informed decisions about planting, irrigation, fertilization, pest control, and harvesting, maximizing efficiency and minimizing environmental impact across all aspects of their operations. The development of precision agriculture platforms, which integrate data from various sources and provide farmers with user-friendly dashboards and decision-support tools, facilitates the adoption of AI-driven sustainable practices.

However, it's vital to acknowledge the challenges that accompany this technological revolution. The adoption of AI-powered agricultural technologies requires significant investment in infrastructure, equipment, and training. Access to high-speed internet, reliable power sources, and the expertise to operate and interpret the data from these systems are essential for successful implementation. Data security and privacy are also critical concerns, as these systems often collect sensitive data about farm operations. The development of robust data security protocols and ethical guidelines is paramount to ensuring the responsible use of these technologies. Addressing these challenges through public-private partnerships, targeted investment, and effective regulations is crucial for widespread adoption and the realization of AI's full potential in driving sustainable agriculture.

In conclusion, the integration of AI in agriculture signifies a transformative shift towards sustainable farming practices. From precision irrigation and targeted fertilizer application to predictive modeling and drone-based monitoring, AI empowers farmers to optimize their operations, minimize environmental impact, and enhance food security. While challenges remain in terms of accessibility and infrastructure, the potential of AI to revolutionize agriculture and build a more sustainable food system is undeniable. The ongoing development of user-friendly platforms, coupled with increased awareness and investment, will ensure the widespread adoption of these technologies, paving the way for a future where agriculture is both productive and environmentally responsible. The continuous refinement of AI algorithms, the integration of advanced sensor technologies, and the development of robust data management systems will further enhance the efficiency and sustainability of agricultural practices, ensuring food security while minimizing the ecological footprint of farming. The future of farming is intelligent, precise, and sustainable—a testament to the transformative power of artificial intelligence.

Ethical Considerations in AI for Environmental Applications

The integration of AI into environmental applications, while promising immense benefits, necessitates a careful examination of the ethical implications inherent in its deployment. The power of AI to analyze vast datasets, predict environmental changes, and optimize resource management comes with a responsibility to ensure its use aligns with ethical principles and avoids unintended consequences. One of the most pressing concerns revolves around data privacy. Many AI systems rely on the collection and analysis of substantial amounts of environmental data, including information on sensitive ecosystems, wildlife populations, and human activities. This data, if mishandled or misused, could compromise the privacy of individuals or organizations, leading to potential harm. For instance, data collected from smart grids monitoring energy consumption could reveal sensitive information about individual households or businesses, potentially leading to targeted advertising or discrimination. Similarly, data from environmental sensors tracking wildlife movements could be misused for poaching or habitat destruction.

To mitigate these risks, robust data security protocols and anonymization techniques must be implemented. Data encryption, secure storage, and access control mechanisms are crucial to protect sensitive information from unauthorized access or disclosure.

Furthermore, the development of anonymization techniques, which remove or mask personally identifiable information while preserving the utility of the data for AI analysis, is essential.

Openness and transparency in data management practices, including clear communication about how data is collected, used, and protected, are vital for building trust and ensuring public acceptance of AI-powered environmental applications. Moreover, the establishment of clear legal frameworks and regulatory oversight is necessary to address data privacy concerns and ensure accountability in the use of environmental data. This includes adhering to existing data protection regulations, such as GDPR in Europe and CCPA in California, and the development of specific guidelines for the use of environmental data in AI systems.

Another critical ethical consideration is the potential for bias in AI models. AI algorithms are trained on data, and if that data reflects existing societal biases, the resulting AI systems can perpetuate or even amplify those biases. In environmental applications, biased AI models can lead to unfair or discriminatory outcomes. For example, an AI system designed to allocate resources for environmental remediation could inadvertently prioritize certain areas or communities over others based on biased training data. This bias could stem from historical data reflecting past inequities in environmental policy or resource allocation. Similarly, AI models used for predicting the impact of climate change could produce inaccurate or misleading results if the training data does not adequately represent the diverse range of vulnerabilities across different regions or populations.

Addressing bias in AI models requires careful consideration of the data used for training. This includes auditing datasets for biases, using techniques to mitigate biases during the training process, and evaluating the fairness and equity of the resulting AI systems.

Furthermore, the development of diverse and inclusive teams working on the design and implementation of AI systems is essential for identifying and addressing potential biases. Engaging with affected communities and incorporating their perspectives throughout the AI development lifecycle can help ensure that AI systems are equitable and just. The ongoing monitoring and evaluation of AI systems for bias is also crucial, requiring mechanisms for feedback and adjustments to address any emerging biases over time. Transparency in the design, training, and deployment of AI systems is key to fostering accountability and building public trust.

Transparency in AI systems extends beyond data and algorithmic biases to encompass the entire AI development and deployment process. This includes clearly documenting the data sources, algorithms used, and decision-making processes involved in developing and deploying AI systems. Providing clear explanations of how AI systems arrive at their predictions or recommendations is crucial for building trust and ensuring accountability. "Explainable AI" (XAI) techniques, which focus on making the decision-making processes of AI systems more understandable to humans, are essential in this regard. For instance, when an AI system recommends a particular environmental policy, it should be able to provide clear and understandable justifications for its recommendations, allowing stakeholders to assess the rationale behind the decisions. The use of visualisations, intuitive dashboards, and natural language explanations can improve the accessibility and comprehensibility of AI decision-making processes, enhancing trust and facilitating informed decision-making.

Accountability is another cornerstone of ethical AI development. When AI systems make decisions with significant environmental consequences, clear lines of responsibility must be established. Determining who is responsible when an AI system makes an error or produces an unintended negative outcome is crucial for addressing potential harms and deterring irresponsible use of AI technology. This accountability framework should include mechanisms for redress and remedies in case of harmful consequences resulting from AI systems. This requires a multi-faceted approach, encompassing individual accountability for developers and deployers, organizational accountability for institutions responsible for deploying AI systems, and regulatory accountability for governmental bodies overseeing the use of AI technology. The development of ethical guidelines and standards for the development and deployment of AI systems, coupled with robust regulatory oversight, will help create a framework that promotes responsible innovation and mitigates the risks associated with AI deployment.

The environmental challenges facing our planet demand innovative solutions, and AI has the potential to play a transformative role. However, it's crucial to acknowledge and address the ethical considerations inherent in the use of AI in environmental applications. Data privacy, algorithmic bias, transparency, and accountability are not merely technical issues; they are fundamental ethical considerations that must be addressed to ensure that AI serves as a force for good in environmental protection and sustainability. By adopting ethical principles throughout the entire AI lifecycle, from data collection and algorithm design to deployment and ongoing monitoring, we can harness the power of AI while mitigating its potential risks and ensuring a more sustainable and equitable future. The ongoing dialogue between AI developers, environmental experts, policymakers, and the public will be instrumental in shaping responsible AI practices and maximizing the benefits while minimizing the potential harms. The ultimate success of AI in addressing environmental challenges hinges on the development and implementation of strong ethical frameworks that prioritize transparency, accountability, and fairness.

Bias and Fairness in AI Systems

The pervasive influence of data in shaping AI systems necessitates a profound understanding of the potential for bias. AI algorithms, no matter how sophisticated, are fundamentally dependent on the data they are trained upon. If this data reflects existing societal biases –be they conscious or unconscious – the resulting AI system will inevitably inherit and potentially amplify these biases, leading to unfair or discriminatory outcomes. This is not simply a theoretical concern; it's a real-world problem with far-reaching consequences across numerous sectors, including healthcare, finance, and even environmental protection, as previously discussed.

Consider, for instance, the development of an AI system designed to assess loan applications. If the training data predominantly consists of applications from a specific demographic group, the AI might learn to associate certain characteristics of that group with creditworthiness, inadvertently discriminating against applicants from other backgrounds who might be equally or more creditworthy. Similarly, an AI system used in hiring processes might inadvertently favor candidates from specific educational institutions or geographic regions if the training data reflects historical hiring practices that exhibit such biases. The consequences can be profound, perpetuating and even exacerbating existing inequalities.

The problem of bias in AI extends beyond simple demographic factors. Biases can also stem from subtle aspects of the data, such as the language used, the imagery depicted, or the implicit assumptions embedded within the data collection process. For example, an AI system trained on text data containing gender stereotypes might perpetuate these stereotypes in its output, reinforcing harmful societal biases. Similarly, an AI system trained on images predominantly featuring individuals from a single ethnic background might struggle to accurately recognize individuals from other backgrounds.

Addressing this challenge requires a multi-faceted approach that encompasses various stages of the AI lifecycle. Firstly, careful attention must be paid to the data used for training. This involves rigorously auditing datasets for biases, identifying potential sources of bias, and developing strategies for mitigating their impact. This might entail techniques like data augmentation, which involves adding synthetic data to balance out underrepresented groups, or re-weighting the training data to give more importance to samples from underrepresented groups. However, these methods should be employed with caution, as poorly implemented techniques can inadvertently introduce new biases.

Beyond data preprocessing, the design of the algorithms themselves plays a crucial role in mitigating bias. Researchers are actively developing algorithms that are inherently more robust to biases in the data. For example, techniques like adversarial debiasing aim to train AI models that are less susceptible to the influence of biased features in the data. These methods typically involve introducing a "discriminator" component that tries to identify biased predictions, effectively forcing the AI model to learn to make fairer predictions.

However, even with careful data preprocessing and algorithm design, ensuring fairness requires ongoing monitoring and evaluation. Once an AI system is deployed, it's crucial to regularly assess its performance across different demographic groups to identify any potential biases that might emerge over time. This requires the development of effective metrics for evaluating fairness, which themselves can be subject to debate and require careful consideration of the specific context. Furthermore, mechanisms for feedback and adjustment are necessary to address emerging biases and ensure the ongoing fairness of the AI system. Transparency in the design, training, and deployment of AI systems is crucial for enabling this ongoing assessment and accountability.

The question of fairness in AI is not just a technical challenge; it's fundamentally an ethical one. Developing AI systems that are both accurate and fair demands a commitment to ethical principles and a recognition of the societal impact of these technologies. This requires collaboration between AI researchers, ethicists, policymakers, and members of the affected communities. It necessitates a careful examination of the values that should guide the development and deployment of AI systems, ensuring that these values align with principles of justice, equity, and inclusivity.

Furthermore, the legal and regulatory landscape surrounding AI is still developing, and it's crucial that laws and regulations are created to prevent and address algorithmic bias. This requires careful consideration of the technical complexities of AI, as well as the ethical and societal implications of these technologies. A strong legal framework can provide a crucial layer of accountability, holding developers and deployers of AI systems responsible for ensuring fairness. It can also establish mechanisms for redress in cases of discrimination resulting from biased AI systems.

The development of explainable AI (XAI) is also pivotal in addressing bias and enhancing fairness. XAI aims to make the decision-making processes of AI systems more transparent and understandable. This allows for scrutiny of the reasoning behind the AI's decisions, revealing potential biases that might otherwise remain hidden. By providing insights into the internal workings of an AI system, XAI can facilitate a more nuanced understanding of its limitations and biases, empowering users to interpret the AI's output critically and identify instances of unfairness. Techniques like LIME (Local Interpretable Model-agnostic Explanations) and SHAP (SHapley Additive exPlanations) are examples of XAI methods that offer explanations for individual predictions, providing valuable insights into the factors contributing to an AI's decision-making process.

The challenge of bias and fairness in AI is an ongoing one, requiring continuous research, development, and evaluation. It's a field where interdisciplinary collaboration between computer scientists, ethicists, social scientists, and policymakers is crucial to navigate the complex ethical and societal implications. Only through a concerted effort to understand, mitigate, and monitor bias can we harness the transformative potential of AI while simultaneously ensuring that its benefits are shared equitably and its harms are minimized. This necessitates a commitment to transparency, accountability, and ongoing dialogue among all stakeholders involved in the AI ecosystem. The future of AI hinges on its ability to not only improve efficiency and productivity but also to promote fairness and justice for all members of society. A future where AI perpetuates existing inequalities is not a future worth pursuing.

Privacy and Data Security in the Age of AI

The preceding discussion highlighted the critical issue of bias in AI systems, stemming from the data used to train them. However, the very foundation of AI's power – its reliance on massive datasets – introduces another equally significant ethical concern: privacy and data security. The ability of AI to learn and make predictions is directly proportional to the volume and quality of data it can access. This creates a potent tension: the more data available, the more effective the AI, but the greater the risk to individual privacy and the potential for misuse.

The sheer scale of data collection required for advanced AI systems is unprecedented. We are witnessing a paradigm shift, moving from an era where data was a relatively scarce resource to one of data abundance, sometimes described as "data lakes" or "data oceans." This abundance, however, doesn't come without significant cost. Every online interaction, every purchase, every social media post, every medical record, even seemingly innocuous data points like location information gathered through mobile phones, contributes to the ever-growing pools of data used to train AI. The aggregation of this data, often across disparate sources, allows AI systems to construct detailed profiles of individuals, revealing patterns and insights that would be impossible to discern through traditional methods.

This raises immediate concerns about privacy. The ability of AI to infer sensitive information from seemingly innocuous data is a significant threat. For instance, an AI trained on purchasing habits might infer an individual's health status, financial difficulties, or even political affiliations, potentially leading to discrimination or manipulation. Similarly, AI-powered facial recognition systems, while capable of impressive feats of identification, raise serious concerns about surveillance and the potential for abuse by authoritarian regimes or even corporations. The lack of transparency in how these systems operate further exacerbates these concerns, creating a "black box" effect where individuals have little understanding of how their data is being used and the implications of that use.

Furthermore, the security of this vast amount of data is paramount.

AI systems are vulnerable to various attacks, including data breaches and adversarial attacks. Data breaches can expose sensitive personal information to malicious actors, leading to identity theft, financial fraud, and reputational damage. Adversarial attacks, on the other hand, involve manipulating the input data to induce the AI system to make incorrect or malicious predictions. For example, a self-driving car might be tricked into misinterpreting a stop sign through a carefully crafted adversarial perturbation, leading to a serious accident. The complexity of these AI systems makes it challenging to identify and prevent such attacks, demanding sophisticated security measures and continuous monitoring.

Protecting sensitive data and ensuring compliance with privacy regulations requires a multi-pronged approach. This starts with responsible data collection practices. Organizations must be transparent about what data they are collecting, why they are collecting it, and how they will use it. This includes obtaining informed consent from individuals before collecting their data, and providing clear and accessible privacy policies. Data minimization is also crucial, collecting only the data necessary for the intended purpose and avoiding the collection of sensitive data unless absolutely essential. Data anonymization and pseudonymization techniques can help to protect the identity of individuals while still allowing the data to be used for AI training. These techniques involve removing or replacing identifying information with pseudonyms, making it difficult to link the data back to specific individuals.

However, even with these techniques, the potential for re-identification remains a concern. Advanced AI systems are increasingly capable of inferring sensitive information from seemingly anonymous datasets. This highlights the need for strong encryption and access control mechanisms to protect data from unauthorized access. Furthermore, differential privacy, a technique that adds carefully calibrated noise to data before analysis, can offer a strong guarantee of privacy even when aggregated data is released. While it may reduce the accuracy of the AI system slightly, it provides a stronger guarantee of individual privacy.

The legal and regulatory landscape around data privacy is evolving rapidly, with regulations like the General Data Protection Regulation (GDPR) in Europe and the California Consumer Privacy Act (CCPA) in the United States setting new standards for data protection. These regulations require organizations to implement robust data protection measures and to be transparent about their data processing practices. Compliance with these regulations is not merely a legal requirement but a crucial aspect of building trust with users and maintaining ethical standards in AI development.

Furthermore, the development of privacy-preserving AI techniques is an active area of research. Federated learning, for example, allows AI models to be trained on decentralized data sources without the need to centralize the data, reducing the risk of data breaches and enhancing privacy. Homomorphic encryption enables computations to be performed on encrypted data without decrypting it, further enhancing data security. These and other privacy-enhancing technologies are essential for enabling the development of AI systems that both respect individual privacy and harness the power of data.

Finally, fostering a culture of data ethics within organizations is paramount. This involves educating employees about data privacy and security best practices, establishing clear guidelines and procedures for data handling, and implementing robust mechanisms for reporting and investigating data breaches. It requires a commitment from the leadership to prioritize privacy and security, integrating these considerations into all aspects of AI development and deployment.

The ethical implications of data collection and use in AI extend beyond legal compliance and technical solutions. They touch upon fundamental questions of human autonomy, societal trust, and the potential for misuse. As AI becomes increasingly integrated into our daily lives, addressing these issues is not merely an optional extra, but a fundamental prerequisite for building a future where AI serves humanity ethically and responsibly. The path forward necessitates continuous innovation in both technological and ethical frameworks, ensuring that the immense potential of AI is realized while safeguarding individual rights and societal well-being. The journey towards responsible AI is a collaborative one, requiring the input of computer scientists, ethicists, policymakers, and the public at large.

Accountability and Transparency in AI DecisionMaking

The preceding discussion underscored the critical role of data in shaping AI systems and the inherent risks to privacy and security. However, the ethical considerations extend far beyond data management; they encompass the very core of AI decision-making processes. Establishing accountability and transparency in AI systems, especially when their decisions have profound consequences for individuals and society, presents a formidable challenge. The "black box" nature of many complex AI algorithms obscures the reasoning behind their outputs, making it difficult to understand why a specific decision was made. This lack of transparency undermines trust and makes it challenging to identify and correct errors or biases.

Consider, for example, the use of AI in loan applications. An AI system might deny a loan application without providing a clear explanation, leaving the applicant bewildered and frustrated. The opacity of the AI's decision-making process makes it difficult for the applicant to understand the reasons for rejection, potentially leading to unfair or discriminatory outcomes. Without transparency, there is no recourse for the applicant, no opportunity to challenge the decision or demonstrate that the AI's assessment was flawed. This lack of accountability not only affects individuals but also erodes public trust in AI systems.

This issue is amplified in high-stakes scenarios, such as those involving healthcare or criminal justice. An AI-powered diagnostic tool that misdiagnoses a patient's condition or a predictive policing algorithm that unfairly targets a particular demographic can have devastating consequences. The inability to scrutinize the AI's decision-making process makes it difficult to determine the source of the error or bias, hindering efforts to improve the system and prevent future incidents. The absence of clear lines of responsibility further compounds the problem, leaving individuals with little recourse when harmed by AI-driven decisions.

The challenge of establishing accountability necessitates a multifaceted approach. Firstly, there is a pressing need for greater transparency in the design and development of AI systems. This involves making the algorithms and data used in AI systems more accessible and understandable. While complete transparency may not always be feasible due to intellectual property concerns or the complexity of some algorithms, efforts to explain the decision-making process in a comprehensible way, even if it's a simplified explanation, are vital. Explainable AI (XAI) is a rapidly evolving field dedicated to developing methods to make AI decisions more transparent and interpretable. Techniques like LIME (Local Interpretable Model-agnostic Explanations) and SHAP (SHapley Additive exPlanations) aim to provide insights into the factors that influence AI predictions.

However, XAI is not a panacea. While it can provide some insight into the decision-making process, it may not always fully reveal the underlying mechanisms, especially in highly complex deep learning models. This highlights the importance of accompanying AI systems with comprehensive documentation detailing their purpose, design, data sources, limitations, and potential biases. Such documentation can help users understand the context and limitations of the AI system, making them more informed consumers and allowing them to assess the reliability and trustworthiness of the AI's output. Furthermore, rigorous testing and validation are crucial to identify and mitigate biases and errors before deployment. This includes testing the system on diverse datasets to ensure it performs equitably across different groups and scenarios.

Beyond technical solutions, accountability also necessitates a legal and regulatory framework that assigns clear responsibility for the actions of AI systems. The question of liability in cases of AI-caused harm remains a complex legal challenge. Is the developer, the user, or the AI itself responsible when an AI system causes damage?

Existing legal frameworks are often ill-equipped to handle these novel situations, necessitating the development of new legal precedents and regulations. This requires collaboration between legal experts, policymakers, and AI developers to create a legal landscape that promotes responsible AI development and provides clear mechanisms for redress in case of AI-related harm.

Furthermore, the creation of independent oversight bodies and auditing mechanisms is critical for ensuring accountability. These bodies could review the design, development, and deployment of AI systems, ensuring compliance with ethical standards and legal regulations. They could also investigate incidents where AI systems cause harm, determining the root cause and recommending corrective actions. Such independent oversight is crucial for maintaining public trust and ensuring that AI systems are developed and used responsibly.

The concept of algorithmic auditing, the process of systematically reviewing algorithms for biases and flaws, is gaining traction. Algorithmic audits can provide valuable insights into the potential for discrimination or harm embedded within AI systems. They can help identify areas where the system needs improvement and ensure that it is meeting ethical standards. However, the effectiveness of algorithmic auditing depends on the availability of appropriate data and the expertise of the auditors.

Establishing transparency and accountability also requires a cultural shift within the AI industry. A culture that prioritizes ethical considerations alongside technical performance is essential. This involves incorporating ethical principles into the entire AI lifecycle, from design and development to deployment and monitoring. It also necessitates educating AI developers about ethical implications and best practices, equipping them with the knowledge and tools to develop and deploy AI responsibly. This includes fostering a culture of open discussion and critical self-reflection within organizations, encouraging developers to scrutinize their work and identify potential ethical pitfalls.

The path towards responsible AI development is an ongoing journey, requiring constant adaptation and refinement. It is a collaborative effort that demands the engagement of researchers, developers, policymakers, ethicists, and the public at large.

Technological innovation in areas like XAI and algorithmic auditing is essential, but equally crucial is the creation of effective legal and regulatory frameworks, the establishment of independent oversight bodies, and the fostering of a culture that prioritizes ethics and accountability in AI. Only through a coordinated and multi-pronged approach can we harness the transformative potential of AI while mitigating its inherent risks and ensuring it serves humanity ethically and responsibly. The failure to address these issues will not only hinder the progress of AI but also compromise the well-being and trust within society as a whole.

The Impact of AI on Employment and the Workforce

The ethical considerations surrounding artificial intelligence extend beyond data privacy and algorithmic transparency; they reach deeply into the very fabric of the workforce and the future of employment. The rapid advancement of AI and its increasing integration into various sectors raise profound questions about the future of work and the need for proactive strategies to mitigate potential job displacement and foster a more equitable transition.

While AI undoubtedly offers unprecedented opportunities for productivity gains and economic growth, its impact on employment presents a significant ethical challenge requiring careful consideration and proactive intervention.

One of the most pressing concerns is the potential for widespread job displacement. Automation driven by AI and machine learning is already transforming industries, automating tasks previously performed by human workers. This trend is likely to accelerate in the coming years, affecting a wide range of occupations, from manufacturing and transportation to customer service and even certain areas of white-collar work. While some argue that AI will create new jobs in areas such as AI development, data science, and AI-related services, the net effect on employment remains a subject of intense debate. The fear is that the pace of job displacement may outpace the creation of new jobs, leading to significant unemployment and social unrest.

The impact of AI on employment is not uniform across all sectors and skill levels. Workers in routine-based, repetitive jobs are particularly vulnerable to automation. Manufacturing workers, truck drivers, and data entry clerks, for example, are likely to experience significant job losses as AI-powered robots and automated systems take over their tasks. However, the impact extends beyond manual labor. AI is also beginning to automate certain aspects of white-collar jobs, such as financial analysis, legal research, and even aspects of medical diagnosis. This raises concerns about the potential for job displacement among highly skilled professionals as well.

The ethical implications of this potential job displacement are substantial. The economic consequences of widespread unemployment could be devastating, leading to increased inequality, social unrest, and a decline in overall well-being. The psychological impact on individuals who lose their jobs due to automation is also significant, potentially leading to feelings of anxiety, depression, and loss of purpose. The challenge lies in ensuring a just and equitable transition for those affected by AI-driven job displacement.

Addressing this challenge requires a multifaceted approach, encompassing several key strategies. Firstly, there is a crucial need for proactive retraining and reskilling initiatives. Governments, educational institutions, and businesses must collaborate to develop programs that equip workers with the skills needed to thrive in an AI-driven economy. This involves investing in education and training programs focused on emerging technologies such as AI, data science, and cybersecurity, as well as developing programs that focus on skills that are less susceptible to automation, such as critical thinking, problem-solving, creativity, and emotional intelligence. These programs must be accessible to all workers, regardless of their background or education level, to ensure an equitable transition.

Furthermore, the development of social safety nets is paramount. Governments need to strengthen unemployment benefits, provide income support for workers displaced by automation, and explore alternative models such as universal basic income (UBI) to ensure a basic standard of living for everyone. These measures are crucial to mitigate the economic hardship that can result from job displacement and to provide individuals with the time and resources needed to acquire new skills.

Beyond individual retraining and social safety nets, the ethical considerations also extend to the design and deployment of AI systems themselves. AI systems should be designed and implemented in a way that minimizes job displacement and maximizes human-machine collaboration. This could involve focusing on AI applications that augment human capabilities rather than replacing them entirely, creating opportunities for human-AI teamwork and fostering a more symbiotic relationship between humans and machines.

The transition to an AI-driven economy also requires a shift in mindset and societal values. We need to move away from a narrow focus on productivity and economic growth at all costs and embrace a more holistic approach that values human well-being and social justice. This involves creating a system that values human work and ensures that the benefits of technological progress are shared more equitably. This may involve exploring alternative economic models, such as shorter workweeks or a shift towards a more leisure-oriented society, to adapt to the potential decrease in overall working hours as AI takes over more tasks.

Moreover, open discussions are needed about the implications of AI on work. These discussions must engage policymakers, industry leaders, educators, and the public at large to explore different approaches for managing the transition and building a more equitable and just future of work. Transparent and inclusive discussions are crucial to address concerns, build consensus, and develop policies that support workers in navigating this transformation.

The creation of a just and equitable future of work in the age of AI demands a proactive and comprehensive approach. It necessitates investments in education and training, the development of robust social safety nets, ethical considerations in AI design and implementation, a shift in societal values, and inclusive, transparent dialogues. Failure to address these challenges risks exacerbating existing inequalities, leading to social unrest, and hindering the full realization of AI's potential benefits. The ethical responsibility extends beyond merely developing AI; it encompasses ensuring a responsible and just transition for all members of society. The focus must be not only on technological advancement but also on human well-being and social justice in shaping the future of work. This necessitates a collaborative effort between governments, businesses, educational institutions, and individuals, working together to navigate this transformative period and ensure a future where AI benefits all of humanity. Ignoring this ethical imperative will not only result in widespread social and economic disruption, but it will also erode public trust in technology and impede its potential to improve lives worldwide. The challenge is not to stop progress but to steer it towards a future that is both technologically advanced and ethically sound.

The Future of Work and the HumanAI Partnership

The prospect of a future profoundly shaped by artificial intelligence necessitates a careful examination of its impact on the workforce. While anxieties about widespread job displacement are understandable, the narrative shouldn't be solely focused on replacement. A more nuanced perspective reveals a potential for a transformative human-AI partnership, a collaborative ecosystem where human ingenuity and AI's computational power synergistically drive progress. This partnership, however, requires strategic planning, ethical considerations, and a proactive approach to managing the transition.

One key element of this partnership is the concept of "augmentation" rather than "replacement." AI excels at processing vast datasets, identifying patterns, and performing repetitive tasks with speed and accuracy far exceeding human capabilities. Instead of viewing AI as a direct replacement for human workers, we should envision it as a powerful tool that augments human skills and capabilities. Consider, for instance, the medical field. AI can analyze medical images with incredible precision, detecting subtle anomalies that might elude the human eye, thereby assisting physicians in making more accurate diagnoses. This doesn't replace the doctor; it empowers them with advanced analytical tools, allowing them to focus on the critical aspects of patient care: empathy, nuanced judgment, and the human touch.

Similarly, in manufacturing, AI-powered robots can handle repetitive, physically demanding tasks, freeing up human workers to focus on more complex, creative, and strategic aspects of the production process. This shift from manual labor to higher-level cognitive tasks necessitates a substantial investment in reskilling and upskilling initiatives. Governments, educational institutions, and businesses must collaborate to create robust programs that equip workers with the skills needed to navigate this evolving landscape. This isn't simply about teaching coding; it's about fostering adaptability, critical thinking, problem-solving, and creative skills – areas where human intelligence remains irreplaceable.

The ethical dimensions of this transition are paramount. Ensuring equitable access to reskilling programs is crucial to prevent the exacerbation of existing inequalities. Those disproportionately affected by automation, often those in lower-skill, lower-wage jobs, need targeted support to bridge the skills gap and access new opportunities. This requires a commitment to lifelong learning, with readily available and affordable retraining programs that meet the evolving demands of the job market. Further, the design and deployment of AI systems should be guided by ethical principles.

Transparency and explainability in AI algorithms are crucial to building trust and ensuring fairness. Understanding how AI systems make decisions is essential for identifying and mitigating biases that could lead to unfair or discriminatory outcomes in the workplace.

Beyond individual retraining, the role of government and social safety nets cannot be overstated. Robust unemployment benefits, income support programs, and even exploration of alternative models like universal basic income (UBI) are necessary to provide a safety net for workers during the transition period. These measures aren't merely welfare provisions; they are crucial investments in social stability and the overall well-being of the population. They provide individuals with the time and resources needed to adapt, acquire new skills, and re-enter the workforce in a meaningful way.

Moreover, a robust social safety net encourages innovation and entrepreneurship by reducing the fear of risk associated with retraining or starting a new business.

The transition to a human-AI partnership also requires a shift in societal values and perspectives. The focus shouldn't solely be on maximizing productivity at all costs. A more holistic approach is needed, one that values human well-being, social justice, and a balanced lifestyle. This might involve exploring new work models, such as shorter workweeks, flexible work arrangements, and a greater emphasis on work-life balance. As AI takes on more routine tasks, it opens up the possibility of reducing overall working hours, allowing individuals to dedicate more time to personal pursuits, family, and community engagement. This potential shift warrants serious consideration and could lead to a more fulfilling and equitable society.

The legal and regulatory frameworks surrounding AI in the workplace also need careful consideration. Laws and regulations should be designed to protect workers' rights, ensure fair compensation, and promote ethical AI development and deployment. This necessitates close collaboration between policymakers, AI developers, and labor unions to create a regulatory landscape that encourages innovation while safeguarding workers' interests. This collaborative process is crucial to building public trust and ensuring a smooth transition to an AI-powered economy.

Further complicating the picture is the issue of AI bias. AI systems are trained on data, and if that data reflects existing societal biases, the AI system will inevitably perpetuate those biases. This can lead to discriminatory outcomes in hiring, promotion, and performance evaluations. Mitigating AI bias requires careful attention to data quality and algorithmic fairness, as well as ongoing monitoring and evaluation of AI systems to identify and correct biases.

Transparency in AI algorithms is essential to allow for scrutiny and accountability, ensuring that AI systems are not used to reinforce or exacerbate existing inequalities.

Furthermore, the increasing prevalence of AI raises questions about the nature of work itself. The traditional definition of work, centered around repetitive tasks and rigid schedules, may become obsolete in an AI-driven world. New forms of work might emerge, characterized by creativity, problem-solving, and human-AI collaboration. This requires a re-evaluation of how we value and compensate work, moving beyond a purely economic perspective to encompass the intrinsic value of human contributions. This could include recognizing the value of caregiving, artistic expression, and community engagement, areas that are less susceptible to automation.

Finally, fostering open and inclusive dialogue is crucial. Discussions involving policymakers, industry leaders, workers, and AI experts are essential to navigate the complexities of the transition and build consensus on strategies for managing the impact of AI on the workforce. Transparency and inclusivity are key to building public trust and ensuring that the benefits of AI are shared equitably. Ignoring these ethical considerations risks creating a future where the benefits of AI are concentrated in the hands of a few, while the majority struggle with job displacement and economic insecurity.

The future of work in an age of AI is not predetermined. It's a future that we shape through our choices and actions today. By embracing a human-AI partnership, investing in education and reskilling, strengthening social safety nets, promoting ethical AI development, and fostering open dialogue, we can navigate this transformative period and create a future where AI benefits all members of society. The challenge is not to resist technological progress but to harness its potential for good, creating a more equitable, prosperous, and fulfilling future for all.

AIDriven Productivity Growth and Economic Impacts

The integration of artificial intelligence (AI) into the global economy is not merely a technological shift; it's a fundamental reshaping of the very fabric of production, consumption, and wealth distribution. While the anxieties surrounding job displacement remain valid concerns requiring careful consideration, the broader picture reveals a far more complex and multifaceted impact on productivity growth and overall economic output. AI's influence spans across numerous sectors, fostering innovation, streamlining processes, and creating unprecedented opportunities for economic expansion.

One of the most significant contributions of AI lies in its ability to drastically enhance productivity. AI-powered automation, particularly in manufacturing and logistics, has led to significant increases in efficiency and output. Repetitive tasks, previously performed by human workers, are now handled by robots and algorithms with greater speed, precision, and consistency. This increase in output per unit of labor translates directly into higher productivity levels for businesses, ultimately boosting economic growth. For example, consider the automotive industry, where AI-powered robotic systems assemble vehicles with remarkable speed and accuracy, reducing manufacturing time and costs significantly.

Similarly, in logistics, AI algorithms optimize delivery routes, predict demand, and manage inventory, leading to significant efficiency gains in the supply chain.

Beyond automation, AI is transforming industries by enabling the creation of entirely new products and services. The rise of personalized medicine, fueled by AI's ability to analyze vast amounts of genomic and medical data, is a prime example. AI algorithms can identify patterns and predict disease risks with greater accuracy than traditional methods, leading to more effective diagnoses and personalized treatments. This innovation not only improves healthcare outcomes but also creates new markets and job opportunities in the biotechnology and pharmaceutical sectors.

Furthermore, AI is driving advancements in areas like materials science, drug discovery, and financial modeling, accelerating innovation and creating new economic value.

The impact of AI extends beyond individual industries and influences the global economy on a macro level. Increased productivity, coupled with the creation of new products and services, drives economic growth, leading to higher GDP and increased wealth. However, this growth is not uniformly distributed. While some sectors experience significant expansion, others face disruption and potential job displacement. This necessitates a thoughtful approach to managing the transition, ensuring that the benefits of AI are shared equitably and that workers are supported in adapting to the changing job market.

The creation of new jobs is another key aspect of AI's economic impact. While some jobs are indeed automated, AI also generates new roles and demands for specialized skills. The development, implementation, and maintenance of AI systems require a skilled workforce of data scientists, machine learning engineers, AI ethicists, and cybersecurity professionals. These high-skilled jobs often come with higher salaries and better benefits, contributing to increased income inequality if access to training and education is uneven. Furthermore, AI-driven innovation creates new industries and business opportunities, further expanding the job market. For instance, the development of self-driving cars has created a new sector with associated jobs in software engineering, sensor technology, and vehicle manufacturing.

However, the transition to an AI-driven economy is not without challenges. The displacement of workers from jobs that are automated requires proactive measures to mitigate potential negative consequences. Retraining and upskilling programs are crucial to equip workers with the skills needed to fill the newly created roles in the AI-driven economy. Governments and educational institutions need to collaborate closely with industries to develop effective training programs that meet the evolving demands of the job market. The curriculum must focus not only on technical skills but also on soft skills such as adaptability, critical thinking, and problem-solving, all of which are crucial in an increasingly complex and rapidly changing environment.

Furthermore, the economic implications of AI are intertwined with broader social and ethical considerations. Ensuring equitable access to education and retraining opportunities is vital to prevent the exacerbation of existing inequalities. Those disproportionately affected by automation often belong to vulnerable populations, including low-income workers and minorities. Targeted interventions and support programs are needed to address these disparities and ensure a just transition to an AI-driven future. This might involve subsidies for training, targeted job placement assistance, and even explorations into alternative economic models such as universal basic income.

Another critical aspect is the potential for AI to exacerbate income inequality. The benefits of AI-driven productivity growth might be concentrated among a small group of highly skilled workers and businesses, leading to a wider gap between the rich and the poor. Policy interventions, such as progressive taxation and wealth redistribution mechanisms, are essential to mitigate this risk and ensure that the benefits of technological progress are shared more equitably across society. This also requires a critical examination of existing economic models and exploring alternative frameworks that prioritize social well-being and economic justice.

The ethical considerations surrounding the development and deployment of AI systems are equally critical. Bias in algorithms, which can perpetuate existing societal inequalities, needs to be addressed through improved data collection practices, algorithmic transparency, and rigorous testing and evaluation. The development of ethical guidelines and regulations for AI is essential to ensure that these powerful technologies are used responsibly and for the betterment of society. This requires collaborative efforts between policymakers, researchers, industry leaders, and civil society organizations to establish robust frameworks that promote fairness, transparency, and accountability.

The future of work in an age of AI is not predetermined; it's a future that is shaped by the choices we make today. By proactively addressing the challenges and opportunities presented by AI, investing in education and retraining, implementing effective social safety nets, and promoting ethical AI development, we can harness the transformative potential of AI to create a more productive, equitable, and prosperous future for all. Ignoring these challenges will lead to a future marked by technological progress but with significant social and economic instability. A collaborative, forward-thinking approach is vital to navigate the complex landscape of an AI-driven economy, ensuring that the fruits of technological advancement are shared by all members of society, regardless of their socioeconomic status or occupation. The path forward demands a commitment to inclusivity, equity, and the ethical deployment of this transformative technology.

Investment Trends and Funding in the AI Sector

The economic impact of AI isn't solely defined by its productivity gains; it's fundamentally intertwined with the vast flows of capital pouring into the sector. Understanding investment trends is crucial to grasping the trajectory of AI's influence on the global economy. The sheer scale of investment in AI reflects a global consensus: this technology represents a pivotal shift, a transformative force reshaping industries and creating entirely new economic landscapes. This influx of capital is not simply fueling technological advancement; it's shaping the competitive landscape, driving consolidation, and ultimately, determining the future direction of AI development.

Venture capital (VC) has played a pivotal role in nurturing the growth of AI companies. Early-stage funding, often characterized by high risk and high reward, has been instrumental in fostering innovation and providing the necessary resources for startups to develop groundbreaking technologies. The amount of VC funding directed towards AI has experienced exponential growth over the past decade, attracting both established venture firms and specialized AI-focused funds. This surge in investment is evident across various sub-sectors of AI, including machine learning, natural language processing, computer vision, and robotics. Companies developing cutting-edge AI algorithms, platforms, and applications have garnered significant attention from investors seeking substantial returns in this rapidly expanding market. The competitive landscape among VCs is fiercely competitive, with firms vying for opportunities to invest in promising startups before they reach maturity. This intense competition often drives up valuations, reflecting the perceived long-term potential of AI technologies.

Beyond VC, mergers and acquisitions (M&A) have become an increasingly prevalent strategy for established corporations to acquire AI capabilities and talent. Large technology companies, such as Google, Amazon, Microsoft, and Facebook (now Meta), have made substantial acquisitions of AI startups, consolidating market share and bolstering their own AI development efforts. These acquisitions often serve multiple purposes: acquiring proprietary algorithms, integrating talented AI researchers and engineers into their workforce, and eliminating potential competitors. The strategic rationale behind these M&A activities is not only about acquiring cutting-edge technology but also about securing access to a highly skilled workforce that is increasingly in demand. This underscores the importance of human capital in the development and deployment of AI, recognizing that the algorithms themselves are only as effective as the expertise that creates, manages, and maintains them. The costs associated with these acquisitions often represent significant investments, highlighting the high value placed on AI expertise and technological innovation.

The increasing maturity of the AI sector is also evidenced by the rise in initial public offerings (IPOs). Successful AI companies, having achieved significant milestones in terms of revenue generation and market traction, are increasingly choosing to go public, offering their shares on stock exchanges. These IPOs provide a liquidity event for early investors and allow the companies to raise further capital for expansion and growth. The success of these IPOs reflects investor confidence in the long-term viability and profitability of the AI sector, signaling a shift from a primarily venture-backed landscape towards a more mature and publicly traded market. The stock market performance of these publicly traded AI companies serves as a barometer of investor sentiment and market expectations, reflecting the ongoing economic impact of AI technologies and their influence on the broader financial landscape.

However, the investment landscape isn't without its complexities and challenges. The hype surrounding AI can sometimes lead to inflated valuations and investment bubbles, prompting cautious assessments of market realities. Overly optimistic projections of AI's impact can lead to investment decisions based on speculative narratives rather than sound economic fundamentals. The risk of market corrections and the potential for significant losses highlight the importance of rigorous due diligence and a nuanced understanding of the technological and economic realities within the AI sector. Additionally, the ethical considerations surrounding AI development and deployment inevitably influence investor sentiment. Growing concerns about algorithmic bias, data privacy, and the potential for misuse of AI technologies can impact investment decisions, particularly among socially responsible investors who prioritize ethical considerations in their investment strategies.

Another significant aspect of the investment landscape is the geographical distribution of funding. While the United States has historically been the dominant player in AI investment, other regions, particularly China, Europe, and Canada, are emerging as increasingly important players. This global competition for AI talent and innovation is driving significant investment in research and development, fostering a vibrant and dynamic ecosystem for AI development worldwide. The strategic importance of AI to national economies is leading governments to implement policies designed to attract investment and promote domestic AI capabilities. This global competition not only accelerates innovation but also raises important questions about international collaboration, regulatory frameworks, and the global distribution of the economic benefits of AI.

Furthermore, the investment landscape is becoming increasingly specialized. Instead of broad-based investment in the entire AI sector, investors are demonstrating a preference for targeted investments in specific sub-sectors, such as AI in healthcare, fintech, or autonomous vehicles. This specialization reflects a growing understanding of the nuances within the AI field and the potential for significant returns in specific applications. This trend indicates a shift towards a more mature and discerning investment approach, moving beyond generalized enthusiasm for AI to a more sophisticated assessment of specific market opportunities and their associated risks.

In conclusion, the investment trends in the AI sector paint a vibrant picture of a rapidly evolving industry. The substantial influx of capital from various sources, including venture capital, mergers and acquisitions, and IPOs, is driving innovation, fueling competition, and shaping the future of AI. However, the complexity of the investment landscape necessitates a cautious approach, recognizing the potential for market volatility and the critical importance of ethical considerations. The global distribution of investment underscores the international competition for AI supremacy and the need for international cooperation to ensure a balanced and equitable deployment of these powerful technologies.

Understanding these investment patterns is crucial not only for financial investors but also for policymakers, researchers, and businesses seeking to navigate the increasingly complex economic implications of the AI revolution. The ongoing evolution of this investment landscape will continue to shape the trajectory of AI's economic impact, making ongoing analysis essential for those seeking to understand and participate in this transformative technological era.

The Global AI Race Competition and Collaboration

The previous discussion highlighted the massive capital influx driving AI development, shaping a fiercely competitive investment landscape. However, the economic story of AI is not solely confined to financial markets; it's deeply intertwined with a global race for technological dominance. This section explores the international competition and collaboration shaping the AI landscape, examining the distinct strategies employed by various nations and regions to secure a leading role in this transformative technology.

The United States, historically a pioneer in AI research and development, maintains a strong position, fueled by its robust venture capital ecosystem, leading universities, and the presence of major tech giants like Google, Amazon, Microsoft, and Meta. These companies, with their substantial resources and established research arms, are at the forefront of developing cutting-edge AI algorithms and applications. The US government also plays a significant role, through initiatives such as the National Artificial Intelligence Initiative, investing in research, fostering talent development, and shaping national AI strategies. However, the US faces challenges, including concerns about maintaining its technological edge in the face of growing competition from other nations, particularly China, and navigating the ethical and regulatory complexities surrounding AI development. The debate surrounding the appropriate level of government intervention, balancing fostering innovation with addressing ethical concerns and potential societal disruptions, is a defining characteristic of the US approach to the AI race. The ongoing debate about antitrust regulations and the potential for monopolies further complicates the landscape.

China has emerged as a formidable competitor, investing heavily in AI research, infrastructure, and talent development. The Chinese government's ambitious national AI strategy, backed by substantial funding and a focus on integrating AI into various sectors of the economy, has driven remarkable progress. Chinese companies like Alibaba, Tencent, and Baidu are actively developing and deploying AI technologies, often leveraging their vast datasets and large domestic markets. China's approach often emphasizes centralized planning and government support, contrasting with the more market-driven approach of the US. This difference presents both opportunities and risks: while it can lead to rapid advancements in specific areas, it can also stifle innovation outside of government-defined priorities. Furthermore, China's focus on AI's role in surveillance and social control raises significant ethical concerns and geopolitical tensions. Concerns surrounding data privacy, potential for misuse, and lack of transparency present a stark counterpoint to the rapid technological advancements. The potential for AI-driven geopolitical conflict is a considerable aspect of the global race.

Europe is pursuing a distinct path, emphasizing ethical considerations and regulatory frameworks as central to its AI strategy. The European Union's AI Act, a landmark piece of legislation, aims to create a trustworthy and ethical AI ecosystem by establishing strict guidelines for the development and deployment of AI systems. This approach prioritizes transparency, accountability, and human oversight, aiming to mitigate risks and ensure fairness. While this regulatory focus may appear to slow down innovation compared to the less regulated markets of the US and China, it could ultimately foster greater public trust and wider acceptance of AI technologies. European countries are also investing in AI research and development, with initiatives focusing on collaboration between universities, research institutions, and industry. However, Europe faces challenges in attracting and retaining top AI talent, often competing with the more lucrative opportunities offered by companies in the US and China. The fragmented nature of the European Union, with differing national priorities and regulations, can also pose obstacles to creating a unified and effective AI strategy.

Other regions are also actively participating in the global AI race. Canada, with its strong research institutions and a focus on AI ethics, has become a hub for AI talent and innovation. Countries in Asia, such as South Korea, Japan, and Singapore, are investing heavily in AI research and development, often focusing on specific applications such as robotics and healthcare. These nations are leveraging their technological expertise and economic strengths to establish a foothold in the global AI landscape. The growing participation of these nations highlights the increasingly global nature of the competition and collaboration in AI. Success will not only depend on technological prowess but also on the ability to attract and retain top talent, nurture a vibrant ecosystem of innovation, and navigate the complex ethical and regulatory landscape.

The global AI race isn't solely a competition; it's also characterized by significant collaboration. International research collaborations, partnerships between universities and research institutions across borders, are common. These collaborations often focus on addressing shared challenges, pooling resources, and accelerating the pace of AI research. However, the geopolitical landscape significantly influences the extent and nature of such cooperation.

Concerns about intellectual property, national security, and the potential misuse of AI technologies can limit the scope of collaborations, especially in sensitive areas of research. The tension between the desire for open collaboration to accelerate progress and the need to protect national interests is a key dynamic in shaping international AI relations.

Furthermore, the global distribution of AI's economic benefits is a major concern. The concentration of AI talent and resources in a few leading nations could exacerbate existing economic inequalities. Ensuring equitable access to AI technologies and their benefits is crucial for promoting global development and preventing a widening gap between developed and developing countries.

International cooperation is essential to address this challenge, fostering technology transfer, capacity building, and inclusive growth strategies. The ethical dimensions of AI, such as algorithmic bias and data privacy, are not confined by national borders, highlighting the necessity for global standards and collaborative solutions. The potential for AI to exacerbate existing social and economic inequalities makes addressing this issue paramount to ensure a truly transformative, rather than divisive, impact.

The future of the global AI race is uncertain, contingent upon various factors such as the pace of technological advancement, the evolution of geopolitical dynamics, and the effectiveness of regulatory frameworks. Competition will likely remain fierce, with nations vying for dominance in key areas of AI research and development. However, collaboration will also play a vital role, particularly in addressing shared challenges such as ethical considerations, safety concerns, and the equitable distribution of AI's benefits. The balance between competition and collaboration will define the trajectory of the global AI landscape, shaping the economic, social, and geopolitical ramifications of this transformative technology for years to come. Understanding the complex interplay of these forces is essential for navigating the challenges and harnessing the opportunities presented by the ongoing AI revolution. The future will belong to those who can effectively manage this intricate balance, fostering innovation while simultaneously addressing the profound ethical and societal implications of this powerful technology. The future of AI is not just a technological race; it's a global challenge requiring both competition and cooperation to ensure a responsible and equitable future.

AI and Inequality Economic Disparities and Social Impacts

The preceding discussion detailed the intense global competition and collaboration shaping the AI landscape. However, the economic impact of AI extends far beyond national rivalries, reaching deeply into the fabric of societies, potentially exacerbating existing inequalities and creating new ones. The transformative power of AI, while promising unprecedented economic growth, carries the risk of widening the gap between the wealthy and the poor, both within and between nations. This disparity arises from several interwoven factors.

One key factor is the uneven distribution of AI's economic benefits.

The creation and deployment of AI systems require significant capital investment, expertise, and infrastructure. Consequently, the financial rewards, in the form of increased profits, enhanced productivity, and new market opportunities, tend to accrue disproportionately to those who already possess these resources. Large corporations, particularly tech giants, are best positioned to leverage AI's potential, often leading to increased concentration of wealth and power in the hands of a few. This phenomenon, sometimes referred to as "AI-driven winner-takes-all dynamics," can create a self-reinforcing cycle, where the advantages of early AI adoption enable further accumulation of capital, expertise, and data, further widening the gap with those lagging behind.

Furthermore, the nature of AI-driven job displacement further contributes to economic inequality. While AI is expected to create new jobs, these often demand higher levels of education and specialized skills, leaving many workers, particularly those in low-skill occupations, vulnerable to automation. This displacement can lead to unemployment, wage stagnation, and a decline in economic opportunities for those unable to adapt to the changing job market.

The resulting skills gap, combined with the potentially unequal access to retraining and upskilling opportunities, can further exacerbate existing inequalities. For example, blue-collar workers in manufacturing industries or call centers might find their jobs automated, forcing them to compete for fewer jobs requiring different skill sets. Similarly, routine office tasks performed by administrative staff are increasingly being handled by AI-powered systems, resulting in job losses in these sectors. The lack of widespread, readily available, and affordable reskilling programs compounds the problem.

The geographical distribution of AI's benefits also plays a crucial role in generating economic disparity. AI development and deployment are concentrated in specific regions, predominantly in advanced economies like the United States, China, and parts of Europe. This concentration of resources, expertise, and investment creates a significant gap between developed and developing countries. Developing nations may lack the necessary infrastructure, skilled workforce, and financial resources to effectively participate in the AI revolution, further widening the global economic divide. They often lack access to the computational power and high-quality data needed to train sophisticated AI models, making it difficult to compete with wealthier nations in the development and deployment of AI technologies. This digital divide inhibits their ability to leverage AI for economic growth and social development, perpetuating existing global inequalities.

Another crucial aspect of AI and inequality involves the potential for algorithmic bias. AI systems are trained on massive datasets, and if these datasets reflect existing societal biases, the resulting AI models will likely perpetuate and even amplify those biases. This can lead to discriminatory outcomes in various applications, such as loan approvals, hiring processes, and criminal justice. For instance, an AI system trained on data that over-represents certain demographics might unfairly disadvantage individuals from underrepresented groups in loan applications or job interviews, further exacerbating existing economic and social inequalities.

Addressing algorithmic bias requires careful attention to data quality, fairness-aware algorithms, and rigorous testing and evaluation of AI systems. The need for transparency and explainability in AI systems is paramount to allow for auditing and identification of potential biases.

The potential for AI to exacerbate existing inequalities demands proactive measures. Addressing this requires a multi-pronged strategy that includes investing in education and retraining programs to equip workers with the skills needed for the jobs of the future. This necessitates not only technical training but also development of broader skills, such as critical thinking, problem-solving, and creativity, which are less susceptible to automation.

Governments and educational institutions should collaborate to ensure that education systems are adapted to prepare the workforce for an AI-driven economy. These programs should be accessible to all segments of the population, especially those disproportionately affected by automation.

Furthermore, policies aimed at promoting inclusive growth and equitable distribution of AI's benefits are essential. This includes initiatives to support small and medium-sized enterprises (SMEs) in adopting AI technologies, providing incentives for AI development and deployment in underserved communities, and investing in infrastructure to bridge the digital divide. Governments can play a vital role in promoting ethical AI development and deployment through regulations, standards, and guidelines that ensure fairness, transparency, and accountability. This also includes measures to mitigate algorithmic bias and prevent the misuse of AI technologies.

International cooperation is also critical in addressing the global economic disparities arising from AI. Developed countries should collaborate with developing nations to promote technology transfer, capacity building, and knowledge sharing. This includes providing technical assistance, educational resources, and financial support to help developing countries develop their own AI capabilities and benefit from this transformative technology. The focus should be on creating an enabling environment that fosters innovation and inclusivity, ensuring that the benefits of AI are shared broadly.

International collaborations in AI research and development can also help to address shared challenges, such as algorithmic bias and data privacy, while simultaneously fostering the creation of global standards and best practices.

In conclusion, the economic implications of AI are far-reaching and complex. While AI presents significant opportunities for economic growth and development, it also carries the risk of exacerbating existing inequalities and creating new ones. Addressing this challenge requires a concerted effort from governments, businesses, educational institutions, and individuals to ensure that the benefits of AI are shared broadly and equitably. This requires proactive policies promoting inclusive growth, addressing the skills gap, mitigating algorithmic bias, and fostering international collaboration. Only through a holistic and collaborative approach can we harness the transformative potential of AI while mitigating its risks and ensuring a more equitable and prosperous future for all. The future of AI is not merely a technological advancement; it is a societal project demanding responsible stewardship and a commitment to fairness and inclusivity.

The Future of the Global Economy in the Age of AI

The preceding analysis highlighted the potential for AI to exacerbate existing economic inequalities, both within and between nations. However, the story doesn't end there. Looking ahead, the long-term impact of AI on the global economy promises to be even more profound and multifaceted, demanding a nuanced understanding of its transformative power. While challenges are significant, the opportunities presented by AI are equally vast, offering pathways to unprecedented levels of economic growth and societal well-being – provided we navigate the transition strategically and responsibly.

One of the most significant long-term impacts will be the reshaping of industries and the creation of entirely new economic sectors. The automation of routine tasks, facilitated by AI, will continue to disrupt traditional industries, leading to job displacement in certain sectors. However, this disruption will simultaneously create opportunities for innovation and the emergence of new industries that we can only begin to imagine today. Consider, for example, the rise of the sharing economy, which has been significantly augmented by AI-powered platforms. This is just a glimpse into the potential for AI to spawn new economic models, business structures, and job categories that didn't exist before.

The development of AI itself will become a significant driver of economic growth. The AI industry is already a multi-billion dollar sector, attracting massive investments from both public and private sources. This investment fuels further innovation, creating a positive feedback loop that propels economic expansion. The demand for AI-related expertise will continue to grow, creating high-paying jobs in areas such as AI research, development, engineering, and deployment. This will necessitate a significant shift in educational priorities, with a focus on STEM fields and the development of critical thinking skills to complement AI's capabilities.

However, the distribution of these benefits will remain a critical concern. The potential for AI to further concentrate wealth in the hands of a few remains a significant risk. This is particularly true in the context of the global economy, where developing nations may lack the resources and infrastructure to fully participate in the AI revolution. Bridging this digital divide will require significant international cooperation and investment in infrastructure, education, and technology transfer. Without concerted efforts to address this disparity, the AI-driven economy could exacerbate existing inequalities on a global scale.

Beyond the direct economic impact, AI will have far-reaching consequences for productivity and efficiency. The automation of tasks will lead to significant gains in productivity across various sectors, potentially boosting economic growth. This increase in efficiency can translate into lower production costs, increased output, and higher overall economic output. However, this increase in productivity must be managed carefully. It's crucial to ensure that the gains are distributed fairly, preventing a scenario where increased productivity leads to job losses without commensurate benefits for workers.

The impact of AI on employment will undoubtedly remain a focal point of discussion and debate. While some jobs will undoubtedly be lost to automation, the overall impact on employment is likely to be more complex. AI will likely create new job opportunities in areas such as AI development, maintenance, and oversight.

Moreover, AI can augment human capabilities, allowing workers to be more efficient and productive in their roles. However, this requires significant investment in retraining and upskilling programs to prepare the workforce for the changing demands of the job market. These programs need to be targeted and inclusive, focusing on providing the necessary skills and support for those most vulnerable to job displacement.

Furthermore, the ethical considerations surrounding AI will increasingly shape its economic impact. Issues of algorithmic bias, data privacy, and job displacement require careful consideration and proactive measures to mitigate potential risks. Regulations and policies will play a crucial role in ensuring that AI is developed and deployed responsibly, promoting fairness, transparency, and accountability. This will involve not only technical solutions but also broader societal conversations about the ethical implications of AI and the need for responsible innovation.

The future of the global economy in the age of AI is not predetermined. The path we take will depend on the choices we make today. Investing in education, research, and development is crucial to harnessing the transformative potential of AI. Likewise, establishing clear ethical guidelines and regulatory frameworks will be essential to mitigating potential risks. International cooperation will be paramount in ensuring that the benefits of AI are shared globally and that the transition is equitable and inclusive.

Consider the potential impact on healthcare. AI-powered diagnostic tools can revolutionize healthcare delivery, leading to more accurate and timely diagnoses, improved patient outcomes, and reduced healthcare costs. This could lead to a significant boost in productivity and efficiency within the healthcare sector. However, the equitable access to these advanced technologies remains a challenge, particularly in developing nations with limited resources.

In the financial sector, AI-powered systems are already transforming financial services, from fraud detection and risk management to algorithmic trading and personalized financial advice. This increased efficiency can lead to significant cost savings for financial institutions and improved services for customers. However, concerns about algorithmic bias and the potential for AI-driven financial instability require careful regulation and oversight.

The manufacturing industry is undergoing a significant transformation driven by AI-powered automation. Robotics, machine learning, and computer vision are revolutionizing production processes, leading to increased efficiency, higher quality products, and reduced labor costs. However, this automation also poses challenges to workers in manufacturing jobs, requiring retraining and upskilling programs to adapt to the changing demands of the industry.

The agricultural sector is also being transformed by AI, with AI-powered systems optimizing crop yields, reducing resource consumption, and improving efficiency. Precision agriculture, enabled by AI, can lead to significant increases in food production, reducing food insecurity and addressing climate change challenges. However, the deployment of these technologies requires access to infrastructure and technical expertise, which may pose challenges in developing nations.

The transportation sector is witnessing the advent of autonomous vehicles, driven by AI-powered systems. Self-driving cars have the potential to revolutionize transportation, improving safety, reducing traffic congestion, and enhancing efficiency. However, the development and deployment of autonomous vehicles require substantial investments in infrastructure and the resolution of ethical and safety concerns.

Looking beyond these specific examples, the future of the global economy in the age of AI will hinge on several key factors. The pace of technological advancement, the effectiveness of policy interventions, and the degree of international cooperation will all play a critical role in shaping the future. The ability to adapt to a rapidly changing economic landscape will be essential for individuals, businesses, and governments alike. Proactive strategies for workforce development, technological innovation, and ethical governance will be critical in maximizing the benefits of AI while minimizing its potential risks. The future is not predetermined; it is a future we will collectively shape through our actions and choices.

The promise of an AI-driven global economy is one of unprecedented growth and opportunity, but the realization of that promise requires a commitment to responsible innovation, equity, and global collaboration. The journey ahead demands careful navigation, but the potential rewards are immense, promising a future of prosperity and well-being for all.

The Global Race for AI Supremacy

The previous discussion illuminated AI's potential to reshape global economics, creating both immense opportunities and significant challenges. However, the very development and deployment of AI are becoming key battlegrounds in a new era of geopolitical competition. The global race for AI supremacy is not merely a technological contest; it's a struggle for economic dominance, military advantage, and ultimately, global influence. This competition is shaping international relations in profound and often unpredictable ways.

Several nations have emerged as clear frontrunners in this race. The United States, with its robust private sector innovation and substantial government investment in research and development, maintains a strong position. Silicon Valley, in particular, has become a global hub for AI research and development, attracting top talent from around the world. However, the US faces challenges, including concerns about data privacy, regulatory hurdles, and the potential for a brain drain to other countries offering more attractive research environments or financial incentives.

China, on the other hand, has adopted a more centrally planned approach, investing heavily in AI research and development through national initiatives and strategic partnerships between government and industry. Its vast data resources, stemming from a large population and ubiquitous digital infrastructure, provide a significant advantage. The Chinese government has set ambitious goals for AI dominance, aiming to become a global leader in the field by 2030. This ambition is coupled with a focus on integrating AI across various sectors, from surveillance and security to manufacturing and transportation, leading to concerns about potential misuse of the technology and its implications for human rights.

The European Union, while not possessing the same scale of resources as the US or China, is pursuing a strategy focused on ethical AI development and regulation. The EU's emphasis on data privacy, algorithmic transparency, and responsible innovation aims to create a framework for AI that prioritizes human rights and societal well-being. However, this approach risks slowing the pace of technological advancement compared to less regulated environments, potentially impacting its competitiveness in the global AI race.

Beyond these major players, other countries are making significant strides in specific areas of AI research and development. Countries like Canada, the United Kingdom, Israel, and several nations in Asia are investing heavily in talent acquisition, research infrastructure, and the creation of supportive ecosystems for AI startups. These countries often focus on niche areas where they can achieve a competitive advantage, such as specific applications of AI in healthcare, finance, or defense.

The competition is not merely about national prowess; it also plays out at the level of individual companies. Global tech giants like Google, Microsoft, Amazon, and Facebook (Meta) are engaged in intense competition to develop and deploy advanced AI technologies. This competition fuels rapid innovation but also raises concerns about market concentration, monopolies, and the potential for misuse of powerful AI systems. Furthermore, the talent war for skilled AI researchers and engineers is fierce, with these companies competing for the best minds globally, often with lucrative salaries and research opportunities.

This global race has significant geopolitical implications. The ability to develop and deploy advanced AI technologies is increasingly viewed as a key determinant of national power and influence. AI is not only transforming economic activities but also revolutionizing military capabilities, leading to the development of autonomous weapons systems and advanced surveillance technologies. The strategic implications of AI in warfare are profound, raising ethical concerns and increasing the potential for miscalculation and escalation.

The competition for AI talent is a crucial aspect of this geopolitical struggle. Nations are vying to attract and retain the best AI researchers and engineers, often offering generous incentives, including research grants, funding for startups, and immigration policies designed to attract skilled workers. This competition for talent exacerbates existing inequalities between developed and developing countries, as the latter may lack the resources to compete effectively for top AI talent.

The ethical considerations surrounding AI are also becoming increasingly important in the geopolitical context. Concerns about algorithmic bias, data privacy, and the potential for AI-driven surveillance are leading to calls for international cooperation and the development of global norms and regulations to govern the development and deployment of AI. However, the divergence in values and priorities among nations makes achieving consensus on these issues a significant challenge.

The future of this global competition remains uncertain. The pace of technological advancement, the evolving geopolitical landscape, and the choices made by individual nations and companies will all play a significant role in shaping the outcome. However, it's clear that AI is rapidly transforming the global power balance, with far-reaching consequences for international relations, economic development, and global security.

The strategic importance of AI is also reflected in the increasing investment in AI research and development by governments worldwide. Many countries have launched national AI strategies with ambitious goals for AI development and deployment. These strategies often include significant funding for research, the creation of AI-focused institutions, and the development of national AI talent pools. However, the success of these strategies depends on a multitude of factors, including the availability of skilled talent, access to data, and the creation of supportive regulatory environments.

Furthermore, international cooperation is crucial for navigating the challenges and opportunities presented by AI. The development of global standards and norms for AI governance, data sharing, and ethical considerations is essential to ensure the responsible development and deployment of AI technologies. International collaborations on AI research and development can also foster innovation and prevent duplication of effort. However, achieving international consensus on AI governance remains a significant challenge, given the differing priorities and interests of nations.

One crucial area where international cooperation is needed is the development of AI safety guidelines. As AI systems become more powerful and autonomous, the potential for unintended consequences increases. International collaboration is crucial to develop safety standards and best practices to mitigate these risks. This includes the development of robust testing and verification procedures, as well as mechanisms for identifying and addressing potential biases in AI systems.

The geopolitical landscape of AI is dynamic and constantly evolving. New players are emerging, and existing power dynamics are shifting. The race for AI supremacy is not a zero-sum game; collaboration and cooperation are as crucial as competition. Nations must find ways to balance the pursuit of national interests with the need for global cooperation to ensure that AI benefits all of humanity. The responsible development and deployment of AI will require a multifaceted approach that considers not only technological advancements but also ethical considerations, geopolitical implications, and the need for international cooperation. The future of AI and its impact on global power dynamics remains a subject of intense debate and speculation, but it is clear that this technology will play a central role in shaping the world in the years to come. The choices made today will determine whether AI empowers humanity or exacerbates existing inequalities and conflicts.

AI and National Security

The integration of artificial intelligence into national security strategies is rapidly transforming the landscape of global power dynamics. No longer a futuristic concept, AI is actively reshaping defense systems, intelligence operations, and cybersecurity protocols, creating both unprecedented opportunities and profound challenges. The development and deployment of AI-powered weaponry, in particular, presents a critical ethical and strategic dilemma with potentially catastrophic consequences.

One of the most significant implications of AI in national security lies in its potential to revolutionize military capabilities.

Autonomous weapons systems (AWS), often referred to as lethal autonomous weapons (LAWs), represent a paradigm shift in warfare. These systems, capable of selecting and engaging targets without human intervention, raise profound ethical concerns about accountability, proportionality, and the potential for unintended escalation. The absence of human control raises questions about who is responsible when an AWS malfunctions or makes an erroneous decision resulting in civilian casualties or unintended conflict. This lack of human oversight is a major point of contention internationally, with numerous nations calling for a preemptive ban on the development and deployment of LAWS. The debate is far from settled, however, with proponents arguing that AWS can enhance precision, reduce collateral damage, and improve battlefield decision-making, ultimately leading to a more humane form of warfare. This assertion, however, is highly contested, with many experts warning of the potential for these systems to be easily hacked, misused, or employed in unpredictable ways, potentially destabilizing global security.

Beyond autonomous weapons, AI is transforming other aspects of military operations. AI-powered surveillance systems are becoming increasingly sophisticated, capable of analyzing vast amounts of data to identify potential threats and predict future actions. These systems can analyze satellite imagery, social media feeds, and other data sources to detect patterns and anomalies indicative of terrorist activity, criminal networks, or potential military deployments.

While such capabilities enhance intelligence gathering and situational awareness, they also raise concerns about mass surveillance, privacy violations, and the potential for bias in algorithmic decision-making. The ability to track individuals without their knowledge or consent raises serious ethical questions about government overreach and the erosion of civil liberties.

Moreover, the reliance on algorithms trained on biased data sets can lead to inaccurate or discriminatory outcomes, exacerbating existing inequalities and potentially leading to misidentification and unjust targeting of individuals or groups.

The application of AI in cybersecurity is another critical area of national security. AI algorithms are increasingly being used to detect and respond to cyberattacks, analyzing network traffic and identifying malicious activity in real-time. This capability is crucial in defending against increasingly sophisticated cyber threats, which can target critical infrastructure, financial institutions, and government agencies. AI-powered systems can learn and adapt to evolving attack patterns, making them more effective than traditional security measures. However, the use of AI in cybersecurity also presents challenges. As AI-powered attack systems become more sophisticated, a cyber arms race is emerging, with both attackers and defenders leveraging AI to gain an advantage. This escalation necessitates a continual evolution of defensive AI systems to counter the ever-changing threat landscape.

Furthermore, the use of AI in disinformation and propaganda campaigns poses a significant threat to national security.

Sophisticated AI algorithms can generate realistic-looking fake videos, images, and audio recordings known as "deepfakes," which can be used to manipulate public opinion, spread misinformation, and sow discord. These deepfakes, easily disseminated through social media and other online platforms, can undermine trust in institutions, exacerbate societal divisions, and potentially influence the outcome of elections or other important events. Combating this form of information warfare requires the development of advanced AI-powered detection systems that can identify and flag deepfakes and other forms of disinformation. However, the development of these detection systems lags behind the ability to create deepfakes, necessitating a constant effort to stay ahead of the curve.

The development and deployment of AI in national security also require careful consideration of the legal and regulatory frameworks governing its use. The lack of clear international norms and regulations governing AI weaponry raises significant concerns about accountability, transparency, and the potential for unintended escalation. The development of internationally recognized standards and protocols for the responsible use of AI in national security is crucial to prevent the proliferation of dangerous AI-powered weapons and to mitigate the risks associated with its use. These frameworks should address issues such as accountability for autonomous weapon systems, data privacy, algorithmic bias, and the protection of human rights in the context of AI-powered surveillance.

International cooperation is paramount in addressing the challenges posed by AI in national security. The development and deployment of AI-powered weapons and surveillance systems are not limited to a select few nations; the technology is rapidly diffusing globally.

This necessitates international dialogue and collaboration to establish common standards, share best practices, and prevent a global arms race fueled by AI. Building trust and fostering open communication between nations are crucial steps in ensuring that AI technologies are used responsibly and ethically in the realm of national security. The failure to achieve international cooperation could lead to an unstable and unpredictable global security landscape, characterized by mistrust, escalation, and potentially devastating consequences.

The future of AI in national security is uncertain but holds immense potential for both progress and peril. Careful consideration of the ethical, legal, and strategic implications of AI technologies is essential to ensure their responsible development and deployment.

Investing in research and development of AI safety and security protocols is crucial to mitigating the risks associated with AI-powered weapons and surveillance systems. Promoting international cooperation and dialogue is equally crucial in shaping a future where AI serves to enhance global security rather than to exacerbate conflict. The path forward requires a concerted effort from governments, researchers, and the international community to work together to harness the benefits of AI while mitigating its potential harms. Only through collaborative efforts can we hope to create a future where AI contributes to a more secure and just world. The potential for misuse, however, requires constant vigilance and a proactive approach to regulating and controlling the technology's deployment. The long-term implications are complex and require ongoing analysis and adaptation.

AI and International Relations

The rise of artificial intelligence (AI) is profoundly reshaping the landscape of international relations, extending far beyond its impact on national security. AI's influence is now felt across diplomacy, conflict resolution, and international cooperation, presenting both unprecedented opportunities and significant challenges. The ability of AI systems to process vast amounts of data, identify patterns, and predict future trends offers the potential to improve decision-making in international affairs, fostering more effective diplomacy and conflict prevention. However, this potential is intertwined with significant risks, including the potential for algorithmic bias, the erosion of trust, and the exacerbation of existing geopolitical tensions.

One critical area where AI is impacting international relations is diplomacy. AI-powered tools are increasingly being used to analyze diplomatic communications, identify potential points of conflict, and facilitate negotiations. Natural language processing (NLP) technologies can translate languages in real-time, breaking down communication barriers and fostering more effective dialogue between nations. Furthermore, AI systems can track and analyze global events, providing policymakers with real-time insights into evolving geopolitical situations. This enhanced situational awareness can enable quicker and more informed responses to international crises. For instance, AI-powered systems can monitor social media and news outlets for indicators of unrest or escalating tensions, providing early warning signals that can help prevent conflict. This capacity to anticipate and mitigate crises represents a significant potential benefit of AI in the realm of international relations.

However, the use of AI in diplomacy is not without its pitfalls. The reliance on algorithms trained on historical data can lead to biased predictions and recommendations, potentially perpetuating existing power imbalances and reinforcing discriminatory outcomes. For example, AI systems trained on data reflecting historical patterns of conflict may overestimate the likelihood of conflict in certain regions or between particular nations, while overlooking potential opportunities for peacebuilding. This risk of algorithmic bias underscores the need for careful oversight and ethical considerations in the development and deployment of AI tools in diplomatic settings. It highlights the importance of human-in-the-loop systems where human judgment and oversight play a critical role in guiding algorithmic decision-making. This ensures that AI complements, rather than replaces, human expertise and judgment in the complex field of international diplomacy.

AI also holds significant potential in the area of conflict resolution. AI-powered tools can analyze conflict dynamics, identify key actors, and simulate various scenarios to predict the potential outcomes of different interventions. This can help policymakers to develop more effective strategies for peacebuilding and conflict resolution. For example, AI could be used to analyze the root causes of conflict, such as resource scarcity, ethnic tensions, or political grievances, providing policymakers with valuable insights to address the underlying issues fueling the conflict. Additionally, AI can support negotiations by identifying common ground between conflicting parties and suggesting potential compromises. This ability to simulate different scenarios and explore potential solutions can facilitate more constructive and effective negotiations, contributing to more peaceful outcomes.

Despite its potential benefits, the use of AI in conflict resolution also poses significant risks. The reliance on AI systems for decision-making in conflict zones raises concerns about accountability and transparency. In instances where AI systems make errors or contribute to unintended consequences, determining responsibility becomes challenging. Furthermore, the use of AI in conflict resolution could lead to a shift in power dynamics, where certain nations with advanced AI capabilities have an undue advantage in shaping the outcome of conflicts. This uneven access to powerful AI tools raises concerns about equity and fairness in the application of AI to conflict resolution. Addressing these concerns requires robust international regulations, frameworks, and guidelines to ensure that AI is used responsibly and ethically to enhance rather than impede conflict resolution efforts. A lack of proper regulations and oversight could potentially worsen the situation.

The increasing integration of AI into international relations also highlights the critical need for international norms and regulations to govern its use. The lack of global governance in this area creates a significant risk of a global AI arms race, where nations compete to develop and deploy increasingly sophisticated AI-powered weapons and surveillance systems. This could lead to an escalation of tensions, mistrust, and ultimately, conflict. Establishing international norms and regulations is therefore crucial to ensure that AI is used responsibly and ethically in the global arena. These regulations should address key issues such as algorithmic transparency, accountability for AI-powered systems, data privacy, and the prevention of the development of autonomous weapons systems. These regulations would ensure the responsible use of AI systems within international relations and avoid potential problems associated with their misuse.

International cooperation is paramount in developing and implementing these regulations. Given the global nature of AI development and deployment, a collaborative approach is essential to prevent a fragmentation of standards and avoid a situation where different nations have conflicting rules governing the use of AI.

International organizations such as the United Nations and other multilateral bodies have a crucial role to play in facilitating dialogue, building consensus, and developing global standards for the responsible use of AI in international relations. This collaboration is not merely desirable but essential for mitigating the potential risks and harnessing the benefits of AI in the international arena, ensuring a future where AI empowers diplomacy, fosters cooperation, and ultimately contributes to a more peaceful and prosperous world. The absence of international cooperation could severely undermine global security and stability.

In conclusion, AI is rapidly transforming the international landscape, impacting diplomacy, conflict resolution, and international cooperation in profound ways. While AI offers significant opportunities for improved decision-making, conflict prevention, and peacebuilding, it also poses significant risks. The potential for algorithmic bias, the erosion of trust, and the exacerbation of geopolitical tensions necessitate the development of international norms and regulations to govern the responsible use of

AI. International cooperation is crucial in establishing these regulations, ensuring equitable access to AI technologies, and fostering a global environment where AI contributes to peace and stability. The future of international relations hinges on the ability of the global community to navigate the opportunities and challenges presented by AI in a collaborative and ethical manner. Ignoring these crucial aspects could have catastrophic consequences on the global stage. The need for proactive and comprehensive international regulation cannot be overstated.

AI and Global Governance

The preceding discussion highlighted the profound impact of AI on international relations, focusing on its implications for diplomacy and conflict resolution. However, the very real potential for AI to exacerbate existing inequalities and create new sources of global instability necessitates a robust framework of global governance. The absence of such a framework leaves us vulnerable to a future where AI benefits are unevenly distributed, leading to power imbalances and increased tensions. Creating effective global governance for AI is a monumental task, demanding international cooperation on an unprecedented scale.

One of the most pressing challenges lies in establishing internationally recognized standards for data privacy. AI systems thrive on data, and the sheer volume of data collected and analyzed by these systems raises significant privacy concerns. The potential for misuse of personal data is particularly acute, with implications for individual rights, national security, and international relations.

Different nations have varying approaches to data privacy, with some exhibiting far stricter regulations than others. The lack of harmonization in these regulations creates a fragmented and inconsistent landscape, hindering cross-border data flows and potentially stifling innovation. A crucial step towards effective global governance is the development of internationally recognized standards for data privacy that balance the needs of AI development with the protection of fundamental rights. This requires careful consideration of data anonymization techniques, secure data storage practices, and mechanisms for user consent and data control. A global standard could establish a baseline level of data protection, preventing a "race to the bottom" where nations compete to attract AI development by offering lax privacy regulations.

Algorithmic accountability is another crucial area requiring global attention. As AI systems become increasingly sophisticated and autonomous, the ability to understand and explain their decision-making processes becomes paramount. This "black box" problem poses significant challenges for accountability, particularly when AI systems are used in high-stakes contexts such as criminal justice, healthcare, or national security. Without transparency and explainability, it becomes difficult, if not impossible, to identify and correct biases embedded within algorithms, or to determine responsibility when AI systems make mistakes with potentially harmful consequences. Global governance frameworks should prioritize the development of techniques and standards for algorithmic transparency and accountability, enabling stakeholders to understand how AI systems arrive at their decisions and hold developers and users responsible for any adverse outcomes. This could involve developing standardized methods for auditing algorithms, requiring greater documentation of the data used to train AI models, and establishing clear lines of responsibility for algorithmic errors. International collaboration will be essential in determining the specific technical standards and regulatory mechanisms required to achieve this goal.

The prevention of harmful uses of AI constitutes another critical aspect of global governance. The potential for AI to be used for malicious purposes is significant and growing. This ranges from the development of autonomous weapons systems (AWS) that can select and engage targets without human intervention, to the use of AI for mass surveillance, disinformation campaigns, and cyberattacks. The proliferation of these technologies poses a serious threat to global stability and security. International cooperation is urgently needed to establish norms and regulations that prohibit or severely restrict the development and deployment of harmful AI applications. This requires careful consideration of the ethical implications of different AI technologies and the development of mechanisms for enforcing international standards. Given the potential for a global AI arms race, the establishment of international treaties or agreements is likely necessary to prevent the proliferation of dangerous AI weapons. The establishment of a global body that is responsible for overseeing the development and implementation of these international treaties would be crucial to ensuring their effectiveness.

Beyond these specific challenges, effective global governance for AI requires a broad and inclusive approach that incorporates the voices and perspectives of diverse stakeholders. This includes not only governments and international organizations but also researchers, developers, civil society groups, and the wider public. A participatory and transparent process is essential to ensure that AI governance frameworks are legitimate, effective, and equitable. Global governance should also foster international cooperation in AI research and development, promoting the sharing of knowledge and best practices, whilst establishing mechanisms for international cooperation and information-sharing to ensure a proactive approach to managing the risks associated with AI. The failure to establish effective global governance in AI could have severe consequences on global stability and security.

Establishing global norms for AI is a complex undertaking, requiring international consensus on principles, standards, and mechanisms. This process is likely to be iterative, adapting and evolving as AI technologies continue to advance. However, the urgency of the task cannot be overstated. The rapid pace of AI development demands proactive, preemptive measures to prevent the worst-case scenarios. International organizations like the UN play a vital role in facilitating dialogue, coordinating efforts, and establishing platforms for international collaboration. However, the success of these efforts ultimately depends on the commitment and cooperation of individual nations, a commitment that must be grounded in a shared understanding of the potential risks and benefits of AI, and a shared responsibility to ensure its responsible and beneficial deployment.

The future of AI and its impact on the global stage will depend largely on the success of international efforts to build a robust framework for governance. This framework needs to address a broad range of issues, including, but not limited to, algorithmic transparency, data privacy, ethical guidelines for AI development and deployment, mechanisms for accountability and redress, and restrictions on the development and use of autonomous weapons systems. The establishment of a dedicated international body, perhaps under the auspices of the UN, could provide a critical focal point for coordination and collaboration. This body could be
responsible for monitoring the development and deployment of AI technologies, setting global standards, conducting assessments of potential risks, and fostering dialogue between governments,

industry, and civil society. Effective global governance of AI demands more than simple regulations; it requires a fundamental shift in global cooperation and a shared commitment to responsible innovation. The challenge is immense, but the stakes are even higher. The future of global security, prosperity, and even humanity itself, may well depend on our ability to rise to this challenge. The path forward requires a sustained effort to balance the extraordinary potential of AI with the need to protect human values and safeguard against its potential harms. The task before us is not merely to manage the technological progress; it is to shape the future of global governance itself. The consequences of inaction are too severe to contemplate.

The Future of Geopolitics in an AIDriven World

The preceding discussion emphasized the urgent need for global governance in AI, focusing on data privacy, algorithmic accountability, and the prevention of harmful uses. However, the ramifications of AI extend far beyond these crucial areas, profoundly shaping the future landscape of geopolitics. The integration of AI into military strategies, economic policies, and diplomatic processes will fundamentally alter the dynamics of international relations, potentially leading to both unprecedented opportunities and significant challenges.

One of the most significant shifts will be in the balance of power. The development and deployment of advanced AI technologies are not evenly distributed across the globe. A small number of nations, primarily the United States, China, and a handful of other technologically advanced countries, currently hold a significant advantage in AI capabilities. This technological asymmetry could exacerbate existing power imbalances, creating new sources of tension and conflict. Nations with superior AI capabilities might gain a decisive edge in military operations, economic competition, and even political influence. The ability to leverage AI for sophisticated surveillance, targeted disinformation campaigns, or the development of autonomous weapons systems could significantly alter the calculus of international relations, potentially leading to a new era of great power competition defined not by conventional military strength, but by technological supremacy.

The economic implications are equally profound. AI-driven automation could disrupt global supply chains, shift patterns of economic growth, and reshape the global labor market. Nations that successfully adapt to this technological revolution will likely prosper, while those that fail to do so may face significant economic hardship and social unrest. This could further exacerbate existing inequalities between developed and developing nations, leading to increased migration pressures and potentially even conflict.

Furthermore, the proliferation of AI-enabled autonomous weapons systems (AWS) presents a particularly grave threat to global security. AWS, sometimes referred to as "killer robots," are capable of selecting and engaging targets without human intervention. The development and deployment of such systems raise profound ethical and security concerns. The lack of human control over these weapons could lead to unintended escalation, accidental conflict, or even the complete erosion of human control over military operations. The potential for misuse by rogue states or non-state actors adds further complexity and risk. International cooperation is essential to prevent an AI arms race and establish clear norms and regulations governing the development and use of AWS. However, reaching a global consensus on this issue is likely to be exceedingly challenging, given the divergent interests and perspectives of various nations.

The future of international cooperation will also be significantly influenced by AI. While AI can enhance communication and facilitate collaboration, its potential for misuse in manipulating public opinion, spreading disinformation, and undermining democratic processes poses a significant threat to international stability. The use of AI-powered deepfakes, for instance, could erode public trust in information sources, making it increasingly difficult to distinguish truth from falsehood. This could have devastating consequences for international diplomacy, as misunderstandings and mistrust could easily escalate into conflict.

The development of robust mechanisms for detecting and countering AI-enabled disinformation will be crucial for maintaining trust and cooperation in an AI-driven world.

Beyond these immediate concerns, the long-term implications of AI for geopolitics are difficult to predict with certainty. However, several scenarios are worth considering. One scenario suggests a future characterized by increased competition and conflict, as nations vie for technological dominance and struggle to adapt to the rapid changes brought about by AI. This scenario could lead to a more fragmented and unstable international system, with heightened risks of conflict and great power rivalry. Another scenario, however, envisions a more cooperative future, where nations recognize the shared challenges posed by AI and work together to establish global governance frameworks, promoting responsible innovation and mitigating the risks of AI. This scenario assumes a greater level of international collaboration and trust, something that is by no means guaranteed.

The success of either scenario will depend, in large part, on the choices made by individual nations and the international community as a whole. Investing in AI research and development is crucial for nations to compete in the global arena. However, this must be coupled with a strong ethical framework and robust regulatory mechanisms to ensure the responsible development and deployment of AI technologies. International cooperation will be essential in this process, enabling nations to share best practices, establish common standards, and coordinate responses to shared challenges.

The role of international organizations such as the United Nations will become increasingly important in navigating the complexities of AI and geopolitics. The UN could provide a platform for dialogue, collaboration, and the development of international norms and standards for AI. However, the effectiveness of the UN, and other international bodies, will depend on the commitment of individual member states to work collaboratively and address the challenges posed by AI in a proactive and effective manner. The potential for AI to disrupt existing power structures, exacerbate inequalities, and destabilize international relations is undeniable. However, AI also presents enormous opportunities for improving human lives and promoting global development. The challenge lies in harnessing the potential benefits of AI while mitigating its potential harms. This requires a fundamental shift in how nations approach international cooperation and global governance.

The development of effective global governance frameworks for AI will require a multi-faceted approach. First, there is a need for international collaboration on setting ethical standards and guidelines for the development and use of AI. These standards should address issues such as algorithmic bias, data privacy, and accountability. Second, effective mechanisms for enforcement are necessary. This could involve a combination of international treaties, national regulations, and industry self-regulation. Third, international cooperation is crucial in sharing knowledge and best practices in AI research and development. A global effort to foster responsible innovation is critical in ensuring that AI benefits all of humanity, rather than only a select few.

The path forward is not without significant obstacles. Differing national interests, technological disparities, and a lack of trust between nations can hinder international cooperation. However, the potential risks associated with unchecked AI development are too great to ignore. The international community must recognize the urgent need for collaborative action, fostering a shared
understanding of the challenges and opportunities posed by AI, and working together to create a future where AI serves as a force for good in the world. The stakes are high. The future of geopolitics, and indeed the future of humanity, may well depend on our ability to navigate this transformative technological era with wisdom, foresight, and a commitment to global cooperation. The time for decisive action is now. Failure to address these challenges
proactively could lead to unforeseen and potentially devastating consequences for global stability and security. The development and deployment of AI technologies are moving at an unprecedented pace. The international community must move with equal speed and resolve to create a future where AI serves as a force for
progress and peace.

Adapting to an AIDriven Workforce

The previous sections highlighted the profound geopolitical implications of AI, underscoring the urgency for global cooperation in navigating its transformative power. However, the impact of AI extends far beyond international relations; it is fundamentally reshaping the very nature of work and the skills required to thrive in the modern economy. For individuals, adapting to an AI-driven workforce necessitates a proactive and strategic approach, focusing on acquiring new skills, embracing lifelong learning, and cultivating capabilities that complement, rather than compete with, artificial intelligence.

The most immediate challenge for many workers is the potential displacement of jobs due to automation. AI-powered systems are increasingly capable of performing tasks previously handled by humans, particularly in sectors like manufacturing, transportation, and customer service. While some fear widespread unemployment, the reality is likely more nuanced. While certain jobs may become obsolete, others will emerge, demanding new skills and expertise.

This necessitates a shift in mindset—from focusing on a single career path to embracing lifelong learning and adaptability as core competencies. The traditional notion of a linear career trajectory, with steady progression within a single company, is becoming increasingly outdated. Instead, individuals should prepare for a more fluid and dynamic career path, characterized by continuous learning, skill development, and potentially multiple career transitions throughout their working lives.

This necessitates a proactive approach to skill acquisition. Rather than passively waiting for job opportunities to arise, individuals should actively identify skills in demand and acquire them proactively. This might involve taking online courses, attending workshops, pursuing further education, or engaging in self-directed learning. The abundance of online learning resources, from Massive Open Online Courses (MOOCs) offered by platforms like Coursera and edX to specialized training programs provided by companies and professional organizations, presents unprecedented opportunities for continuous skill development. Individuals should leverage these resources to acquire technical skills that are complementary to AI, such as data analysis, programming, and cybersecurity. They should also develop softer skills, such as critical thinking, problem-solving, creativity, and communication, which are less easily automated.

A critical element of adapting to an AI-driven workforce is focusing on developing skills that uniquely leverage human capabilities. AI excels at repetitive tasks, data processing, and pattern recognition, but it lags behind in areas requiring creativity, critical thinking, emotional intelligence, and complex problem-solving. These uniquely human attributes will become increasingly valuable in an AI-driven world. Individuals should actively cultivate these skills through various experiences, including project-based learning, collaborative work, and mentorship programs. The ability to work effectively in teams, communicate ideas persuasively, and demonstrate emotional intelligence will be crucial for success in a collaborative environment where humans and AI work side-by-side.

This emphasizes the importance of lifelong learning. The pace of technological change is accelerating, rendering many skills obsolete far quicker than in previous eras. To remain competitive in the job market, individuals must embrace a culture of continuous learning, actively seeking out new knowledge and skills throughout their careers. This is not simply about obtaining formal qualifications; it also includes informal learning through online courses, workshops, networking events, and self-directed projects. The ability to learn quickly and adapt to new technologies will be a crucial differentiator in the future job market. This requires a proactive mindset, a willingness to step outside of one's comfort zone, and a commitment to continuous self-improvement.

In addition to acquiring new skills, individuals need to develop an understanding of how AI works and its potential impact on their respective industries. This does not necessarily require becoming a computer scientist, but a basic understanding of AI principles and its applications is essential for making informed career choices and adapting to the changing job market. This knowledge can help individuals identify emerging opportunities and proactively position themselves for future success. Staying informed about technological trends through reading industry publications, attending conferences, and networking with professionals in the field is crucial for maintaining a competitive edge.

Furthermore, individuals should focus on developing strong communication and interpersonal skills. As AI systems become more sophisticated, the ability to effectively communicate with machines and other humans will become even more critical. This includes the ability to articulate complex ideas clearly, actively listen to others, and work collaboratively in diverse teams. These skills are essential for working effectively alongside AI and navigating the complexities of the future workplace. Developing a strong network of professional contacts can also be beneficial, allowing individuals to learn from others, share knowledge, and access new opportunities.

The transition to an AI-driven workforce will also necessitate adapting to new work arrangements. The rise of remote work, gig economy, and freelance opportunities presents both challenges and opportunities for individuals. Embracing flexibility and adaptability is crucial for navigating these changes successfully. This may involve acquiring skills in project management, self-organization, and virtual collaboration. Individuals need to be comfortable managing their own time, setting priorities, and working effectively in virtual teams.

Governments and educational institutions have a crucial role to play in facilitating this adaptation. They need to invest in training and education programs that equip individuals with the skills needed to thrive in an AI-driven economy. This includes promoting STEM education, fostering digital literacy, and providing opportunities for reskilling and upskilling workers displaced by automation. Government policies that support lifelong learning and encourage workforce adaptability are essential for ensuring a smooth transition to an AI-driven future.

The transition to an AI-driven workforce is not without its challenges. Concerns about job displacement, income inequality, and the ethical implications of AI are valid and need to be addressed proactively. However, by embracing lifelong learning, developing complementary skills, and adapting to new work arrangements, individuals can not only navigate these challenges but also harness the opportunities presented by this transformative technology. The future of work is not about humans versus AI; it's about humans and AI working together to achieve greater productivity and innovation. By proactively acquiring the necessary skills and embracing adaptability, individuals can secure their place in this evolving landscape and contribute to a more prosperous and equitable future. The key is recognizing that adaptation is not a one-time event but a continuous process that requires ongoing learning, critical thinking, and proactive engagement with the changing technological landscape. The individuals who embrace this mindset will be best positioned to thrive in the age of AI.

Harnessing AI for Business Growth and Innovation

The transition to an AI-driven world presents not just challenges, but also unprecedented opportunities for businesses. The companies that successfully integrate AI into their operations will likely be the ones that thrive in this new landscape, achieving significant growth and fostering unparalleled innovation. However, the path to AI-driven success requires a strategic and phased approach, recognizing both the potential rewards and the inherent risks.

One of the first steps is identifying areas where AI can deliver the most significant impact. This involves a thorough assessment of the business's current operations, identifying bottlenecks, inefficiencies, and areas ripe for automation or enhancement. This assessment shouldn't be limited to operational processes; it should also consider opportunities for improved customer engagement, product development, and market expansion. For example, a manufacturing company might identify AI-powered predictive maintenance to reduce downtime, while a retail company might utilize AI-powered recommendation engines to enhance customer experience and increase sales. A financial institution could employ AI for fraud detection and risk management, while a healthcare provider could use AI for diagnostics and personalized treatment plans. The key is to focus on specific, measurable, achievable, relevant, and time-bound (SMART) goals, aligning AI initiatives with broader business objectives.

Once promising areas for AI implementation are identified, the next step is to carefully select the appropriate AI solutions. This requires a deep understanding of various AI techniques, including machine learning, deep learning, natural language processing, and computer vision. Different AI tools are best suited for different tasks, and selecting the right one is critical for achieving the desired outcomes. A company might choose to develop custom AI solutions in-house, leveraging its existing data and expertise. However, this path can be resource-intensive and time-consuming, requiring specialized technical skills and significant investment. Alternatively, companies can choose from a range of off-the-shelf AI solutions provided by cloud providers and technology vendors. This approach offers faster deployment and often lower initial costs, but may require adapting business processes to fit the capabilities of the chosen solution. Careful consideration must also be given to data privacy and security concerns, especially when using third-party AI solutions.

The successful implementation of AI requires not only the right technology but also the right people. Businesses need to invest in upskilling and reskilling their workforce to manage and effectively utilize AI tools. This may involve providing training in data science, machine learning, AI ethics, and data management. It's crucial to foster a culture of data literacy across the organization, empowering employees to understand and interpret AI-generated insights.

Furthermore, building a strong team of data scientists, engineers, and AI specialists is essential for designing, implementing, and maintaining AI systems. This may involve recruiting new talent or developing existing employees' skills through internal training programs and mentorship opportunities.

Moreover, businesses must establish robust data management practices. AI systems are only as good as the data they are trained on. High-quality, accurate, and representative data is essential for building effective AI models. This requires investing in data collection, cleaning, and storage infrastructure. Implementing strong data governance policies is also crucial, ensuring data privacy and security compliance. Furthermore, businesses need to establish processes for monitoring and evaluating AI model performance, continually refining and improving models based on real-world data and feedback.

The adoption of AI is not without risks. One significant concern is the potential for bias in AI algorithms. If the data used to train an AI model reflects existing societal biases, the model may perpetuate or even amplify these biases, leading to unfair or discriminatory outcomes. Businesses must actively work to mitigate bias in their AI systems, using techniques such as data augmentation, algorithmic fairness testing, and human-in-the-loop oversight. Another risk is the potential for job displacement due to automation. While AI can significantly improve productivity and efficiency, it can also lead to job losses in certain sectors. Businesses need to carefully manage this transition, providing retraining and reskilling opportunities for employees whose roles are affected by automation. Transparency and open communication with employees are crucial for navigating this process effectively.

Furthermore, the ethical implications of AI must be carefully considered. The use of AI raises questions regarding data privacy, accountability, and the potential for misuse. Businesses need to establish ethical guidelines for the development and deployment of AI systems, ensuring compliance with relevant regulations and adhering to high ethical standards. Regular ethical reviews of AI projects are essential, ensuring that they align with the company's values and societal expectations. This includes considering the impact of AI on various stakeholders, such as employees, customers, and the wider community.

The successful integration of AI requires a holistic approach that encompasses technological, organizational, and ethical considerations. Businesses must develop a clear AI strategy that aligns with their overall business goals, outlining specific objectives, key performance indicators (KPIs), and a phased implementation plan. This plan should include resource allocation, timelines, risk management strategies, and a process for continuous monitoring and improvement. Regular evaluations and adjustments are essential to ensure the AI strategy remains aligned with evolving business needs and technological advancements.

Beyond the immediate operational changes, AI can also drive significant innovation. By analyzing large datasets, AI systems can identify trends and patterns that human analysts might miss, leading to the development of new products, services, and business models. For example, AI-powered sentiment analysis can provide valuable insights into customer opinions, enabling businesses to tailor products and services to meet evolving demands. AI can also facilitate the development of personalized experiences, offering customized recommendations and targeted advertising. In the research and development sector, AI can significantly accelerate the pace of innovation by analyzing vast amounts of scientific data and identifying potential breakthroughs. This can lead to the development of new materials, medicines, and technologies. The ability to anticipate market trends and customer preferences through AI-driven insights offers a significant competitive advantage.

Furthermore, AI can help companies optimize their supply chains, reducing costs and improving efficiency. By predicting demand fluctuations and optimizing logistics, AI can minimize waste and streamline operations. AI-powered robots and automation systems can improve productivity in manufacturing and other sectors, while AI-driven analytics can help businesses make better decisions regarding inventory management and resource allocation. The increased efficiency and cost savings translate into a stronger bottom line and enhanced competitiveness.

Finally, successful AI adoption requires a culture of continuous learning and experimentation. Businesses should encourage experimentation with new AI technologies and approaches, fostering a culture of innovation and risk-taking. This involves investing in research and development, participating in industry events and conferences, and collaborating with AI experts and researchers. The ability to adapt quickly to new technologies and incorporate lessons learned is crucial for sustained success in the age of AI. The companies that embrace a continuous learning approach, adapting to the ever-evolving AI landscape, will be best positioned to lead the way in this transformative era. The integration of AI is not a one-time project; it's an ongoing process of adaptation and improvement. By embracing this mindset, businesses can harness the full potential of AI to achieve substantial growth and drive lasting innovation.

Investing in AI and Emerging Technologies

Investing wisely in AI and related emerging technologies requires a nuanced understanding of the market, a careful assessment of risk, and a long-term perspective. The rapid pace of innovation means that technologies deemed cutting-edge today might become obsolete relatively quickly. This necessitates a strategy that balances high-growth potential with manageable risk, recognizing that not all AI investments are created equal.

One primary avenue for investment lies in publicly traded companies actively involved in AI development and implementation. This could encompass established tech giants heavily investing in AI research and product development, or smaller, more specialized companies focused on specific AI applications like machine learning, natural language processing, or computer vision. Thorough due diligence is crucial here. Analyzing a company's financial performance, competitive landscape, intellectual property portfolio, and management team is paramount before committing capital. Looking beyond immediate returns and focusing on long-term growth potential is essential, particularly given the inherent volatility of the tech sector. Industry analysts' reports, financial news, and company filings can offer valuable insights into a company's prospects and risks.

Venture capital (VC) and private equity (PE) represent another significant pathway for investing in AI. VC firms often target early-stage companies with high-growth potential, while PE firms tend to invest in more mature companies seeking expansion or restructuring. This route typically involves a higher degree of risk compared to publicly traded equities, as the returns are less predictable and liquidity can be limited. However, the potential rewards can be significantly higher, especially for early-stage investments in disruptive technologies. Accessing these investment opportunities usually requires a considerable investment amount and a sophisticated understanding of the VC/PE landscape.

Networks and relationships within the industry can also play a critical role in gaining access to promising deals.

Direct investment in AI startups can be particularly lucrative but also carries substantial risk. Many startups fail, even those with promising initial technologies. Careful evaluation of the startup's team, technology, market potential, and business model is critical.

Assessing the strength of the team's expertise, the defensibility of their intellectual property, and their ability to execute their business plan are all essential components of this due diligence.

Furthermore, understanding the competitive landscape and identifying potential barriers to entry are crucial. Before committing funds, a comprehensive analysis of the startup's financial projections, funding rounds, and overall trajectory is essential.

Accessing this level of information might require leveraging established networks and partnerships within the industry.

Beyond direct equity investments, there are alternative ways to participate in the AI revolution's growth. Exchange-traded funds (ETFs) focused on technology or AI-related stocks provide a diversified approach to investment, reducing the risk associated with investing in individual companies. These ETFs offer broad exposure to the sector, minimizing the impact of individual company failures. Similarly, investing in companies that utilize AI to improve their own operations, even if they aren't explicitly AI companies, can provide a less direct but potentially less risky exposure to the industry's growth. This might involve companies leveraging AI for improved efficiency, automation, or enhanced customer experience.

Furthermore, the burgeoning field of AI-powered financial instruments offers new investment avenues. AI algorithms are increasingly used to manage portfolios, predict market trends, and execute trades. Robo-advisors, for example, offer automated investment management services based on AI-powered algorithms. While this can offer convenience and potentially improved returns, it's essential to understand the underlying algorithms and risk factors involved. Transparency and clear disclosure of the algorithms' limitations are vital for informed decision-making.

The ethical considerations surrounding AI investments should never be overlooked. Investing in companies that prioritize ethical AI development and deployment is not just morally responsible but can also be financially advantageous in the long run. Consumers and investors are increasingly demanding transparency and accountability from companies involved in AI, and those that fail to meet these expectations risk reputational damage and financial losses. Therefore, choosing to invest in companies that prioritize ethical AI development should be a key criterion in any investment strategy.

Beyond the financial aspects, investing in AI also involves understanding the broader societal implications. The potential for job displacement, algorithmic bias, and misuse of AI technologies are significant concerns that investors should consider. Supporting companies committed to responsible AI development and deployment can mitigate these risks and contribute to a more equitable and beneficial future for all. Understanding the potential social and economic impacts of AI is essential for making informed and responsible investment decisions.

The landscape of AI investment is constantly evolving, with new technologies and business models emerging regularly. Staying informed about the latest developments in the field is therefore crucial for successful investment. Regularly reviewing industry publications, attending conferences, and networking with experts can provide valuable insights and help investors adapt to the changing market dynamics. Continuous learning and adaptation are key to navigating the complexities of the AI investment landscape and capitalizing on its transformative potential.

Another critical aspect of investing in AI is recognizing the interconnectedness of different technologies. AI often synergizes with other emerging technologies, such as blockchain, quantum computing, and the Internet of Things (IoT), creating even more powerful and transformative capabilities. Investing in companies that effectively integrate these technologies can yield substantial returns. Understanding the interplay between AI and these other emerging technologies is crucial for identifying high-growth opportunities.

Finally, it's crucial to acknowledge the uncertainties inherent in investing in any emerging technology, including AI. Market fluctuations, technological disruptions, and unforeseen regulatory changes can all significantly impact investment returns. A well-diversified investment portfolio, risk management strategies, and a long-term investment horizon are essential for mitigating these risks and maximizing long-term returns. Remember, patience and persistence are key attributes for investors in the dynamic world of AI. The rewards can be substantial, but they often require time and a tolerance for uncertainty. A thoughtful, well-researched approach, coupled with a long-term perspective and an understanding of both the financial and ethical aspects, is the cornerstone of successful investment in AI and emerging technologies.

Building an AIReady Organization

Building a successful AI strategy isn't simply about acquiring the latest technology; it's fundamentally about transforming the very fabric of an organization. It demands a holistic approach that encompasses talent acquisition, cultural adaptation, ethical considerations, and a robust infrastructure capable of supporting the complexities of AI implementation. This transition requires a long-term commitment, significant investment, and a willingness to embrace change. Failing to address these crucial elements will likely result in suboptimal AI adoption and potentially missed opportunities.

The cornerstone of any AI-ready organization lies in its human capital. Attracting, retaining, and developing AI talent is paramount. This goes beyond simply hiring data scientists and machine learning engineers. It requires building a multidisciplinary team that includes statisticians, domain experts, ethicists, and project managers, all capable of working collaboratively to define problems, develop solutions, and deploy AI systems responsibly. A crucial aspect of this talent acquisition is fostering a culture of continuous learning. The rapid evolution of AI necessitates ongoing upskilling and reskilling initiatives for existing employees to adapt to the changing technological landscape. This could involve internal training programs, online courses, workshops, and collaborations with universities or research institutions. Moreover, organizations should look to attract diverse talent, as diversity of thought and experience is crucial for developing robust and unbiased AI systems. Blind spots in data sets and biases inherent in algorithms are often the product of a lack of diversity in the development teams.

Cultivating an AI-friendly culture extends beyond simply hiring the right people. It requires a shift in mindset, a move away from traditional hierarchical structures toward a more agile and collaborative environment. AI projects often require cross-functional collaboration, involving engineers, marketers, sales teams, and even legal departments. A culture that fosters open communication, knowledge sharing, and risk-taking is crucial for successful AI implementation. This culture should encourage experimentation, learning from failures, and a willingness to embrace iterative development processes. Encouraging a culture of innovation is crucial. AI projects are inherently complex, and it is necessary to build a culture that rewards creativity and novel approaches while minimizing the fear of failure. This may involve establishing dedicated AI innovation labs or partnering with external research institutions to enhance innovation and promote creative solutions.

Ethical considerations are no longer an optional add-on but a fundamental requirement for responsible AI development and deployment. Organizations must establish clear ethical guidelines and governance structures for their AI initiatives. These guidelines should address issues such as data privacy, algorithmic bias, transparency, and accountability. An ethical framework should be integrated into the entire AI lifecycle, from data collection and model training to deployment and monitoring. Regular audits and ethical reviews of AI systems are crucial to ensure adherence to these guidelines. Furthermore, building mechanisms for transparency in decision-making is essential. Users and stakeholders must be able to understand how AI systems arrive at their conclusions, especially when those conclusions have significant implications. Transparency builds trust and helps to identify and mitigate biases and errors.

The infrastructural needs of an AI-ready organization are substantial. This includes investing in high-performance computing resources, robust data storage and management systems, and secure networks capable of handling the vast amounts of data required for AI model training and deployment. Organizations also need to consider the need for specialized AI software and tools, and the integration of these systems with existing IT infrastructure. This investment goes beyond hardware and software; it encompasses the development of data pipelines, algorithms for data cleaning and preparation, and tools for model monitoring and evaluation.

Furthermore, investment in cybersecurity is crucial, given the potential vulnerabilities of AI systems to cyberattacks. Robust security measures must be implemented to protect sensitive data and ensure the integrity of AI systems. The integration of AI tools with existing infrastructure often requires considerable effort in terms of data migration and software customization. This necessitates a phased approach, starting with pilot projects before expanding to larger-scale deployment.

Beyond the technical aspects, an AI-ready organization needs to invest in the development of robust data governance frameworks.

This involves establishing clear procedures for data collection, storage, and use, ensuring compliance with relevant regulations like GDPR and CCPA. Data quality is paramount, and organizations must establish processes to ensure data accuracy, completeness, and consistency. Effective data governance reduces risks associated with poor quality data and enhances the trustworthiness and reliability of AI models. Moreover, organizations must have systems in place to manage and respond to data breaches, ensuring compliance with relevant regulations and industry best practices.

Finally, measuring the success of AI initiatives is essential.

Organizations need to establish clear metrics for evaluating the performance of AI systems and their impact on the business. These metrics should be aligned with the organization's overall strategic goals and objectives. Tracking key performance indicators (KPIs) like accuracy, efficiency, and cost savings allows for continuous improvement and optimization of AI systems. Regular reporting and monitoring of these KPIs provide crucial feedback and insights into the effectiveness of AI initiatives. Furthermore, this data can be used to identify areas for improvement and guide future investment decisions.

In conclusion, building an AI-ready organization is a multifaceted undertaking that requires a long-term perspective and a commitment to continuous improvement. It involves attracting and developing AI talent, creating a collaborative and ethical work culture, investing in robust infrastructure, establishing effective data governance frameworks, and implementing systems for continuous monitoring and improvement. Organizations that successfully navigate these challenges will be well-positioned to harness the transformative power of AI and thrive in the increasingly AI-driven world. Failing to embrace this transformation risks being left behind, with severe implications for future competitiveness and market viability. The journey requires significant investment, commitment, and a fundamental shift in organizational thinking. However, the potential rewards are vast, potentially leading to improved operational efficiency, enhanced decision-making, innovative products and services, and a more resilient business model.

Preparing for the Future of Work and Society

Preparing for the future of work and society in the age of AI necessitates a proactive and multifaceted approach. While the transformative potential of artificial intelligence is undeniable, its impact on jobs, industries, and societal structures demands careful consideration and strategic planning. The key lies not in fearing AI's advance, but in understanding its capabilities and harnessing its power for responsible innovation and inclusive growth.

One of the most pressing concerns surrounding AI is its potential impact on employment. While some jobs will inevitably be displaced by automation, history shows that technological advancements have historically created new jobs while rendering others obsolete. The Industrial Revolution, for example, witnessed a massive shift from agrarian societies to industrialized ones, leading to job losses in agriculture but significant growth in manufacturing and related sectors. The AI revolution will likely follow a similar pattern. The focus should be on preparing the workforce for these shifts, investing in education and training programs that equip individuals with the skills needed to thrive in an AI-driven economy. This means emphasizing STEM education, but also focusing on skills that are uniquely human – critical thinking, creativity, problem-solving, and emotional intelligence – which are currently difficult to replicate with AI. Reskilling and upskilling initiatives are not just a matter of individual responsibility; governments and businesses have a crucial role to play in providing resources and support for workforce transitions.

Furthermore, the development of AI should not be solely driven by profit maximization. Ethical considerations must be at the forefront of every AI project. Bias in algorithms, data privacy concerns, and the potential for AI to exacerbate existing societal inequalities are all critical issues that require careful attention. Building ethical guidelines and regulatory frameworks is essential to ensure that AI technologies are developed and used responsibly. This includes transparent algorithms, robust data governance frameworks, and mechanisms for accountability. Independent auditing of AI systems can help identify and mitigate potential biases and ensure fairness and equity in their application. The development of ethical AI is not just a technical challenge; it requires a broader societal discussion involving ethicists, policymakers, technologists, and the public. Open dialogue and public engagement are crucial for shaping the ethical landscape of AI and preventing unintended negative consequences.

The potential for AI to exacerbate existing societal inequalities is a serious concern. Access to AI technologies and the benefits they bring are not evenly distributed across society. This creates the potential for widening the gap between the rich and the poor, further marginalizing already vulnerable populations. Efforts to ensure equitable access to AI education, resources, and benefits are therefore critical. Policies that promote digital literacy and bridge the digital divide are necessary to ensure that everyone has the opportunity to participate in the AI-driven economy. Furthermore, careful consideration must be given to the design of AI systems to ensure that they do not perpetuate or amplify existing biases. This requires diverse and inclusive teams involved in AI development, testing, and deployment.

Beyond the workforce and societal equity, the integration of AI into various aspects of life also requires careful consideration.

Autonomous vehicles, for instance, represent a significant technological leap but also pose challenges related to safety, liability, and regulation. The development and deployment of such technologies necessitate careful consideration of these complexities, ensuring that robust safety mechanisms are in place and that appropriate legal and regulatory frameworks are established.

Similarly, the use of AI in healthcare, finance, and criminal justice raises ethical concerns that require careful deliberation and regulation. The potential for algorithmic bias in healthcare, for example, could lead to discriminatory outcomes, while the use of AI in criminal justice raises concerns about privacy and due process.

The future of work in an AI-driven world is not a zero-sum game. While automation will displace some jobs, it will also create new opportunities. The key to navigating this transition successfully lies in proactively adapting to the changing landscape. This includes investing in education and training, fostering a culture of lifelong learning, and developing skills that are uniquely human.

Governments, businesses, and individuals all have a crucial role to play in this process. Governments can invest in education and training programs, provide social safety nets, and develop regulatory frameworks that promote responsible AI development. Businesses can invest in reskilling and upskilling their employees, adopt ethical AI practices, and create new jobs in the emerging AI-related sectors. Individuals can invest in their own education and development, acquire in-demand skills, and adapt to the changing job market.

Moreover, fostering a culture of continuous learning is essential.

The rapid pace of technological advancements necessitates a commitment to lifelong learning and adaptation. Education systems must adapt to the changing demands of the workforce, providing students with the skills and knowledge they need to thrive in an AI-driven world. Businesses should invest in training and development programs for their employees, helping them acquire new skills and adapt to evolving job roles. Individuals must take responsibility for their own learning and development, staying up-to-date with the latest technologies and trends.

In conclusion, preparing for the future of work and society in an AI-driven world requires a comprehensive and proactive approach. It demands a shift in mindset, moving away from fear-based narratives to a future-oriented approach focused on responsible innovation, inclusive growth, and proactive adaptation. Addressing the ethical concerns surrounding AI, promoting equitable access to its benefits, and investing in education and training are all crucial steps in ensuring a future where AI serves humanity and promotes a more just and prosperous society. The journey will require collaboration between governments, businesses, and individuals, a commitment to lifelong learning, and a shared vision for a future shaped by responsible technological advancement. The potential rewards, however, are immense: a more efficient, innovative, and equitable world where human ingenuity and AI capabilities work in concert to solve some of humanity's most pressing challenges.

Appendix

Appendix A: Detailed Timeline of AI Milestones (1956-Present) – This appendix provides a more comprehensive timeline than that presented in Chapter 1, including minor breakthroughs and key publications that contributed to the field's evolution.

Appendix B: Statistical Data on AI Investment and Adoption – This section contains detailed charts and graphs outlining global investment trends in AI research and development, along with data on AI adoption rates across various sectors, providing a more detailed quantitative analysis of the trends discussed.

Appendix C: Ethical Frameworks for AI Development – A summary of prominent ethical guidelines and frameworks for responsible AI development from organizations like the OECD, IEEE, and others, complementing the ethical discussions.

Glossary

Artificial Intelligence (AI): The theory and development of computer systems able to perform tasks that normally require human intelligence, such as visual perception, speech recognition, decision-making, and translation between languages.

Machine Learning (ML): A subset of AI where systems learn from data without explicit programming.

Deep Learning (DL): A subfield of machine learning that uses artificial neural networks with multiple layers to extract higher-level features from raw data.

Neural Network: A computational model inspired by the structure and function of the human brain, used for machine learning.

Algorithm: A set of rules or instructions followed by a computer to solve a problem or perform a task.

Big Data: Extremely large datasets that are difficult to process using traditional data processing applications.

Bias (in AI): Systematic and repeatable errors in a computer system that can lead to unfair or discriminatory outcomes.

Explainable AI (XAI): The development of AI systems whose decisions and processes are transparent and understandable to humans.